TATAMI DAYS

TATAMI DAYS

Getting a Life in Japan

Michael Guest

FURIN CHIME • SYDNEY

Published by Furin Chime Press
Copyright © Michael Guest 2018, 2020

ISBN 978-0-6487517-0-0

Book and cover design by Furin Chime Press, Sydney,
Australia
Furinchime.com

Cover photography by Sora Sagano, Unsplash.com
Interior image used under license from Shutterstock.com

Contents

Preface

Tatami permeates your lifestyle, soothes your senses with the subtle charm of its look, feel and scent. Wear shoes on tatami?—unthinkable, barbaric violation. Minimalist furnishings (where any) transcend our gross Western ones, though many houses and apartments have become Westernized, retaining a single, multi-purpose tatami *washitsu* (Japanese room). Low table; *zabuton* cushion or *zaisu* legless chair for sitting; futons for sleep are shut away during the day. Of standard dimensions—rooms being measured by the number of mats they contain—tatami determines the appearance and proportions of interiors, enhancing them with criss-cross patterns of brocaded edging. People tend to behave more gently, with better grace and humility, as if complementing the tatami.

It was with that charm lingering in my memory as at once symbol and sensuous trace that I wrote *Tatami Days*, a series of sketches from my fifteen years of living and working as a higher educator in Japan, during which time I transitioned from doctoral graduate, through business school lecturer to tenured national university professor. Hence the book offers informed glimpses of the post-secondary education system, which is different in many ways from those in Western countries. Equally, my aim is to capture in a mosaic the unique and multi-dimensioned context for personal exploration and development that Japan offers a long-term expat. Each day brings challenging experiences and realizations—cultural, social, religious and philosophical in nature—some eye-opening in themselves, many minute but ultimately bringing you to question your conventional wisdom. Living as the ultimate outsider—by definition an "outside person" (*gaijin*)—is an existential growth process in which you learn something new every day.

I'm not the first to be fascinated with the play of otherness and topsy-turviness that inflects the foreigner's life in relatively homogeneous Japan. Indeed, the "gaijin memoir" has become a mini-genre, often with an inclination to the bizarre and zany sides of the expat experience, others by authors who have worked in Japanese high schools for a short while or studied in the traditional or martial arts. What I believe distinguishes this book is its reflective, critical focus on cross-cultural adaptation in the context of long-term work in higher education, which forms the nexus for layers and offshoots of personal experiences and relationships. I moved to Japan "on spec" at a rudderless time, so life there was for me somewhat a matter of "getting a life." They were gloomy economic times in Australia during the late 80s, with repercussions throughout the arts, and my occupation of a sessional university lecturer and freelance arts writer offered uninspiring prospects. When I graduated with a PhD in arts from the University of Sydney and was offered a job as English language instructor in a Japanese business *senmon gakko* (vocational or professional college), I felt little distress about the prospect of sacrificing them for an uncertain solitary excursion into a curious country and culture about which I knew next to nothing, with no anticipation of the exercise lasting more than a year or two at most.

My narrative begins *in medias res* at a pivotal incident, my acceptance by one of the national universities. The device helps highlight what was required in order to make that step, as well as a contrast between university and senmon gakko cultures, by way of two counterposed job interviews. While mine was a particularly strict senmon gakko, with unusual characteristics from a Western perspective, working there equipped me with skills needed to progress in my career and introduced me to some memorable and admirable individuals. Entering the university, however, opened the way to an expanded, deeper, longer-term engagement with Japan.

Chapters 1 and 2 establish in practice my method for exploring my Japanese surroundings, my tacit use of a figure of the *flâneur*—which is basically a type of narrative persona, someone who "saunters" about town observing and interpreting meanings in the things around him. A kind of flâneur mask informs the storytelling technique throughout (if sometimes mounted on a bicycle), most literally in Chapters 9, Main Street Middle Japan; 16, Married Life; 17, Downtime; and 12, Cold Garden of Ryoanji. Chapters 3–7 deal with acclimatizing to the country and the system of the senmon gakko. Chapters 8–22 are based on working life as a university teacher and researcher.

At one level *Tatami Days* traces out a path of development, a process of acculturation in which every act of adaptation becomes a kind of growth node. At the same time, I wished to develop a more "objective" or detached impression of the country. I try to accomplish both aims by exploring the Japanese historical, social and cultural context. Chapter 1, Spirits of Atsuta, for example, incorporates an excursus into some of the history and legend surrounding the famous shrine where the framing action takes place. Accounts of the exploits of the warlord Oda Nobunaga and his successors, who unified Japan after the era of warring states, and reflections on the gods (*kami*) in legendary and contemporary worlds, enrich and inform the context in an authentic way: history, tradition and religion lurk ever behind the scenes in contemporary Japanese life, spilling out into it. In Japan there is a story behind everything, waiting to be uncovered.

Historical themes are taken up subsequently (especially in Chapter 11, Old Ego Dies Hard) in explaining the significance and character of "middle Japan" (Tokyo, Shizuoka, Nagoya, Kyoto, etc.) including the "Tokaido megalopolis," the main economic artery of the nation, which provides the overall geographical and demographic setting.

A main theme of cultural reflection further underpins narrated incidents. My own story of adaptation is a specimen of the kinds of challenges encountered by many expatriates. The term "culture" is used to encompass everyday norms and social behaviors, as well as to refer in the traditional way to "higher" cultural values generally associated with the arts. Specific characteristics of a culture affect such socio-psychological considerations as relations between individuals, the effects of hierarchies and power relations, "groupism," and culturally specific modes of communication (see in particular Chapters 19, Music City Blues; 20, Gaijin House; and 22, Weightless). A range of everyday customs and behaviors, often decidedly minute but equally fascinating, also falls within the culturally reflective scope, as do experiences extracted from some of my cross-border projects in arts, literature and media.

I wrote *Tatami Days* to be entertaining, informative, and intellectually stimulating. It is a work of creative nonfiction, based on memory and research. Events and experiences in the book are real, or at least as I remember them, though except for some public figures, the names of most characters, and where appropriate some enterprises, have been changed to maintain the privacy of the individuals portrayed.

Michael Guest
February 3, 2018, Sydney

Spirits of Atsuta

Undertakings bring good fortune.
I Ching

Late in the afternoon I stepped from the subway car, climbed the stairs to the street and made my way furtively to the Atsuta Shrine. I wore my brand new suit, the most elegant I could afford, a style called the "New Yorker" in deep charcoal with faint maroon pinstripes. I couldn't go straight home, because at this time of day I'd be likely to meet other instructors from my college on their way home via the Atsuta Jingumae railway station. Disastrous to be seen in the vicinity just now. I entered the grounds and made for the main sanctuary, loitering by the turtle pool. In this quiet part of the day the turtles were huddled together in repose, a collective organism of muscle and shell. A single turtle shuddered to readjust itself, initiating a minor chain reaction, a wave motion of agitation, re-settling and calm.

One semi-submerged beast, forequarters and the shoulder portion of its shell dry, strained to haul itself up a fraction more out of the water onto a rock platform. The platform itself was rough-hewn in the shape of a turtle, assembled from natural slabs and boulders. Turtles resting on turtles, upon turtle shaped rock, upon the turtle-like earth itself: a living tableau of infinite regression. Turtles upon turtles, all the way down. "A crane lives a thousand years, a turtle ten thousand," says a Japanese proverb — an ancient one, so it should know. A small shop along the street specialized in turtle products. You could buy canned flesh and bottled essences to help you live for a hundred years. Abstaining from these tonics, I'd be content with a shorter life.

Coming to the main sanctuary, I tossed three five-yen coins into the offerings box. The *kami*, the gods of Shinto, preferred these because they had a square hole in the middle, so I usually set some aside for them. Who can decipher the partialities of the gods? I clapped my hands to awaken them, bowed my head and shut my eyes, pressing my palms together in a gesture of prayer. An incision in time, the hand-clap has echoed in the back of my memory ever since, along with the rustling leaves, birdsong, chirping insects and the trickling of a stream.

Felt the breeze touch my face, heard the distant hum of traffic, focused my mind on the here and now. Bowing to complete the ritual, I moved on, slipped into the wood behind the sanctuary and went down a rough embankment to the stream. Everything here was ancient and auspicious, like the thick moss on an oak against whose trunk I rested my hand. Between two of its roots were an iridescent beetle and a brown spider weaving a web. A pigeon scratched about on the forest floor. I was startled to the realization that these creatures had an awareness of me too—an awareness that manifested the spirituality of the shrine.

Among the deities enshrined here, I imagined, dwelt the spirit of Oda Nobunaga, a great sixteenth century *daimyo* (warlord). I saw him in my mind's eye, his bright warrior's regalia multicolored like the beetle's, his grotesquely sneering black face-mask, bronze horns curving up from the forehead of his iron helmet. Though Nobunaga was not officially enshrined at Atsuta, a spiritual residue must surely permeate the wall he built here in gratitude to the gods for his victory at the Battle of Okehazama, a heroic and epoch-making event . . .

SUMMER OF 1560. Full of contempt for Nobunaga, Imagawa Yoshimoto, one of Japan's mightiest daimyo, was on his way to Kyoto from Sumpu (present-day Shizuoka) with an army rumored forty thousand strong, trespassing through Nobunaga's territory in Owari province. Holed up in his base at Kiyosu Castle, Nobunaga tried to sleep but could not abide the affront. He arose and sang his favorite lines from a famous noh drama, Zeami's *Atsumori*:

> *Compared to eternity*
> *Our human span of fifty years*
> *Is a dream.*

> *Having received life*
> *Does anyone live forever?*

Believing that reports had exaggerated the size of

Imagawa's army, which was in all probability no greater than a mere twenty-five thousand men, he rode out with a contingent of two hundred samurai to engage them, rallying three thousand more warriors along the way and stopping here at the shrine to pray for victory.

Imagawa's soldiers were camped near the village of Okehazama, drinking and reveling in celebration over some recent triumphs. Just as Nobunaga arrived with his army, a torrential downpour set in, concealing their approach. The storm lifted miraculously at the right time, allowing them to surprise the vastly superior force and rout it in a mere two hours. Later he returned to the Atsuta Shrine and erected the wall.

Nobunaga's power grew so much in that era of warring states that he entertained an ambition to bring Japan under the one sword. He could not accomplish the deed alone in his lifetime, but he set in motion a chain of events through which he, his general Toyotomi Hideyoshi (who had risen from being no more than Nobunaga's personal sandal-bearer at the Battle of Okehazama), and Hideyoshi's general in turn, Tokugawa Ieyasu, unified Japan. All this took place during the period between 1568 and 1603, the year Ieyasu became shogun, military dictator over the whole country. There is a saying that Nobunaga cooked the rice cake and Hideyoshi shaped it, but only Ieyasu tasted it.

These heroes of Japanese unification were very different types. Once, legend has it, the three powerful warlords discussed what to do with a songbird that refused to sing:

"Kill it," said the most ruthless of them, Nobunaga.

"Make it sing," said the coercive Hideyoshi.

"Wait for it to sing," said the wise and patient Ieyasu.

* * *

FADING DAYLIGHT, but I was still not prepared to risk running into my workmates from the other departments. My only absence during my year and a half teaching at the college—and on false pretenses.

In the morning, I'd telephoned my boss Sogabé from the Shinkansen (bullet train), en route to Shizuoka City, capital of Shizuoka Prefecture, for a job interview at the national university there. I lied that a friend from Australia got into a scrape in Tokyo and I had to go there to help her out. A flimsy story but the best I could dream up. Simply to call in ill would not have been safe: someone might see me at the station or on the Shinkansen, and anyway, there was every chance Sogabé would go to my apartment to check up on me.

Indeed, the next time I saw my friend and workmate Yanagi, he said that when I failed to turn up an hour after clock-on time, Sogabé ordered him to go with him to my place to make sure I was all right. When they rang the doorbell and no one answered, Sogabé produced a key and told him to go inside and investigate, but he refused, arguing that that would be breaking the law.

If the bosses learned I was absent to go to a job interview, or if I couldn't provide them with any proof of my story, they would fire me on the spot. They had me in an awkward position. Almost time to renew my visa, and with no contract, no guarantor, I would have to leave the country.

I'd had enough of hanging around the shrine, and the Fantastic Shop should be open by now. It took fifteen minutes to hurry through the grounds, some forest fowl scurrying away from my feet. I went through the gates and over the wide pedestrian crossing in front of my apartment building. Passing by the bus depot, where commuters were milling about, I kept my eyes fixed straight ahead.

The slender Chinese woman, Ko, was tending bar, wearing jeans and a crimson Chinese blouse, her long black hair tied in a ponytail.

"Just got back from an interview at Shizuoka University," I said to her in Japanese. "I have to telephone them at seven o'clock for the result."

"You are going to leave Nagoya?"

"Well, if I get the job I'll move to Shizuoka."

The shop owner, whom everyone knew by the generic barkeeper's name of "Master," came in from his kitchenette and Ko related to him what I'd been saying.

"Shizuoka University is a pretty good one—a national university," he said, impressed. He made a level with his hand, waving it above his head. "If Tokyo University is up here, Shizuoka University ranks about here." His other hand was around chest level. "Ko-chan's university is very small. Not so good. Way down here," he said, laughing and lowering his hand. She gave him a dark look and turned away.

"I don't think I passed the interview, anyway," I said, convinced of it.

Master switched to English. "Shizuoka izzu *inaka*," he said, reaching for his dictionary. "Ru-raru . . ." He had a hard time getting out the word. ". . . Za kantorii. Fujisan!"

"Rural," I said. "Yes, the country. Mount Fuji. It's smaller than Nagoya but quite a pleasant city." I wrote down the population on a slip of paper, unable to do the translation immediately in my head: to name big numbers in Japanese, you put a comma before every four zeros, not three. "*Gojumannin gurai*," I said. "About half a million people."

MY APPLICATIONS had attracted some nibbles: a short-listing by a university from Hokkaido in the far north, another from Okinawa in the far south, and the one from Shizuoka, less than an hour from Nagoya by Shinkansen and about the same from Tokyo. My little publications appeared to be paying off, but I realized I would never be able to wangle any days off for attending interviews. Of the three universities, Shizuoka was the best. Fortunately, they were interviewing soonest. If I were successful first up, I'd have nothing to worry about.

I decided to buy myself a new suit for the occasion, so the next Saturday afternoon after I received their letter, I caught the subway to a stop at Motoyama, a suburb of Nagoya. Nearby was Grandback, a menswear store that specialized in large sizes and was thus an invaluable resource for foreigners. An agreeable walk up a hill to get there, past Nanzan University. Togan-ji was on the way, a Buddhist temple whose grounds housed a giant buddha and a pet cemetery. I often took the trip here on the weekend and burned some incense sticks in memory of some dear departed canine friends. This time, I lit the incense for good luck too, sensing that my fate may be unfolding in a favorable direction.

The traditional tea ceremony is supposed to have an effect of making the events that surround it in time assume significance: in retrospect, it is as though everything leads up to and radiates out from it. That was how I felt then: each incident had an auspicious glow.

My New Yorker hung on the rack at Grandback, perfect in cut, material and fit. Too bad that a nice garment like this demonstrated the flaw of most suits sold in Japan: just half a lining hanging down the inside back of the coat. Since most everyone wore them, however, it made no difference. I agreed to buy it, so the saleswoman had me sit down at a special purchasing customer's table, treating me to a cup of coffee and a cream wafer biscuit while I waited for her to prepare the account—another satisfied customer.

Come the eve of the interview, I laid out my new suit, set my alarm clock and mentally rehearsed my escape plot. Timing was critical, because I had to catch an early morning Nagoya-bound train while avoiding running into my colleagues. In the middle of the night, I was awakened by the screams of a motorcycle gang tearing past: *bosozoku* ("speed tribes"). They drove everyone mad. The gang members were *yakuza* gangster hopefuls who souped up their bikes so they made earsplitting bursts and blasts of noise like Screaming Mimis. Wearing kamikaze-style outfits—baggy pants tucked into their boots, jackets emblazoned with slogans, fluttering headbands and sashes—they wove erratically through traffic, carrying baseball-bat wielding pillion passengers, intimidating motorists and creating as much noise and havoc as they could. Being the home of the country's colossal automotive industry, in which many of the bosozoku worked, Nagoya had more than its fair share of them.

The night quietened, and when I opened my eyes the sun had barely risen. I was dressed and ready to go when the trains arrived carrying the bulk of commuters headed for the college. I waited unseen on the landing until they passed beneath me; then I skulked down the stairway and went to the station. When the next Nagoya-bound train came, I stepped on board, staring straight ahead, expecting to come face to face with one of my bosses, but it did not happen. In fifteen minutes I had reached Nagoya station and was sitting on the bullet train, headed for Shizuoka.

APPROACHING by taxi, I looked up at the rectangular gray-white concrete buildings of the university, which was set on a picture-postcard wooded hillside. Parallel blocks thrusting out imposingly into space, a character-istic architectural style for institutions located on elevated sites like this. One rooftop was crowned with the white dome of a modest astronomical observatory. The campus teemed with greenery; quadrangles and footpaths were adorned with cherry blossom trees, pre-sently dormant, awaiting springtime. A road snaked up through the campus, branching off to access various groupings of tallish buildings. Mount Fuji was in her full snow-capped glory to the northeast, and to the south-east the panorama stretched to a coastline—a low density urban environment with houses and rice paddies, traversed by a straight, elevated roadway, the Tomei Expressway to Tokyo. I had time to kill, so I found the place where the interview was to be held and then wandered for about half an hour, taking in the scene: the buildings and cafeterias, the earthen sports fields, enormous gymnasium and library. A lump rose in my throat at the thought that here I was with a shot at a proper university job, along with the misgiving that it was all too good to be true.

Outside the interview room, a suave gentleman

wearing a tweed coat introduced himself to me in perfect English. Fine features, a twinkle in his eye and a mane of gray hair that hung down past the collar.

"I am Kuniyoshi Munakata, a professor here, and a student of noh theater and Shakespeare." Flashed me a charismatic smile.

"Is that so?" I said. "Drama is one of my specialties, too. I wrote my doctoral thesis on Samuel Beckett."

"I know—I read your resume, of course." Again that smile spontaneously animated his face and shone through his steady intellectual gaze.

He handed me his card, which announced him as Professor in the Faculty of Liberal Arts and Leader of the Noh Shakespeare Company of Japan. Wishing me luck, he made a sweeping motion to the room and followed me in. A panel of six men—Munakata, four other Japanese and a Brit—greeted me warmly. We seated ourselves on comfortable low armchairs placed around a broad, low table. I had one side to myself, and the interviewers arranged themselves around the other three. The chairperson sat across from me. He had his back to a window, the rays of the midday sun lending him a halo, an effect that enhanced the brightness of his open smile, the sheen of his straight black hair and the glint of his intelligent eyes. He introduced himself to me as Associate Professor Tokui.

"The interview will be in three parts English and, later, one part Japanese," he said, and my heart sank. They took turns asking me questions about my research and teaching experience. A young man sitting on my left had copies of the publications I submitted; he had highlighted several passages and he quizzed me on some fine details. Then he wanted to know how much I contributed to a co-authored article on the Coppola film *Apocalypse Now*. That fazed me: I was dubious about my own integrity in having taken on board a bogus co-author—the principal of my college—purely to have the thing published, and I wondered what they would make of it.

"I wrote the essay and adjusted the content to accord with the co-author's perceptions and outlook," I said, embroidering a smidgen. I had cut a minor reference to drug use in the film, in case he bothered to have someone translate the piece for him—I knew that he would not be pleased to be associated with such a theme and there would be unpleasant repercussions if he were.

"So in fact you wrote it by yourself?" the young man asked, without a hint of reproof or surprise.

"Yes," I replied, and he jotted something in his note-pad. I was glad to have that out in the open.

"Now, you will understand that the successful candidate must speak Japanese," said Tokui smiling, "so we will conduct the next session in *Nihongo*."

I thought, well, here goes nothing. I entertained little hope of managing. One thing to get by at my local "red lantern" drinking house in pidgin Japanese, another to express myself convincingly in front of a panel of university academics. I prayed that what I lacked in formal training I might compensate for with the communicative competence I had built up over the past eighteen months.

I gave all my concentration to the task of listening. I had acquired the essential communicative skill of being able to identify a question, which generally had the grammatical particle *ka* added on at the end as a kind of verbal question mark. You could be riding merrily along in a taxi, having with a few well-chosen phrases convinced the driver you knew enough Japanese for him to be contentedly raving on to you. But if you missed that *ka* and continued grinning and nodding at him in the rear-view mirror, the illusion was dispelled. On the other hand, if you picked up on the *ka*, even if you had not precisely comprehended what he said, at least you could show him you realized he had asked you something. You might try reformulating the phrase he used just before his question marker, or a word or two of it, to seek clarification. He would not mind repeating himself, perhaps using plainer words; so you would have taken part in a meaningful exchange even before you fully understood his question.

As the interview progressed, I was surprised to find I could follow what was being said: questions to put me at my ease, about where I came from, how I liked Japan, how I found Japanese students and Japanese food. As the questions became more difficult, my comprehension let me down at some points, and I was certain they must have found my ability wanting. The mood in the room, however, grew ever more jovial as the interview went on. They could have tripped me up if they wished but were inclined to help me along, at times laughing and commenting to each other, remarking on my answers. We were having a grand old time, and I did my best to encourage the conviviality by settling into my comfort zone, rather than trying to wow them with my limited book study of Japanese—refraining, for example, from attempting more polite forms of speech I'd studied but had little opportunity to practice. Foreigners were forgiven lapses in politeness that would mark out a Japanese as ill-refined.

Professor Munakata brought the proceedings back to English.

"I think we should ask Michael whether he would want to accept the position if we were to offer it to him."

I didn't hesitate. "Oh yes," I said, with heartfelt sincerity. "I want this more than anything."

As I was leaving, he approached me again and shook my hand.

"That seemed to go very well," he said, with his engaging smile.

"Thanks, I do hope so."

Arriving back at Shizuoka Station, I had coffee and a sandwich while replaying the interview over in my mind. One instant, I was overjoyed at how well things had gone, the next, I began to sink into dejection. I had misread everything: they couldn't miss the severe limitations of my Japanese proficiency, but concealed that to spare my feelings. I shuddered at how poorly I'd followed the Japanese portion of the interview and how ungrammatical, even infantile, some of my responses were. The panel had simply been keeping the mood positive. And what about Munakata's question about whether I would want to accept their job offer if they made one? They must ask everyone the same thing as a matter of form.

On my way to the Shinkansen platform, I put a one-hundred yen piece into a fortune telling machine. A fierce looking, fiery-skinned automaton with jewels for eyes and a turban on its head stared out from a glass case attached to a solid metal base. When my coin dropped into the slot, the demon emitted a menacing laugh, lights flashed on and off behind its eyes, and my fortune fell out into a cavity in the base—a folded up paper resembling an *omikuji* (fortune telling slip) from a Shinto shrine. I recalled a conversation I had with Sogabé, when he commented wryly on Japanese superstitiousness.

"We read the omikuji," he was saying, "and tie it to a tree. If it says something good is going to happen, we pray it will come true. If it says something bad is going to happen, then we pray it won't come true. Ha ha ha!"

Worshipers leave hundreds of these omikuji slips tied to pine trees in the grounds of the Atsuta Shrine in the hope that the bad luck they predict will wait at the tree, because the Japanese words for "wait" and "pine" sound identical: *matsu*. When I looked at this one, I felt another pang of despair, unable to work out much of what it said. Surely that was its brutal, transparent omen.

"FIVE TO seven, better go make the call," I said to Ko. Master was waving his arms and holding forth excitedly to two customers at the other end of the bar. I drained my glass of whisky and went outside, heart pounding. Across the road, over near the bus station, was a telephone booth. No point wasting time. I took Tokui's business card from my wallet and dialed his number. He picked up immediately.

"Thank you very much for calling," he said. "Our selection committee met today after the interviews, to decide on the successful candidate. I am sorry"—*Thump!* Thud of vain hopes hitting the concrete floor—"sorry we could not give you the news sooner than this."

"No, that's fine," I said, controlling the tightness in my voice.

"We decided that we want to offer you the position at Shizuoka University. Would you like to accept it?"

"Oh yes," I said, scarcely believing my ears. "Yes."

I was free. I headed straight for the subway, where I knew was an international pay phone. I wanted to let Isabella know straight away. Jubilant, I wound my way through waves of homeward bound commuters as though my feet had wings. Suddenly there appeared before me a lecturer from the college, a friendly big fellow with a round face, who worked in the Travel Department. He broke into an enormous grin when he saw me and pointed his finger straight at me. Unmistakable wordless message: "Gotcha!"

"*Komban wa!*" ("Good evening!") I laughed, slapping him on the shoulder as we passed each other by.

2

Color of a Gray Rat

My first trip to Japan was nearly two years before, in 1991, to apply for a job as an English instructor at Central Japan Business College. I had no particular interest in Japan, nothing more than mild curiosity in an exotic country about which I knew extremely little. Though I was in my thirties, lack of money and the demands of work and study had so far prevented me from traveling outside Australia, so when they wanted to interview me, I accepted the free return flight thankfully, but less with a sense of optimism than the notion that I had nothing to lose.

During my first couple of years living in Japan, I landed at Nagoya airport a few times. I preferred the evening descent. It offered a fine-spun neon light-show, a glistening web, as though an image of cool, pulsing computer circuitry gradually appeared on the fading scene. Among the twinkling gems aligning themselves with rows of streets, buildings and flows of traffic, zapping electrons traced thin pink and turquoise lines around the top of a building here and there. A neon ray would surge and in an instant wrap itself up and around the four walls several times, climaxing in a starburst of silent luminous fireworks, then retract to nothing, withdrawing into itself like a robotic *anime* snake. What the hell were they?

Another mystery, looking up. Searchlights still raked the night sky as they had during the Second World War—American airmen termed Nagoya Bay "Flak Alley"—and I couldn't figure out what they were for nowadays. Perhaps they embodied some kind of collective paranoia rooted in the trauma of the devastating bombings, which the presence of heavy industry, including aircraft factories, had attracted? A couple of nights, I sat alone on a grassy mound in a deserted park, gazing up, taking sips from a can of ulon tea and pondering my theory, the warmth of the atmosphere and the nocturnal symphony of the city covering me like a blanket.

My urbane friend Mr. Amachi chuckled when I asked him about those searchlights one day. Three of us were sitting around a wobbly wooden table lunching on *gyudon*—boiled rice topped with shredded beef and onion—in an eatery annexed to a vegetable market, somewhere in the tangle of residential lanes behind our college.

"If you follow one of those beams of light down to the end, you will find a pachinko parlor," he explained.

Mr. Onoé glanced up from his bowl, narrowed his eyes and nodded mirthfully. His cheek, bluish from a perpetual five o'clock shadow, bulged as he chewed on his rice, his disposable *hashi* (chopsticks) poised to scoop in the next mouthful. The thick black hairs amassed together across his cranium threatened to shoot out like porcupine quills.

"It is the 'pot on the end of the rainbow,'" Mr. Amachi continued, smiling, unintentionally revitalizing the cliché for me. I smiled back. Mr. Onoé grunted approval midway through a swallow.

"Pachinko was invented here in Nagoya, so Nagoya people love pachinko *very maarch*," he said mirthfully.

The neon light-show one saw from the plane was another element in a clever wordless advertising strategy of the parlors, which appropriated the night sky for its medium. *Pachinko!* The word echoed the jangling rattle of metal balls dropping through berserk contraptions resembling small pinball machines stood on their ends, setting off a blaring electronic commotion as they fell.

The silver balls crashed against bumpers and spinning cogs, interrupted and scattered in their fall by craftily inserted pins, which specialist technicians had tapped into position using little hammers, with the solemn concentration of a surgeon. Cigarette-smoking gamblers — including full-time professionals — set their wits against the expertise of the technicians, focusing their willpower through the control dial used to fire the balls up into the machine. They perched on stools, row upon row of them, facing the long lines of machines.

If a player was skillful or lucky enough on the day, the silver balls multiplied and spewed out into a tray. He'd shoot them into the machine again, with hopes of increasing the flow a hundred-fold, collecting the balls in plastic baskets, which attendants stacked up for him like silver bullion. He could exchange these for prizes — cigarettes, alcohol, chocolates, toys or electronics. Or else, when he was finished playing, he went out to a nondescript shop in an alleyway behind the parlor and cashed in a voucher for a monetary prize. Gambling was illegal, hence this hedge: the shop in the alleyway, reputedly operated by the Japanese mafia, the yakuza, bought his prizes from him and then resold them to the parlor—so not, *technically speaking*, gambling.

Pachinko parlors gave me a headache just walking along the pavement in front of them; the automatic doors would open and a toxic cacophony spill out. Garish signs and banners and big multicolored plastic floral wreaths adorned the street fronts for good luck. A certain stamp of men and women thrived on their electronic din and cigarette smoke, and if, as I had read, a quarter of the population indulged in the game, they appeared to be the less inspiring proportion. Occasionally during midsummer, a parent caught by the lure of pachinko would accidentally leave a toddler to suffocate in the family car.

ON A MORNING approach, however, you would be treated to a gray urban sprawl and a chaos of oblong buildings like blocks scattered by a child. "Japan is the color of a gray rat," a Japanese woman once complained to me after vacationing in Spain. Some visitors, too, found the view repulsively dull, others intriguingly haphazard. To me it seemed, as I landed in Japan that first time, an inscrutable face of indeterminate possibilities, a glimpse of a future most likely not to be.

Hardly any Australians were to be seen among the disembarkees. Most were Japanese returning from holidays and business trips, and they moved familiarly through the gates assigned to them. We foreigners stood in our own line, and it took the customs officers longer to look us over and question us. They did so efficiently, though, with poker faces and heavily accented English. Noise in the terminal rose no higher than a busy hum.

The alienating spectacle—channeled flows of bodies and the all-pervasive Japanese speech—stimulated in me a new sense of my own ethnicity, of being one among a tiny but visible minority. I was excited to set foot in a foreign country and glad to be out of that infernal aluminum tube, with its incessant humming, flimsy floor and sense of suspended time—of being physically trapped in the moment. I'm someone in whom flying stirs up an insecure feeling, peaking in gruesome fantasies and anxieties about death, heights and closed spaces, all combined in a single imagined catastrophe.

A crowd was gathered at the final roped-off exit to greet the arrivals. Several people held up cardboard signs bearing the names of passengers they were there to meet. Suddenly I saw mine in black marker. A strong looking, square-jawed fellow in his mid-thirties, of medium height, held the card. He wore rectangular glasses and a plain light-gray suit, with a necktie held in place by a silver tie clip. His hair was combed back impeccably in a style reminiscent of an old-fashioned TV newsreader's.

"My name is Masaru Sogabé," he said. "I am a head teacher at Central Japan Business College." We shook hands and he handed me a business card. He spoke good English with a touch of an American drawl and a nasal intonation.

He asked me whether I had visited Japan before and I told him no, this was my first time.

"Really? I didn't know that. Well then . . . welcome to Japan. You had better call me Mister Sogabé, I think, rather than Masaru. Usually, unless we know each other closely, we Japanese don't use each other's personal name." He gave a friendly snort and patted my shoulder. A smile spread over his face, underneath what struck me as rather impassive eyes.

He guided me confidently through the building. The interior was most unremarkable — almost remarkably so. The yellowy brown of the walls seemed to infuse the atmosphere, infecting not only the building but the people in it with a drab mood of sameness and conservatism. Among the crowd milling around were several men wearing tie clips. One elderly gentleman had on a bola or "string tie," the kind that wealthy ranchers or Texan oilmen wear in the movies, a cord fastened with an ornamental clasp.

The odd 1950s aura was most unlike what I expected of a first impression of Japan. The ordinariness became surreal as we moved through the terminal. Individual features of people milling around me seemed lost in a blur of ethnic homogeneity and conservative style. Two women in pastel kimonos tripped along, twittering gaily. One businessman greeted another, a mirror image, jet-black hair slicked down and briefcase in hand. They executed brisk formal bows and rattled off volleys of Japanese.

Sogabé stowed my bag in the trunk of his Nissan and hung his coat on a hook in the back.

"Let me take yours too, it's so damn hot," he said, referring to my trusty, well-worn sports coat. He held out his hand when we got in the car.

"Can you show me your passport, please?"

There must be some official reason, I guessed, if just to confirm my identity, so I handed it to him. His white business shirt was faultlessly pressed, and the fact that his singlet showed through the material in distinct lines did not detract in the slightest from his self-important air.

"Oh, you drive on the left too," I noted as we pulled out of the parking lot. "So do we. For some reason, I thought it would be the same here as in America."

We passed through suburbs with rice paddies tucked away incongruously in urban streets. I couldn't fathom what one oddity in the urban landscape might be: enormous skeletal metal structures supporting sheets of green netting. Giant aviaries? Sogabé explained that these were driving ranges for golf, multiple stories high. At some newer, automated ranges, the balls returned to the golfers through a system of pipes, washed and polished along the way. At other places, an attendant drove around in a protected vehicle, mechanically scooping them up.

"Do you play?" I asked.

He turned down his mouth and snorted.

"Nah, too boring. I like to work out." Rolled his head to loosen his neck.

I became absorbed in trying to isolate whatever it was that made the highway seem quite unusual to me: from some indefinable peculiarity of the flashing red lights on a temporary roadwork sign, to the gigantic concrete pylons supporting the elevated train tracks that reared up high above us as we came farther into the city. Trivial details merged in a disorientating undertone of difference that washed through my perceptions, just as it radiated out in all directions.

"I will take you to your hotel," he said. "And then, tomorrow morning I will pick you up and show you the college, and you will meet the president of the academy, Mr. Harada. He does not speak very much English so I will act as interpreter at your interview—I am your driver *and* your interpreter." He glanced at me sideways and gave me his friendly, cold-eyed, laughing snort.

"That'll be good—I'm looking forward to meeting him."

Traffic flowed smoothly along the highway. All the cars were immaculately clean and all late models, including sleek new ones I hadn't seen on Australian roads.

"Shit!" he burst out.

A car crossed into the lane in front of us, though not terribly recklessly, unless I'd missed something. But Sogabé looked at me agape, shaking his head in amazement as if to say, "Can you believe this idiot?" He repeated the word with a chortle—"Shi-yit . . ."—savoring its sound and his ability to apply it in the context. I shook my head and rolled my eyes in a show of sympathy—"Tsk-tsk." Starting to like Mr. Sogabé quite well: the first Japanese I had ever met, but we were connecting. I was an appreciative audience for his personal little theater, and he seemed to gather that. Good, how the cultural gulf between us eliminated the minutiae of communication, forcing all the expressions into clear, broad strokes.

After an increasingly congested journey, we pulled up in a winding lane, before the glass facade of a narrow building, evidently a hotel. Sogabé ushered me in and gave the man at the reception desk the details of my stay. Then he showed me to a modest room on the third floor and left me with instructions to relax for the rest of the day and meet him next morning in the lobby.

* * *

LOOKED OUT through an open window, over rusty corrugated iron rooftops of some adjacent buildings. A colony of cats of assorted genes basked in the afternoon sun, stirring occasionally to stretch or look around. Battle-scarred ginger tom with a stub for a tail looked back at me and yawned.

A deserted alley stretched out below, leading toward the hectic city jumble. Small buildings crammed together lining both sides, some sporting inert neon signs and dull red lanterns painted with thick, black Japanese characters. No garbage anywhere, but the alley was not exactly spick and span, either. Reminded me of a dusty light globe with a broken filament, such as one might find in the back of a drawer in an old shed.

From somewhere beyond drifted the buzz of traffic and, superimposed upon this murmur, the periodic whine of a high-speed train, escalating from zero to a scream, an invisible demon wind speeding through, before diminishing in seconds to a distant clatter. I heard other trains slow down to a standstill amid the squeal and hissing of brakes, suspension and sliding doors. A jangle of warning bells heralded the approach of each one.

Textured weaving of sounds of the human world, carrying through space and vibrating directly from the window frame into my fingertips. Amplified the desolation of the alley. Deaf to the symphony of life that floated on the breeze, insensitive to its pulse, blind to the sunny afternoon. Seemed not to exist, this zone that registered on the cats' retinas and mine.

Minutes later, I felt them peering down as I trespassed

through their eerie domain. Progressing through a maze of interconnected alleyways, I came to a thoroughfare with traffic and pedestrians. To my right ran a multilane highway, a pedestrian crossing and an imposing entrance to what looked like a big tree-filled city park. The street I stood in joined the highway at an angle. To my left were multiple sets of train tracks traversed by a railway crossing about fifty meters wide.

Public transport hub. Lanes from the highway fed covered stations with buses and cabs, and past the crossing was a railway station. I walked toward the park and turned a corner. Sidewalk went straight along, covered by a continuous awning. Line of homely, old-fashioned shops offered up diverse goods for leisurely walkers to peruse: clothing, shoes, cigarettes, second-hand furniture, personal seals, souvenirs and ornate wooden carvings. I spent some time looking inside the stores and poking around idly through the merchandise displayed on tables out front. Elderly shopkeeper would regard my activity casually from the gloom in the back of the store; in other places, no one bothered to make an appearance.

I turned toward the station, merging with a stream of pedestrians. The pronounced sibilant and staccato effects of their utterances combined in impossible sounding cadences. I was uplifted, even though the situation etched me out as an abnormal entity, uncomprehending yet walking as one with them. Sun shining on my face as we entered the broad railway crossing, I felt a tingle of elation—my fresh awareness of existing as a complete outsider.

Next instant an urgent clanging of bells shattered my daydream. Far across the expanse of ground in front of me, a black and yellow striped boom gate was descending, a row of red lights attached along its length flashing frantically. I realized I was among a small group of stragglers caught in a strip of empty ground separating the two central sets of tracks. I froze for a moment, flustered about whether it would be better to go forward or retreat over the tracks I had already crossed—long enough for the others to desert me and hoof it over no-man's land to safety. Not knowing which direction the train was coming from, or on which set of tracks, I bolted after them for about twenty meters, acutely aware of my mortality as I crossed the last track and ducked under the boom gate, just as two express trains sped through in opposite directions.

SAFELY ENSCONCED in my hotel room, I reflected on my narrow escape, determined to spend the evening relaxing and preparing for my interview by studying some English language teaching textbooks I'd bought at a Sydney bookshop the month before. The fact was I had scant knowledge about language teaching apart from having read these. I turned on the television, found a bottle of orange juice in the mini-bar and sat down on the edge of the bed, which was hard as a board. The variety show that came on was so bizarre that I ended up watching it all the way through, making some notes and sketches in my diary to show Isabella when I got home.

Outside, the light had dimmed. I put down my textbook and moved to the window. Nearly all the cats on the rooftops had disappeared, and those still there were alert and peering down into the alley. Occasionally an ear or the tip of a tail would twitch, a face turn upward or a head sway, mesmerized by the trace of an aroma.

The alley was undergoing a transformation with the changing light, coming to life as evening fell. Two big red paper lanterns were alight, their painted black symbols vibrantly foregrounded. Neon signs flickered on, one of which drew my eye: hoist up above an entrance door, the single word JOY shed pink and purple rays onto a white, windowless shopfront. Businessmen carrying briefcases and shoulder bags strolled in pairs and small groups, laughing and chatting, coming from the direction of the station. Shopkeepers were opening their establishments for dinner. More like stalls than restaurants, with a row of stools along a counter for customers to sit facing inside, where a cook stood grilling. Narrow curtains adorned with symbols hung from above doorways and counters.

A beguiling scene. The sky deepened to blue-black, while the street grew brighter and livelier with every passing minute, in heightening contrast. Then abruptly I returned to the pressing reality of my situation. A lot may depend on this meeting tomorrow, I said to myself, I really need to knuckle down. Sigh. I surveyed the text, lying open where I'd left it on the hard bed . . .

Five minutes later, I rounded a corner into the alley, a slim English-Japanese dictionary concealed in the front pocket of my sports coat. The word "alley" was a misnomer now—it was more of an entertainment quarter. Narrow lanes stemmed off from the main one, dimmer and with a quiet traditional bar or eating-place nestled here and there. The quaint neighborhood had a dusty, honest humility. Lurid neon signs adorned its nightspots. Apart from the one word JOY, they glowed and sparkled with Japanese text.

My surroundings metamorphosed into a social microcosm as the outside world turned dusky all around. The spring evening mingled with the neon, and the atmosphere assumed an eerie incandescence, like that of a luminous aquarium from which I was somehow semi-excluded, standing right there, but at the same time looking on from outside. Genial, tastefully clad fish floated about. The men were mostly in business suits. Some had young women in tow, also dressed for the office and tagging along as though persuaded to come for a drink after work. A pair of businessmen went to open the metal door to the JOY shop as I passed, when a woman in her mid-thirties came out, causing a minor collision with them. She wore a black dress with lace and silver trim, and had her hair piled up on her head, with long curls dangling down the sides of her face like loose springs. Her reaction was out of proportion to the incident; she squealed with laughter and half-collapsed against the men, her legs giving way in embarrassment. She apologized profusely, bowing deeply and repeatedly, giggling and covering her mouth with her hands. The three obviously knew each other well—the men responded with warm baritone utterances and bows meant to dismiss any suggestion of offense and escorted her into the establishment laughing. They noticed me amble by, and I heard the word "international" inserted in what must have been a witticism, since they laughed together in my direction; but not unkindly, so I smiled at them as they disappeared inside JOY, closing the door behind them.

I walked on to the small eateries I had observed from my room, glancing in through an open service window. A cook in an apron, a toweling headband wound tight over his brow to soak up the sweat, was at work at an iron hot plate, basting slices of sizzling meat. It took several minutes and one or two return trips past the shop for me to summon up the courage to go in, dictionary in hand, having quickly looked up and silently rehearsed some vocabulary.

The shop barely had room for two or three small tables and a refrigerator with a glass door, full of bottles. A customer sat at a corner table, an appetizing array of dainty grilled dishes spread out in front of him. He gave a start, before replying with a warm "Haro" to my clumsy *"Komban wa."* From his counter, the cook looked over his shoulder with a clipped "Hoh?!" and called out something incomprehensible but welcoming and hearty.

"Beer *kudasai* (please)," I said, my confidence boosted. The cook pointed to the refrigerator, so I took out a bottle and set it on the counter. He picked it up by the neck and whipped off the cap, plonked a five ounce glass down and filled it.

"Oh, please, please—here, here!" the other customer called to me, gesturing to the empty chair at his table when I went to take a stool by the counter. I shuffled over and squeezed in opposite him, feeling too large in the narrow confines of the shop. We introduced ourselves and raised our miniature glasses.

"Cheers," I said.

"Chiyahzu," he mimicked as he topped up my glass from his bottle.

We struck up a primitive mode of conversation, with me continually consulting my pocket dictionary, brand new in its plastic cover. At times, he conveyed points of interest to the cook, who I presumed must be the proprietor, since my drinking partner addressed him as "Master." He was serving two patrons who were sitting outside, facing in over the window counter and contributing occasional remarks in Japanese. My companion taught me the custom of always topping up your companion's glass, never your own, so as not to be considered an alcoholic who can't get enough fast enough; and he introduced me to some spicy morsels from the hotplate. We established that I was from Sydney— *Shidonii*—Australia, and this was my first day in Japan; kangaroos and koalas lived in Australia, but not in Sydney, except in the zoo; now Australia was in autumn, the opposite season to that in Japan, as it was in the southern hemisphere.

Rudimentary as the content of our talk was, the interaction itself was exhilarating and somehow liberating. I felt like an anonymous speck, immersed in this enthralling, alien place, some inconsequential corner of a city in central Japan, detached from the world that had produced, structured, tagged and cataloged my identity throughout my life. Our conversation crystallized a psychological aspect of this sense of detachment, reawakening in me a childlike, ego-less state, awed by a vast unknown. Though I have to admit that the overwhelming attraction the alleyway first held for me was tinged with apprehension, I now felt completely safe and secure, more than I would in any vaguely comparable drinking and dining district in an Australian city.

When I took out my wallet, my new friend declined my contribution, though we had consumed a substantial snack and drinks. The more I gesticulated and protested in a flurry of words that neither he nor the proprietor could understand, the more firmly they refused.

"No, no. When we visit you *Osutoraria* (Australia), *you* pay!"

We bowed and shook hands all around and I thanked them from the heart. Outside, night had fallen and the street was dark but for the glow of the neon signs. Two middle-aged businessmen halted in their stride to thrash out a point before laughing and moving by on their way to the station. I ambled to my hotel, tarrying by a night-spot to listen to the strains of amplified music and singing that wafted into the night air. Clearly karaoke, since the vocals muscled into the foreground with the grating metallic sparkle that only a directly amplified microphone can impart. Good-natured, alcohol-fueled applause ornamented appallingly off-key cadenzas. My first exposure to *enka*, the deliciously schmaltzy, fading popular genre: the music oozed nostalgia and drama, with full orchestral accompaniment and romantic, almost Spanish sounding guitar lines. As I sauntered along the lane, music spilled out from multiple clubs, fused in weird oriental treacle.

3

The Contract

Sogabé escorted me to the front steps of one of the two eight-story buildings of Central Japan Business College. In the forecourt two business-men stood bidding each other formal farewells beneath a brilliant sun, performing mutual bows, each one as deep and crisp as the other. I thrilled at the perfection of the iconic ritual, at its physical articulation, which had a precision and clarity beyond that of any imagined image. I experienced a kind of involuntary reflection, as though at a revelation . . . *This is Japan.*

The building aspired to a shiny modernity—abundant glass and stainless steel. Once inside, Sogabé introduced me to the vice-principal, Mr. Mori, who would have been in his mid-forties. He had cold, piercing eyes and slicked down black hair with a razor-sharp part on the side. I made to return his bow, but mine was clumsy and self-conscious. A part of my psyche seemed to rebel and press back against my forehead, permitting me no more than a sheepish downward twist of my upper body. I saw no students anywhere, but some administrative staff were busy in an office area near the front entrance.

"You should remove your shoes and put them in one of these shelves," Sogabé said. "Take a pair of slippers to wear—if you can find any big enough." He chuckled.

The biggest plastic scuffs I could find were indeed on the small side, but I could get the front of my feet in, with the heels hanging over the back. The two men showed me around the building, with Sogabé doing most of the talking. Mori's English was minimal, so Sogabé interpreted his occasional comments about the college.

The foyer sported low couches, gleaming metal columns and a marble-look floor. Attached to the walls were video screens, a map of the world and a row of clocks displaying the time in various world capitals. Sogabé shepherded me into a bathroom to demonstrate how the lights turned themselves on and off automatically when one entered and left; the taps too worked by motion sensor. Such technology, so commonplace today, was new in the early 90s and contributed to my perception of the place as an "intelligent building." So did the split video screens in the office area that showed what was going on in other parts of the building.

Video surveillance was uncommon in those days, not that I had any experience in the sort of workplace that would have used it, so I was more impressed with the technology itself than concerned about the implications for employment relations and privacy. Sogabé and Mori showed me a language laboratory, which I was able to appraise with a knowledgeable air, thanks to my new textbooks. Then we went up by elevator to examine classrooms in one or two of the eight floors. The roof boasted a diminutive golf driving range of its own, with green netting to catch the golf balls. Months later I would learn that this facility was never used except as a selling-point in public relations brochures.

Across the street was a ten or so story building that housed a department of electrical engineering and an administrative center. As Sogabé and I approached, we passed a life-sized bronze statue of a benevolent looking gentleman.

"This is the president of our academy, Mr. Harada," Sogabé informed me casually. Shuffling along in our scuffs, we toured the lower floors. In a teaching laboratory, electronic components cluttered the benches, surrounding some mechanical assemblages of various shapes and sizes up to a couple of feet high.

"Our students designed these robots for a national competition," he said. "They are supposed to get them to play soccer or something." He tilted one over and let it go, so that it wobbled and righted itself. He glanced at me with something between a smile and a smirk.

"That's remarkable," I said, playing it safe.

"Hmm. I don't think they can play soccer very well yet." One orange and silver, three-wheeled robot had a heavily taped antenna. Sogabé felt obliged to investigate and in the process accidentally half-dropped the robot, causing the antenna to hang down limp. "Oops," he said, now with a big embarrassed grin. "Well, they have to learn to fix things like that."

We entered an elegant, dimly lit reception lounge, where he beckoned me to occupy an extremely low, luxuriously upholstered armchair, one of several placed around some long low tables.

"I will be back shortly," he said and left the room.

The furnishings combined class and formality with a premium on comfort. Sinking into the chair, I felt divested of any bodily or social stiffness—a feeling enhanced by the pleasant sensations my feet were experiencing. Freed from their leathery armor, they breathed and cooed to themselves delightedly as I wiggled my toes. I noticed another bronze depicting Harada, a larger than life-sized bust set on a plinth. While I was admiring it, two men carrying briefcases came in and sat down at a table in a far corner. Paying me no heed, they lit up cigarettes and chatted, flicking their ash into a heavy glass ashtray.

Sogabé returned and saw me up a flight of stairs and into a meeting room, where a man sat waiting. Just as we entered, Mr. Harada arrived in the flesh through a different door, accompanied by two more men. Sogabé introduced me to Harada and his two male secretaries who followed him in, one about sixty and the other in his mid-thirties. The other man, Iwasaki, who stood up when the others entered, was, like Sogabé, an instructor and middle ranking executive. Sogabé directed me to take a seat opposite Harada. The others distributed themselves around the three sides of the table facing me. Harada handed me his business card. A stocky man in his fifties, he presented a grand and commanding figure, an effect that the deference his subjects extended served to magnify.

"How do you do? I'm very happy to meet you," he mumbled in a gravelly voice, delivering the rehearsed expression shyly and smiling as he took my hand in a limp handshake—he didn't seem very used to the custom.

"Thank you very much for your hospitality and for flying me over from Australia," I said.

Harada spoke, and when he finished, Sogabé translated.

"When you return to your country, please give his personal regards to Professor Reynolds." Our mutual acquaintance was the director of an English language school at University of Wollongong, an Australian regional university where I studied as an undergraduate and worked as a sessional lecturer. Groups of students from Harada's academy attended intensive English courses there. Reynolds's recommendation was to thank for Harada having me to this interview.

A young woman came in carrying a tray and served us tea. Harada drew out a silver cigarette case from an inside pocket of his double-breasted suit, and by the time he had it open and placed a cigarette in his mouth, three lighters had been shoved at his face. He allowed himself a moment to select the most prominent one and inclined his cigarette to its flame, seeming to make a mental note of the subordinate he had favored. You got the feeling you would not want to be too slow with your lighter too often . . .

Sogabé translated his boss's questions to me.

"If we select you as an instructor, how will you go about teaching our students English conversation?"

Prior to a fortnight ago, I wouldn't have had the foggiest idea how to answer, but by now I had read enough to gain a basic idea of the theory and practice of teaching English as a foreign language. Moreover, I had taken an opportunity to sit in on a class at Professor Reynolds's college, where in addition to receiving a valuable EFL classroom experience—my only one to date—I was warned that I would never manage in Japan without formal teacher training.

"Well," I said to my prospective employers, "I have to say I'm more used to teaching in the traditional university style of lectures and tutorials. For language teaching, though, the teacher needs to engage individually with students in the classroom. I would first introduce a particular idea to them as a group, conduct exercises based on that idea, and then revise the material to debrief and suggest corrections."

"So you would move about the classroom and interact with the students?" Sogabé asked.

"Yes, I would use a student-centered approach—for example, first stand in front of the class to demonstrate an idea and lead a class discussion, then move around among them to facilitate the exercises," I said, as Sogabé translated for Harada.

"What sort of exercises?"

"Divide the class up into pairs and groups, giving everyone a chance to practice simultaneously. Apply what are known as information gap exercises, in which students need to communicate in order to solve a particular problem together."

"Japanese students are very shy about speaking up in class," said Sogabé and laughed sarcastically. "You know, some of them never say *anything*. So how are you going to get them to speak English?"

"Try to be sensitive and approachable. It is important to provide students with material that engages their interest. And I wouldn't correct or criticize them when they were trying to speak—"

"So you wouldn't correct their grammar?" Sogabé looked dubious, with the corners of his mouth turned down.

"Well, some teachers who use the communicative style do advise not to correct grammar at all, because they believe it inhibits the student from speaking. But I do consider it essential to teach your students good grammar, both so they can make themselves understood clearly and as a tool that can continue to help them increase their proficiency. I would make a note of errors and review and correct them after each exercise."

As I was to discover over subsequent years, foreign teachers in Japan apply the so-called "communicative approach" almost exclusively, with the object of activating the passive command of English that students acquire from studying under the "grammar-translation method" throughout their school years. Japanese teachers tend to use this "traditional" method, involving drills and rote learning. Student textbooks published by foreign presses such as Cambridge, Oxford and Macmillan promote the communicative methodology with foreign teachers in mind—naturally enough, since they only need to know their own language to implement it. Domestic texts often gloss English passages with translations. Western texts reflect higher production values, which their Japanese rivals try to imitate, but poorly, since they lack the resources of Western publishers, for whom the teaching of English abroad is a global industry. Just as importantly, domestic publications simply do not "own" the linguistic and cultural schema they purport to impart. The authenticity of Western texts makes them desirable, the same quality that makes the Western teacher a sought-after commodity. In time, I became aware of a certain ideological dimension of English language education, which governs the flow and dissemination of the language according to economies and discourses favorable to it, gathering up the expatriate teachers, educational rationales, methods and materials in its own particular cycle of production, to its own ends. My textbooks initiated me into this system, supplying me with enough key concepts and buzzwords to make me appear quite knowledgeable.

After a short while, Harada drew a breath, turned and said something to Sogabé.

"He wants to offer you the job," Sogabé said. "If you'd like to accept it, we can sign the contract now."

"Yes indeed, I'd absolutely like to," I said, making no effort to conceal my pleasure. Harada's younger secretary placed two identical documents on the table, several pages in a booklet format, printed in Japanese and English. I leafed through my copy.

"The contract is for two years," Sogabé said, indicating the relevant section. "It can be renewed for another two years after that." He pointed out the proposed salary and I agreed to it at once. Much more than I ever earned, it dwarfed the pittance I'd been gleaning from freelance writing and part-time university work since graduating from Sydney University with my arts doctorate. "We will pay for your airline ticket to come to Japan, but you yourself will have to pay when you return to your country after the contract ends," he went on, as we looked over the details. "The job is from eight until four weekdays, and three Saturday mornings per month you will have to work from eight until twelve o'clock."

Harada, Sogabé and one of the secretaries exchanged a few words.

"You will be free on Saturday mornings," Sogabé said to me. "There is no time right now, so they will change that part of the contract later."

"This is all fine," I said and signed the documents. Harada firmly pressed his personal seal onto them, making impressions in red ink.

And that was that. A job in Japan.

The negotiation finished, the whole group walked to a nearby restaurant for a celebratory meal. The menus were startling: photograph albums of raw meat. Sogabé said the restaurant specialized in *shabu shabu*, a dish named for the bubbling and swishing sounds made in the do-it-yourself cooking method. Our table incorporated a gas stove for heating up a big communal pot. The idea was to use your chopsticks to drop thin slices of raw marbled beef into a simmering broth, along with various other morsels: vegetables, spring onions, tofu and delicious, long, thin mushrooms. You allowed your slice of meat only seconds to cook, before retrieving and dipping it in a sauce — either sesame or citrus-flavored. When the meat was gone, you cooked up some thick, chewy *udon* noodles in the enriched broth. Following Harada's lead, everybody loosened up. They slurped up their meat and noodles, and laughed and talked while I ate, drank and enjoyed the spectacle. Occasionally Harada would direct a remark to me, which Sogabé interpreted.

"You are good at using chopsticks."

Harada made a comment in his guttural voice, along with which the company laughed uproariously as one.

"He says you should try to learn some Japanese before you move to Japan. Mr. Iwasaki will accompany you to the bookstore tomorrow to find a book you can study while you wait to come back," Sogabé said.

NEXT MORNING, Iwasaki checked me out of the hotel and we toured another of Harada's institutions, the College of Law and Administration, before heading into central Nagoya. A dazzling sky, periods of sparkling sunlight moistened by light spring showers. We drove through the local government district with its stately architecture—a 1930s fusion of traditional Japanese and Western styles. He parked his car near the classic Nagoya Castle; a white five-story edifice bedecked with a cluster of blue-green roofs, it sat imperiously above subtly curved, sloping stone foundation walls, surrounded by pine trees.

On the topmost roof-ridge were perched a pair of golden figures, facing each other like bookends.

"They are famous statues called *shachi* . . . ten feet tall," Iwasaki said. "The shachi is like a dolphin. But not real, only myth."

Cherry blossoms in bloom, their pink-tinged white petals shimmering—delightful touch to the cityscape. Spring showers fell intermittently, and downtown Nagoya looked like a movie set. Taxicabs picked up and deposited well-heeled clientele, smartly dressed black-haired men and women. The drivers wore peaked caps and white gloves. Their vehicles were immaculate, conservatively styled sedans with sumptuous upholstery and spotless enamel. Tires hissed along the damp streets as they pulled out into the traffic. Iwasaki took me to a multistory bookshop called Maruzen and selected a bulky introductory textbook on conversational Japanese, full of indecipherable characters. Then he proposed an early lunch so we could make it to the airport in plenty of time for my flight home. We took the elevator up to a swank Chinese restaurant on the top floor of a luxury hotel. The atmosphere was quite hushed, few patrons having arrived as yet. Iwasaki was a quiet, serious, somewhat paunchy individual who relished his food as much as I did. So we lunched, occasionally commenting appreciatively on the Cantonese dishes served to us by a young waitress and bow-tied waiter, impeccably clad in black and white.

During a lull in our conversation, the sun came out from behind clouds, flooding the expansive, faint-tinted glass windows across the room with light. Outside, a void, high above the city streets. From where I sat, I could see nothing but the translucent blue-gray of the sky, which, through the misty glass, gave the illusion it surrounded our luxurious zone, as though we were suspended at the center of a crystal sphere. I truly relaxed for the first time since landing, reflecting on the momentous change that had occurred in my life during the course of this day and wondering what the future would bring. Leaning back in my chair, I closed my eyes, pausing to listen to the subdued murmur of a Japanese conversation, until a clink of fine china caused me to open them again.

4

Early Days

My apartment was directly across the road from the main gates of the Atsuta Shrine, what I had thought was a wooded city park, near where I encountered the speeding trains on my earlier visit. This is the second most important Shinto shrine in Japan next to the Isé Shrine, where the sun goddess Amaterasu Omikami, legendary ancestor of the imperial family, is enshrined—that is, housed as an immortal entity with a living, spiritual presence. Atsuta Shrine has attracted throngs of worshipers ever since ancient times. It is due to its presence in Nagoya that the city, now with a population of approximately two million, flourished as a medieval town. Each year, nine million people visit the shrine, a million and a half of them during the New Year, when everyone makes it their business to pay a call on the kami.

The district where I lived was Jingumae, meaning "in front of the shrine." My place was on the fourth floor of a six-story building called Jingumae Corpo, which accommodated small businesses and shops as well as apartments. Harada owned my apartment and perhaps the entire building. His administrators arranged to deduct rent for the apartment automatically from my salary. The arrangement turned out to be a great boon, because for foreigners to find and rent an apartment for themselves was an involved process, definitely beyond the capacities of an absolute novice such as me. A handy head start for life in Japan: a job, an apartment, and in my patron, the wealthy Mr. Harada, a formidable guarantor for a two year work visa as a college instructor.

A beauty parlor and a dental surgery occupied the same level as my apartment, and occasionally a customer or patient would pass by me as I made my way up or down the flights of cement stairs that connected the external landings. The walls of Jingumae Corpo were rough and speckled, coated with a cement-like substance sprayed on about thirty years prior, when the building went up. This rough coating couldn't have been better designed to trap the dust and grime, and I avoided touching the dirty surfaces, for they left a greasy sensation on the skin. The old building swayed and creaked disconcertingly during an earth tremor—sure to disintegrate the instant a decent earthquake struck.

The apartment was a 2DK—two rooms plus a combined dining-kitchen area—in Japan, a lavish amount of space for a single individual. Dank and grubby, with a small lavatory and a bathroom containing a stainless steel bathtub just big enough to hold me, sitting in an upright fetal position with the water up to my chest. The bathroom was the shabbiest room of all, deep cracks in its concrete floor ideal for cockroaches and betraying doubtful structural integrity. Two tatami rooms overlooked the rooftops of neighboring buildings. Sliding glass doors opened onto a balcony, at one end of which stood a decrepit washing machine. A drainage system took the water down off the balcony. I did my washing here and hung it out to dry, like millions of other apartment dwellers. Like them, I draped my futon over the balcony railing for beating and airing, fastening it with giant plastic pegs.

The steel door onto the landing had a chain and peephole and a slot for mail. From the landing, I could just see the tops of the trains as they arrived and departed from Jingumae Station. Like all Japanese homes, the apartment had a *genkan*, a small area immediately inside the doorway, where you left your shoes before stepping up into the apartment proper, a custom that is not solely for domestic cleanliness but demonstrates a spiritual regard for the interior of the home.

Harada's younger secretary moved me in and arranged for me to rent a futon so I would have one right away. That evening, lying supine on my futon I breathed in the wholesome, straw-like smell of the tatami. I reached out my arm and traced the tight weave with my finger—smooth as silk to the touch. Loved these mats. Six of them covered my bedroom floor, placed tightly together in an overlapping pattern. The long edges were trimmed with rich green brocade, making the whole arrangement quite beautiful. The firm tatami was far more comfortable to lie on than a mattress.

Each brand new experience was like a further degree of immersion. My head resting on a small, firm pillow stuffed with rice-chaff, I looked up at the halo-shaped fluorescent light hanging from the ceiling, with its square plastic light-shade and dangling cord. I switched on my pocket radio and listened to the Japanese voices and syrupy pop music, then turned over on my side to admire the Japaneseness of the *oshiire* built-in closets, their sliding doors made from thick paper wrapped taut around light wooden frames. A horizontal olive stripe segmented the doors a little lower than halfway. Sounds of traffic filtered in from the street below. My life felt severed. Removed from familiar contexts and expectations, I was plunged into a fresh new beginning, apprehensive but exhilarated, embarked on an adventure.

Before long my coffers were running low. For some weeks, I subsisted mainly on dehydrated noodles, of which an impressive variety was available at the supermarket, and bought a carton of milk daily. I had brought a single suitcase packed with clothes, along with a plate, knife, fork and spoon, one frying pan and a small saucepan that I now used to heat water for noodles and coffee. My kitchen had a small bench-top gas stove but no other furniture or appliances. When I ran out of money to buy food, I had to ask for an advance on my monthly salary. Harada's older secretary, Mr. Takagi, happened to be the one I approached.

"I am very sorry," he said, "it is not possible to pay you an advance. But I will make you a personal loan if you would accept it." He lent me a sum of about two hundred dollars, for which I signed an IOU; and he returned that to me when I repaid him on receiving my initial salary payment. If he was surprised I was so destitute, he gave no sign of it.

One day I called in to the Meitetsu Depato, an upscale department store near Jingumae Station, close to my apartment. Going up on the escalator, I almost spun out, overwhelmed by the sea of oriental faces that engulfed me. I went to browse for some household items I needed—a soup bowl and a spatula—aiming to diversify my diet away from dehydrated noodles. The cheapest bowl I could find was a red plastic one decorated with a motif of gold cranes, selling for an exorbitant fifteen dollars. Shaky though my finances were, I decided I might as well take it, because for all I knew, that might be the going rate for plastic bowls, and I'd had enough of an excursion for one day. I picked up a spatula with a black coating that resembled teflon. Still, in case it was only for preparing salad, I thought I'd better check with the sales assistant. I pointed at the flat end.

"Not plastic?" I asked.

"*Purasutiku?*" The woman appeared puzzled and guarded.

"Not plastic? Need for cooking," I said, making dumb show gestures and handing her the spatula.

She shook her head alarmingly and made a negative sounding utterance:

"*Ie, ie, ie!* No *purasutiku—tefuron desu.*"

"Ah, teflon?"

"*Hai, tefuron desu,*" she affirmed vigorously, tapping the spatula with her fingernails.

When I arrived home, I tried to remove the price label from the fifteen dollar red bowl by giving it a scrub under the faucet—horrifying to see the red paint come off, leaving a two inch square patch of black. I went to fry up an egg for lunch with the assistance of the spatula, which melted the moment it touched the frying pan. Rather than take on the probably futile challenge of trying to return it to the store, I tossed it into the trash bin in dismay.

* * *

Often I escaped to the Atsuta Shrine. Set in the solemn, sacred Atsuta Forest, its precincts occupied fifty acres. There were trees a thousand years old and a famous giant camphor thirteen hundred years. Gardeners tended all the trees with exceptional care, bandaging damaged or weakened branches and supporting them with timber struts.

Thick straw rope called *shimenawa* encircled venerable trees that hosted deities, denoting their sacredness; *oshide*, paper strips folded into lightning bolts, purified them. Indigenous to Japan, Shinto is an animistic religion, grounded in the belief that individual kami inhabit natural objects and phenomena. Nature is sacred: kami exist within natural elements, animals and some human beings. Shinto shrines are dedicated to the worship of particular kami, whose spirits reside there within sacred objects, which are kept in a place only ever entered by priests on special religious occasions. The sacred objects may be natural, such as branches or stones, or fabricated, such as bells, dishes, mirrors or swords.

On weekends I wandered the grounds; tucked away among lesser shrines were leafy walks among the trees. I would amble in an ancient grove, enveloped in the silence and the solitary feeling of being at one with nature, seeking solace from the subtle sense of alienation I began to notice due to being a *gaijin* — literally an "outside person": a non-Japanese.

By watching the other visitors, I learned to perform the simple Shinto rites of shrine worship. Using a bamboo ladle placed there for the purpose, I rinsed my hands with water in a symbolic act of purification at the *temizuya*—a roofed font—making sure that no water spilled back into the trough but drained away onto the ground. It came to feel natural to bow before the sanctuary housing the sacred objects. To attract the attention of the deity in a shrine, I clapped my hands twice or rang a hanging gong. I assumed the correct posture for prayer, with head bowed and palms together, then bowed deeply.

Meditating like this had a profoundly peaceful effect. Standing erect with my eyes closed and head bowed in the position of prayer, I opened myself to the natural phenomena around me: the cool sensation of the breeze upon my face and arms, the thin chirp of a cricket, the footsteps and quiet babble of other people moving through the shrine. The rite centered me, drew me into the stillness of the moment, into a state of mind that lay beneath my wavering sense of identity in the world outside. I felt I understood the symbolic power of the massive timber *torii* gate I passed through on my approach to the shrine, the power to mark the entrance to the sacred space and separate the womblike, inner spiritual world from the exterior physical one. The shrine preserved and hallowed nature; pivoting on the finite and the infinite, the torii sealed this peaceful domain from the crush and turmoil of the city.

An evocative landscape, the woods stimulated the spirit and imagination—thereby hosting, one might say, a more rarefied sense of reality. It was in such terms that I developed a fondness and respect for the deities of Atsuta. I imagined that I communed with them during my meditations there, but in the sense that the imagination informed the sphere of their existence, their potency. I experienced a sense of belonging, felt thankful for their welcome and their benevolence, so I expressed these feelings in an individualistic form of prayer. You might think me self-deluded, but it was my sincere act of trying to objectify the "spirit" of Japan, with which I felt I needed to establish a relationship.

Conspicuous nationalist symbolism, shades of "state Shinto": resplendent flags bearing the *hinomaru*, the red sun disk on a white field, flapped majestically on high before the entrance of the shrine and above the gracefully curved rooftops of the museum building housed in the grounds. An awe-inspiring sight.

ALONG WITH the other major religion, Buddhism, Shinto is an intrinsic part of everyday life. Most people worship at shrines and take part in activities associated with the Shinto festivals and holidays that regulate the year. Shinto mythology and ceremony inform the significance of the imperial institution. After the Second World War, the perceived divine role of the emperor was transformed into a symbolic one (according to Article 1 of the post-war constitution, to be "the symbol of the state and of the unity of the people"), but that symbolism, derived from ancient folk myths, is very powerful.

The imperial family is the oldest hereditary monarchy in the world, older than the recorded history of Japan; in early literature, its origins meld with folk traditions and creation myths. The earliest extant historical chronicle of Japan is a text called the *Kojiki* (Record of Ancient Matters), compiled in the year 712. The *Kojiki* was devoted to the period from the mythical age of the gods up until the seventh century. The work served to empower the ruling elite of its day, by chronicling a hereditary line that connected the legendary emperors with those who existed in history. Thus historical emperors could claim a divine status.

According to the *Kojiki*, the chief deity, the sun goddess Amaterasu Omikami, sent her grandson Ninigi no Mikoto from heaven, to conquer and rule the islands of Japan. Amaterasu gave Ninigi three sacred objects as symbols of authority: a mirror, a curved jewel and a sword, which he passed on to his descendants. Ninigi's own grandson, Jimmu, became the legendary original emperor, Jimmu-tenno. The three objects, known as the imperial regalia, were handed down from one emperor to the next until the ninth century, when the mirror and sword were enshrined at the Isé and Atsuta shrines and replicas made for the emperor to keep in his personal possession. Since then, the original curved jewel and the replica of the sword have passed to each new emperor as part of the rites of accession to the throne; the most recent ceremony was in 1989, when the present emperor, Akihito, took possession of the regalia after the death of his father, the Showa emperor, Hirohito.

Physical objects with a divine origin, the imperial regalia symbolize and attest to the divine bloodline of emperors. During the war, of course, the militarists applied the mass acceptance of these beliefs to fanatical ends, with catastrophic results. At the end of the war, the emperor Hirohito explicitly renounced his divinity. "The ties between us and our people," he wrote in a New Year's announcement to the nation in 1946, "have always stood upon mutual trust and affection. They do not depend upon mere legends and myths. They are not predicated on the false conception that the Emperor is divine and that the Japanese people are superior to other races and fated to rule the world."

The sword is kept at the Atsuta Shrine away from public view. Its name, Kusanagi no Tsurugi, or "grass cutting sword," comes from another intriguing legend recorded in the *Kojiki*. Carrying the sacred sword for protection, the legendary hero Prince Yamatotakeru, son of the twelfth (legendary) emperor, Keiko, undertook a mission to subjugate the Kumaso, a rebellious tribe from southern Kyushu. Bandits attacked him, trapping him in a grassfire, but he saved himself by using the sword to mow down an area of grass around him and setting another fire to chase them away. Legend has it that Yamatotakeru's consort founded Atsuta Shrine after his death nineteen hundred years ago, for the purpose of enshrining the Kusanagi sword. The name Atsuta means "burning field," in reference to the hero's adventure.

ON WEEKDAYS I awoke to the sound of early morning trains, which sent their shrieks and clatters echoing through the empty streets outside. As I got myself up and ready for work, they sped by with increasing frequency, transporting commuters to the city center. Most paused at Jingumae Station to disgorge crowds of workers and students, whom I would hear pass through the lane behind my building minutes later, many on their way to the college. I dressed, straightened my tie, made sure I had my company badge pinned on my lapel (a strict college rule), and went downstairs to join the ranks of high school and college students advancing purposefully along the wide sidewalk. Students on bicycles wove through the procession. Shouldering a soft leather briefcase on a strap, I walked alone and silent amid the conversation and laughter. High school boys wore black military-style uniforms with a standing collar and metal buttons down the front of their jackets. A few managed to express a rebellious side, growing shaggy hair, wearing sneakers and leaving their shirttails hanging out. The most common uniform for girls was in navy-blue and modeled on a sailor's suit, with a sailor's collar trimmed with three white stripes and a ribbon tied in front, a pleated skirt, long blue or white socks and polished black shoes. Other girls were from a school that had dispensed with the sailor outfit in favor of a tartan skirt, white blouse and maroon or gray blazer.

Some wore what were known as "loose socks," coordinated with a shorter than regulation skirt. Loose socks resembled leg warmers and were bulkier and roomier than the officially ordained knee-high socks, bunching up and sagging over the heel and foot. They stayed aloft to just beneath the knee, often, apparently, stuck to the skin with special "sock glue." I heard that the loose-socks girls' fashion sense was an expression of precocious sexuality. More conservative schools frowned on the garments and banned them during school hours; but their girls would pull them on before and after school hours.

It soon became clear that a certain cut of high school girl was not as innocent as she looked. The schoolgirl was a notorious fetish — to a pornographic degree in numerous *manga* comic books for sale in ordinary 7-Eleven and Circle K convenience stores. High school girls could make substantial disposable incomes and were a driving force in popular culture, determining trends in lucrative areas such as fashion and music. Some were shamelessly acquisitive, and even hired themselves out at night as dates for wayward salarymen. In 1993 three businessmen were arrested for stocking Tokyo vending machines with used underpants, advertised as previously worn by schoolgirls. This spoke significantly, too, about the infantilism of a sector of the male population. Commentators lamented a tendency in contemporary society for males to become increasingly weak and ineffectual and females domineering. They blamed the work culture as a possible cause: many young males supposedly lacked a strong role model because they saw their father for no longer than a few minutes each weeknight when he staggered into the house drunk. Mother was typically the more dominant figure, the one who managed the household and controlled the purse strings.

AFTER THE working day, I wearily retraced my footsteps. A pleasant enough walk, and as I neared home, the aromas drifting from nearby restaurants made my mouth water. Always something to please the senses, if merely the sight of a woman in a beautiful kimono leaving the shrine. One evening, the spectacle of a gigantic sumo wrestler, his long black hair tied up and wearing a blue and white *yukata*, a casual summer kimono, bearing down upon me on his bicycle, froze me to the spot. Then, without notice, he veered off onto the street, unmindful of the cars, which maneuvered to give him maximum leeway. July had arrived, the month of the annual Nagoya *basho* — fitting sounding term for a sumo tournament. A group of wrestlers trained in a ring down the street from the shrine, in sessions open to the public. The hulking men performed their drills, slapping their bare skinned bulk into each other and practicing their falls in the clay ring.

At the foot of my building were a liquor store, a restaurant and a vending machine containing cans of tea, coffee, soft drink and beer. I recall my shock of disappointment when, coming home on a hot day, I first bought a drink from this machine. The Dydo brand can with a cherry motif promised "A gallon of deliciousness in every drop!" making my taste buds quiver in anticipation, before dousing them in unsweetened cold tea. Subsequently I found that downing some chilled tea was a good way to rehydrate after an outing to the shrine or the city on a summer's day. After work, however, I would pick up a can of Kirin or Sapporo beer from the vending machine, or for a lift, Jolt brand cola, advertised as having "Twice the caffeine!"

By now I had a few funds with which to equip my apartment. After learning to negotiate the subway system with its Japanese signs and symbols, I took a trip to the commercial suburb of Sakae and purchased a small black refrigerator, which the store delivered. Then one day, strolling past a row of festival stalls that had been erected in the shrine precincts, I came across a Lilliputian foldable wooden chair for sale, bought and took it home. Farther afield, on an exploratory subway excursion, I acquired a lightweight coffee table with folding legs and lugged it home under my arm. I was beginning to feel easier in my new lifestyle, one so congruous with my simple tastes. I was content in my sparse tatami rooms with the bare essentials, and the process of building up my life from zero in a country so different from my own was very satisfying. Although I had no long term plan to live in Japan—no idea in particular about what to do with my future at all—the longer I was here, the more agreeable grew the customs and the more fulfilling the everyday challenges. I merged increasingly with the flow of life. Even my body language and patterns of thought were beginning to change; and I reacted smugly to the occasional sight of foreign tourists, who stood out conspicuously as they made their ungainly progress along the street or through the subway. I had lived here now for some months, and some foreigners I met—seasoned expats of three or four years—dazzled me with their acquired savoir-faire. Turning Japanese might be an impossible and not necessarily desirable end, but as you adapted and progressed in your initiation into the culture, you accumulated a unique store of social and linguistic expertise through which you were able to form your own niche and foothold.

At night I dedicated myself to the task of learning a new language. Sitting on the tatami, I propped my back against the wall and ticked off exercises in Japanese one by one as I worked through them aloud. The complex writing system was an enduring challenge: two sets of forty-eight phonetic symbols, called the *kana* syllabaries, in addition to more than two thousand Chinese characters, the *kanji*, officially approved for general use. Japanese is at a far remove from the Indo-European family of languages, including English and our traditional second language staples such as French, German, Italian and Spanish. Heavy work, but I reasoned that no language would be more difficult than it needed to be. After I got over the initial hurdles my study became a pleasure, and I came to enjoy practicing the economical grammar and staccato cadences.

Gradually I grew attuned to the foreign world outside my apartment. Solitary life is often held to promote personal growth—perhaps on the model of the religious recluse—but it can be a tough process. Isabella and I had been together for ten years before I came to Japan, but the time and distance of separation, plus the uncertainty of which way the future was going to lead, caused me to wonder about the possibility of sustaining the long-distance relationship. Isabella was a sophisticated and extroverted Russian, who emigrated to Australia via Europe with her parents as a child. Surviving Hitler's invasion of Russia, they were among the second shipload of displaced persons (DPs), attractive, blue eyed, blonde, "assimilable" families, brought to Australia in 1948 to promote a post-war policy of immigration to a chary public. Isabella built a successful career as a physiotherapist and, in her previous marriage, lived abroad and traveled Europe. She had European tastes and I could not imagine her taking to the idiosyncrasies of the Japanese way of life, let alone to my rickety framework within it. We corresponded fervently, but to the extent that I adjusted to Japan, I became detached from my memories of her and the time we shared. I fell into doubt, dwelt on perceived and imagined flaws.

5

Obento Lunchbox

A t my desk in the communal office for instructors, ground floor of Building 1, eating lunch and reading an obituary in the *Japan Times*. Crestfallen that one of my favorite authors, the avant-garde novelist and theater director Abé Kobo, had died.

Lunch was a tasty *obento* — a traditional box lunch — and a bottle of chilled green tea. A neighborhood shop prepared and delivered them to us on a group order. Today the meal consisted of boiled rice sprinkled with poppy seeds, and various side dishes, which were kept separate in individual compartments molded into the plastic box: a small portion of fried tuna; a prawn; a frankfurter; a single meatball with gravy, seated invitingly in a pleated cupcake paper all its own; a slice of yellow pickled daikon radish; boiled bamboo shoot; a baby carrot and teaspoon sized dollop of mashed potato; a slice of orange; and a miniature fish-shaped plastic bottle of soy sauce. Because of the time taken to transport the meal, it was lukewarm when you opened it, but that didn't detract from the taste much. The combination of flavors and the appearance of the food demonstrated an evolved understanding of culinary aesthetics. Obento were a communal pleasure. Each day, their arrival aroused an expectant hum as we removed their paper covers to reveal the dish of the day—always fairly much on the same theme but with enough variety to keep us interested. We would ease off the elastic band that held on the lid and kept the wooden *hashi* in place. I rolled the band over my hand onto my wrist, where it stayed until I'd finished. The atmosphere lightened as the lids came off the plastic boxes, the aroma wafted through the office, and everyone turned their attention to the contents. Sharing our obento induced in us workers a regenerated, even festive, frame of mind.

My workspace was one of nine identical gray metal desks pushed together into a long rectangular worktable, four on each side, with one joined crosswise at the end, where our *kacho* (deputy section chief) sat like the father at the head of a family table, in a position to supervise our activities. His name was Fujita-sensei: it was a college rule to use the more polite honorific suffix of -*sensei* rather than -*san* among the teachers, a mark of the strict regime that governed operations. (The "diminutive suffix," -*chan*, is for informal, intimate use; at the other end of the scale is the extremely polite -*sama*.) Ours was a type of higher education facility known as a *senmon gakko*, a professional or vocational college. Most of our students had failed to enter university and thus wound up here; the mission of the college was to develop them for careers in business—a goal it did not try to achieve by mollycoddling them.

Fujita-sensei was a serious and sober individual and

a practicing Christian. His round face and broad forehead were a little prone to perspire, and he wore
studious, dark rimmed glasses. To my right, next in line
toward the head of the table, and thus one degree more
important than me, was Saza-sensei, a gaunt, fidgety individual whose innately dismal worldview he had
exacerbated with some terrible recent financial invest-
ments, on account of which his family home now
appeared lost. Along from him, Onoé-sensei, short and
thickset, with his shock of thick black hair, forever laughing, loved nothing more in life than eating; and this he
was doing now, digging in voraciously. Facing us across
the table, sitting by Fujita, sat Yanagi-sensei, wiry, ath-
letically built, and a good marathon runner in his high
school years. Frank and forthright. When I had happened to mention I was one-eighth Chinese, he made
a surprised face.

"Really?" he said. "To me you look just like a typical
Anglo-Saxon." How could you take offense?

Outgoing and intelligent though he was, Yanagi-
sensei would sometimes brood, and he was the heaviest
drinker among us.

Beside him sat Amachi-sensei, a pampered individual
endowed with a worldly and cynical wit. Opposite me
Ikari-sensei, in his late twenties younger than the rest
of us, at various stages in our thirties. Tall and good-
looking, quiet and aloof, he had an unusual, tentative
way of performing physical actions, seeming to test the
environment around him with invisible antennae.

We in the English Department shared this office with
the Travel and Secretarial Departments, both deployed
around worktables like ours. Next to us was the secretarial table, occupied by women in their twenties. Next

around the room, the Travel Department's table was home to a group of men our age and older. Each of these groups of tables, along with a further empty one for miscellaneous use, occupied a little less than a quarter of the office. At the head of the rectangle they formed was a big metal desk where Watanabe-sensei sat monitoring affairs: the *bucho* (division-chief), a graying, strongly built, big voiced man in his fifties. He wore a habitual scowl that he could switch off when the occasion demanded and assume a gregarious, backslapping personality; in both guises, he possessed a domineering physical presence. An ex-naval officer, as was the principal, Ikeda Hideo, a short, white-haired man. They governed with a strong hand and a regime calculated to mold the sometimes reluctant students into responsible businesspeople.

Onoé and Amachi bantered over their obento. Amachi was scolding Onoé, when he noticed me watching.

"Onoé-sensei eats too fast, which is why he so often suffers from indigestion."

"And Amachi-sensei suffers every day from his hangover," Onoé riposted, articulating his words through a mouthful of rice.

Fujita-kacho smiled over at them benignly. A good-hearted person, though he felt the need to preserve a distance between him and his subordinates. Saza, who had no time for social niceties at the best of times, shook his head in disgust. Apart from Fujita and him, the others often joked and teased each other with comments that could be close to the bone; but none ever took offense, even when the spotlight happened to fall on one unappealing quirk or another. Sometimes they touched on more of a personal note than would be usual among a Western group of colleagues: once, the others laughed about there being a hole in the wall of Yanagi's apartment, which he had punched in during a solo binge. Westerners tended to keep such details to themselves in my experience, whereas my Japanese colleagues bantered about them carelessly. Of course, Westerners did "take the piss" as well, but here the custom differed in essence. My colleagues were not the slightest bit aggressive in their observations, but somehow affectionate. The channels of communication between the individual and their clique seemed to work quite palpably to provide and foster forms of intimacy and trust that were conducive to a culture of "groupism."

Deru kugi wa utareru, as the saying goes: "The nail that sticks up is hammered down." Our need to communicate publicly in English for my benefit bestowed a modicum of prestige upon my close workmates and enclosed us in a bubble of privacy. We presented a pocket of resistance against a force field that *should* have penetrated all relationships in the organization, subordinating them to the common purpose. We criticized—to each other—the hardline philosophy and tactics of our institution, many repressive and some plain stupid; but although the literal sense of our satirical comments in English went uncomprehended, over time the management formed a general picture of our attitudes and would apply discomfiting stares and coercive pressures as often as they could.

"We had better move away from that surveillance camera," Amachi said nervously one day when he and I had taken refuge in a storeroom and were idly exchanging seditious talk. "I don't want Watanabe-sensei to see me."

"Why, what would he do?"

"We are not supposed to be here. He would get angry and shout at me."

I hadn't witnessed any such heavy-handed treatment of staff. On one occasion, however, four of us went out on the town and all came down with food poisoning. I later heard that the upper managers severely reprimanded my three workmates for taking me to the type of place where such a thing could happen. Unacceptable that our superiors considered their powers to extend beyond business hours, but I was in no position to do anything but tolerate it.

A telephone rang from its wobbly perch on a stack of textbooks and papers that were crammed together in makeshift shelves along the middle of our worktable. Amachi put down his folding fan, reached over and picked up the receiver.

I liked his way of answering the phone—"Amachi *desu ga . . .*"—decisive and businesslike, with the syllable *ga* ("but") an economical means to signify a humble attitude: "But it's only me, Amachi." Next to me, Saza was rummaging in his desk drawer. He came up with a hand mirror and pair of nail scissors and proceeded to trim his nasal hair. Across from us, Ikari and Yanagi had finished their lunch. Ikari had already fired up the word processor; Yanagi was leaning over his shoulder, pointing at the screen.

I was putting my used hashi back into the empty obento box just as Sogabé entered. He turned a blank glance in my direction, evidently to check that I was there, and then in his self-assured manner strutted over for a word with Division-chief Watanabe. I braced myself. A managerial task of Sogabé's was to liaise with

Watanabe and keep his eye on us, but when he came over from the other building especially to see me, his purpose was often to conduct a maneuver in personal politics. Sogabé's approach to "managing" me became clear during a visit that had taken place during my second week. He made his entrance and, after doing a circuit of the office and chatting with Watanabe for a minute, drew a chair over by mine. He adjusted the bottom half of his silk tie so it fell neatly into his lap, and he tilted his head from side to side, limbering the muscles in his neck.

"The weather has been quite cool," he had opened smilingly, articulating the sentence perfectly.

"Yes—nice and sunny though."

"How are you doing with your classes?"

"No problem. Everything's going well, thanks."

"How do you find Japanese students?" he asked with a chuckle.

"We're getting along well," I said. "I've never had such polite students. They're very eager to please."

"Well, they are often embarrassed to speak in English," he reminded me.

"I've heard that," I said. "But I do my best to encourage students and give them as many opportunities to speak as possible."

Then the point of his visit.

"I wonder whether you have forgotten," he said, "that you are supposed to work a half-day on the first three Saturdays of each month?" Not looking straight at me but staring into space. Of course, I had not attended work on my first Saturday, as we agreed during my job interview that I would not be required to work at all on weekends.

"But we discussed that at the interview," I said, "and you said I could have the whole weekend free. They were going to indicate that on the contract later."

He knit his eyebrows affectedly, still looking into space so that I had him in three-quarter profile. He wore an impassive yet at the same time disingenuous look.

"I can't remember that," he said, as simple as that, his jaw set. Futile to answer his bald-faced lie — I knew that my contract would corroborate what he said. I looked him blankly in the eye.

"Oh, I see. All right then." My loyalty to the organization would develop a slow but critical leak.

Now long after that incident, Sogabé drew up the same chair beside me, adjusted his tie, leaned back and crossed one leg over the other. I replaced the lid on my lunchbox and snapped the elastic band back in place to fasten it.

"Gesuto-sensei," he said, in the Japanese fashion of pronouncing my name, Guest, "Principal Ikeda and the senior teachers want to observe your class next week. Every instructor has to — you don't have a problem with that?" Bowing to the inevitable, I gave a shake of my head and shrugged my assent.

He paused a moment or two.

"Have you been keeping in good health? You look like you have lost weight," he said, regarding me expressionlessly. "When you started here, you were . . . quite heavy, but you are a lot thinner now. I am worried that you might not be feeling well."

"Never felt better."

"No problems, living in your apartment?" Trying his utmost to persuade me he was concerned about my well-being, rather than any inconvenience that might arise for the college. I assured him all was well. The physical side to life here hadn't done me any harm at all. I climbed the stairs to my classes in order to avoid the crush of the elevator, and had to check all eight floors at the close of the working day to ensure that all the windows were closed and the electric typewriters shut down. On the weekends, I explored Nagoya on foot and by subway.

"Do you own a TV?" he asked.

"As a matter of fact," I said, "the NHK (national broadcaster) inspector knocked on my door a fortnight ago to collect the license fee and asked me the same thing. He wouldn't believe I didn't own one until I offered to show him in."

"I noticed a spare one in an unoccupied house near here that our college has bought," said Sogabé. "No one wants it, so you can take it home if you like. It will give you something to do in your spare time and help you improve at Japanese."

We went by van to a house half a mile away and found the television on a bench in an empty room on the second floor; the seventeen-inch color set had seen better days but worked when we tested it, so we took it to my apartment. An extraordinary feeling to be out of the office on a workday, and I marveled at what a slavish mentality I was developing. I was warming to Sogabé again in a funny sort of way. He was relentless but disarmingly transparent in the way he soaked up the power and perks with which his job invested him. In any event, I was glad to have taken possession of a free television. I couldn't quite work out who had given it to me or why, whether the college administration in an effort to protect me from the perils of cheap nightspots, or Sogabé himself to instill a feeling of indebtedness.

6

The Fantastic Shop

Out for a walk one hot Saturday afternoon, I
noticed a dusty old place not far from my
apartment. The narrow two-story building
was in a drab row of miscellaneous businesses, on a
corner where the main street to the railway station
intersected with a lane leading into the local entertainment quarter. The most humble station spawns
nearby venues for drinking and carousing, for the
benefit of commuters (read "salarymen") after their
day's work.

An extinguished red paper lantern adorned the shopfront. This type of shop is called an *akachochin*—
literally, a "red lantern"—a basic style of traditional
drinking house. Japanese refer to various kinds of establishments for eating and drinking as "shops" (*misé*)
generically, be they akachochin, *izakaya* ("sit and
drink") or *yatai*, portable noodle stalls, unless they are
up-market or Western enough to warrant the term "restaurant." A bar can be a "shop," as can the different

styles of traditional restaurants, such as those that specialize in soba or ramen noodles or tempura.

The front door stood ajar. I had not yet been into an akachochin or izakaya by myself, fearing them too much of a challenge for my rudimentary language skills. The times I glanced into one, not a word of English was to be seen. The menus were in Japanese script chalked on blackboards or painted on wooden plaques attached to the walls. Chances were slim that anyone would speak English, and I couldn't face going in without an idea of what was on offer, or making a spectacle by having to choose from the wax models of food sometimes on display in the shopfront window (bearing in mind that wax models are not meant primarily for the convenience of illiterate gaijins, but in order to proclaim the mouth-wateringness of the fare—often a counter-productive effort in those more modest dives where the models are amateurish and the windows dusty and dingy). On this day, I heard the tinny strumming of a guitar drifting out from the doorway and took it as a good sign. On an impulse I went in, ducking my head under the lintel and descending a few stone stairs into the dim interior.

Low ceiling, musty odor and a subterranean mood like that of a basement. Six vacant stools in line before an empty wooden bar. Floor of uneven cobblestones smoothed shiny with time. Paintings in oil bedecked the walls: naive portraits of the red lantern's denizens, apparently. The room long and narrow, with hardly any space between the row of stools and a tatami covered platform behind them, a foot or so high, which supported low tables. This raised part of the floor went most of the way around the room, with more low tables by the far wall.

A man sat on the edge of the platform with his feet on the floor, strumming on an unplugged electric guitar. He was in his late thirties and had thick jet-black hair. He stopped and looked up at me, taken aback that a foreigner had come in. A typical response, and I waited to see what the next moments would bring. I had experience of being confronted by the X-sign that some Japanese made when they barred your entry from somewhere, crossing their forearms at you: *"Damé, damé!"* ("No, you mustn't!") The reception would provoke an unpleasant feeling in your gaijin heart, a mixture of sadness and anger. Some proprietors would give advance notice of their attitude by displaying the discreditable sign "Japanese Only"—you didn't feel much better seeing that. The measure was not considered to be racist; it was just that they could not speak a foreign language (together with the presumption that no foreigner could speak theirs), and they wanted to avoid any misunderstandings, to spare their usual clientele any awkwardness that foreigners may cause. Nothing prejudiced about that.

But this fellow before me broke into a wide, white-toothed smile with a glint of gold, put down his guitar and got up to welcome me, beckoning theatrically with his arm.

"Aw. *Irasshai!* ('Come on in!') Puriizu shitto here!"

He ushered me to the counter and supplied me with a glass of water and an *oshibori* (rolled up, moistened hand towel), with which I cleaned my hands and cooled my face, as my workmates had taught me during our social outings. He commenced an exaggerated, rather amusing performance of mine host.

"May I hel-pu you?" he said from behind the counter,

with a big grin and a studied articulation that suggested he was as limited in English to fixed phrases and isolated words as I was in Japanese. I asked for a beer, and he bent down and took out a medium sized bottle from a bar fridge, uncapped it and half-filled a glass for me. Next to it he placed a saucer of short, furry green pods. I tore one open with my fingers and discovered a line of green beans inside, which tasted healthily bland but edible.

"Zissu izzu . . . *edamame*," he said solemnly, indicating the dish with a flourish.

I took another pod, an action that prompted him to demonstrate the proper method for eating them. He placed one near his lips and squeezed the ends with his thumbs and two fingers, deftly firing the beans out into his mouth. After a couple of misfires, I learned the trick. Then he produced a small book from beneath the counter, a dog-eared pocket translation dictionary, and thumbed through it.

"Bean-zu," he said, quoting. "A soybean; a soya bean . . . *re-gu-mi-no-sae* . . ." He indicated a word on the page, Latin for a family of pea plants, *leguminosae*, evidently within which legumes are classified. He looked me in the eye like a professor trying to elicit a response, but I couldn't get his drift.

"Ah, it izzu Ratin. A regumu," he said. "A regumen."

"Beans," I confirmed. "Yes, I see, beans are legumes. Very nice. Delicious."

"Dericious," he said, flipping through to another page. "In Japaneezu, *umai*. 'It taste-*su* good-*do*.'" He quoted an example from the dictionary, following his index finger across the page. "'Naiisu; sayberry; taystii— Quail-*zu* are excerren-*to* eatin-*gu*.' But today no quail-*zu*

—Japaneezu edamame. Regumu-*zu* are excerren-*to* eating-*gu*."

"They are very nice," I agreed. "Mmm." I had another and laughed along with him.

"Yes, berry naiisu." He quoted another example. "I dine-*do* wi-*su* a goo-*do* appetai-*to*. I enjoy-*do* za me-a-*ru*.'" He appended a Japanese syllable to each word, in producing the English consonant. *Do* as in "dog," *su* as in "Sue," *to* as in "top," *ru* as in "kangaroo." He pronounced each of these additional syllables emphatically, so the rhythm was like adding a full stop to nearly every word.

His face was thin and craggy, with kind, dark eyes, his skin like smooth, tanned leather, at the darker brown end of the Japanese spectrum. He amused me with his antics and interest in words, and we shared a conversation full of good cheer, with digressions sparked indiscriminately by linguistic examples in his dictionary. I ordered sashimi, which he prepared in a kitchenette partitioned off at the back of the bar. When I asked him about his music, indicating the scrapbook he'd been playing from when I walked in, he passed it to me; it contained his handwritten lyrics and guitar chords for a collection of "soft rock" tunes. He implored me to sing a verse from one I knew and resumed his spot on the tatami platform. I had a go at "Ziggy Stardust" while he strummed the accompaniment, my performance earning his effusive applause.

"Sankyu, sankyu. You are berry, berry . . . *onchi*," he said, clapping his hands.

"*Onchi*?" I shrugged, wondering how the compliment might translate.

"*Onchi*." He got the dictionary, scanned through some pages and handed it to me, pointing at a definition.

". . . Tone deaf."

"*Onchi!*" he laughed.

I treated us both to a drink, paid his very reasonable bill and we shook hands farewell. He suggested I return one evening when the place was busier, and I assured him I would.

NEXT TIME I called in, he welcomed me like an old friend and told me to call him Master, like everyone else. He was behind the bar working alongside two young women. One of the female bartenders was Ko-san, an exchange student from Shanghai who worked part-time to finance her studies at a private university. Master explained that her Chinese name sounded nothing like "ko," but that was how the kanji character she used to write the name was pronounced in Japanese.

Ko's English was all but non-existent, so Master eagerly interpreted to the extent he could, and the dictionary had a workout. The triangular communication was fun and stimulating, facilitated by the dictionary and pad and pencil, with me explaining English expressions, Ko the nuances of Chinese characters, or Master tutoring her and me on linguistic points at our disparate levels.

I asked him the name of his akachochin.

"Aw," he said, tapping on a framed certificate hanging from a crosspiece above the bar, his license to operate. "Zissu izzu za Fantasutikku Shoppu. Yeeah!" His laugh was slightly hysterical as he gestured to encompass the room. "Za Fantasutikku Shoppu!"

A cross-linguistic portmanteau word combining the verb *nomu* (to drink) and the English noun "communication" referred to an ideal combination of the two: *nommunication*. Having many modest drinking holes across a district instead of a big, centralized pub facilitated plenty of nommunication. Rather like a beehive, with each cell a little Fantastic Shop, each one with its own particular social atmosphere emanating from the shop master and his assistants, whose role was not just to serve alcohol to the six or eight customers sitting there, but also to entertain and bring them together. Then, when groups of customers occupied the low tables on the tatami platforms as well, that communicative goodwill would radiate out through the whole place in a festive buzz. Master would not jam people in to the full capacity of the shop, but he allowed a certain optimum number of places and no more. Guests at the tables could semi-recline and drink, eat, laugh, chat and sing at leisure, their shoes placed in a neat row on the stone floor.

One or two young female bartenders would hold center stage at the bar while Master disappeared out back to look after orders of food and fire out an occasional comment or jibe. The menu consisted mostly of snacks to take the edge off the alcohol; a general principle of the drinking culture was always to include something to eat. You could have a plate of sashimi or a bowl of *asari no ushiojiru*, a clear broth with about a dozen tiny clams in their shells, seasoned with *saké* (rice wine) and soy sauce. The selection was consistent with the simplicity of the place itself, an honest, traditional dive, without the pretensions, glitz and gold neck chains of the more upmarket nightclubs, with their metal doors, gaudy carpets, karaoke and hostesses. I did have many opportunities to explore these as well, however, since the lane outside took one deeper into the local entertainment quarter. One night I walked into an ancient dive full of middle-aged and older customers singing old nationalistic songs to karaoke, with a wartime propaganda film showing on a video screen — naval vessels proudly flying the wartime *kyokujitsu-ki* (rising sun ensign) with its sixteen red rays, and firing their canon. I felt as though I had stepped back in time as I sat there and visualized how the patrons might have appeared during those unfortunate years. They regarded me smugly, with a hint of guilt, like children up to mischief.

Occasionally I took the subway for a visit to one or another of Nagoya's gaijin bars, where I could mix with other foreigners, most often Americans, or else Japanese who went with the express purpose of meeting foreigners. Sometimes Yanagi, Amachi, Onoé and I went out for an evening of entertainment and nommunication. ("We must experience *everything*," Amachi said philosophically as we wove our way from nightclub to bar.)

But the Fantastic Shop became what the Japanese too call my "local," and its crew and I became friends. At least one night during most weeks, its call would lure me from my books. An excellent schoolroom, if an expensive one: as I became an entrenched patron, Master showed me he knew how to charge. I had read about Sufis in the Middle East who speak of a "tavern of ruin," in which one seeks destruction of the ego through becoming intoxicated in the divine aspect of existence. The Fantastic Shop had nothing notably divine about it, but for me it assumed something like that function of "ruin" by becoming a vehicle for losing myself in my new life.

The business had survived the heavy wartime bombings of Nagoya, and Master inherited it from his father.

Thus despite his relative youthfulness, he commanded local respect. One time, a pop group set themselves up in the shop and played Beatles numbers until the early hours, prompting a polite appeal from a delegation of neighbors. His friends and customers included other young shop owners, such as the married couple who owned a ramen shop on the same block and whose son played the drums in a gothic punk band. The Fantastic Shop attracted a respectable clientele who were drawn to the idiosyncratic ways of its proprietor, the wit and sparkle of its female staff, and the wholesome honesty of the venue itself—long established business and in sight of the shrine. The most distinguished regular and the subject of one of Master's portraits was known as JTB-san, a stocky man with thick glasses who wore quality business suits, a high ranking manager in the Nagoya branch of the Japan Travel Bureau.

One night a drunk staggered in and for no reason took to swaying about in front of me in a boxing stance. An instance of the unwanted attention a foreigner could elicit, though Westerners were often conferred a degree of celebrity that could become just as tedious. Master talked him to the door cordially, patted him on the back and bade him adieu:

"Bad nighto!" Master threw me a wide grin and called out again after the man "Yeeah, habba *bad nighto*," and shut the door firmly behind him.

Old dives accumulate apocryphal tales about themselves, which often conclude with a rat taking a sip out of a customer's glass. I came to understand the basis for this myth. The Fantastic Shop was superficially clean, but the hidden presence of rodents became undeniable, if unmentionable, over time, the scuffling of their tiny claws audible through the ceiling of wooden boards. Looking up, I could detect a fine dust of particles suspended in the air. I knew that the progress of this foul dust was down, ever down into my sashimi. I scrutinized the cracks between the boards and visualized what was happening in the dark up there. I was dubious too about the state of sanitation in Master's kitchenette and opted to avoid his sashimi in favor of peanuts and the occasional bowl of clam soup. One evening, a staff member, a nice, wholesome, buxom young woman with long thick hair was behind the bar, leaning against the wall. Suddenly she started to shriek and wriggle as though she was having a fit, imagining that a cockroach had run down her back. Ko divulged to me later that she understood her co-worker's reaction and that she herself showered and washed her hair after every shift she worked.

Then one subsequent evening, I was sitting at the bar alongside JTB-san and another customer while Master was instructing me on some moves in the game of *shogi* (Japanese chess). JTB stopped talking, and I noticed he had inclined his head and was peeking surreptitiously down at the floor behind us, where a brown rat sat nonchalantly grooming its whiskers. It sniffed and blandly returned our look. None of us three customers said a word; the room was fraught with suspense. I turned back to Master, whose face was frozen. He was obviously aware of the apparition but went on determinedly talking about shogi. For someone to dispel the illusion that nothing was there would be unspeakable — the building could come tumbling down around our ears at the very least. I stared again at the rat, and my alcoholically stimulated mind's eye produced an alternative hallucination. The rodent stood up on its back legs and did a little shuffle, before climbing up to the bar, taking a drink out my glass and teleporting himself back over to his place on the floor. The imagination rebelled against our refusal to acknowledge the reality of a universe in which a rat could possibly exist in the Fantastic Shop. As the Japanese saying goes, "Don't take the lid off a smelly cauldron."

A combination of strength of will and obsessive politeness brought us four to a state of denial tantamount to a collective delusion. A psycho-social mechanism, perhaps—similar to the national forgetfulness about the Second World War, a condition so widespread that even the odd university student is surprised to hear that Japan was once at war with the United States.

7

Z Flag and Sparrow's Tear

Each workday morning, I punched a clock and joined the other instructors in the lobby of Building 2, in the area beneath the international clocks, which, while alluding to the glamorous world of international business, actually served no more than an ornamental purpose. All of us from the English Department assembled nonchalantly in the midst of the larger group in readiness for our morning exercises.

"Have you seen how the propaganda pamphlet for the college makes a special mention of those international clocks?" Amachi said quietly. "It is like they are doing their best to make us appear completely stupid." He hated the morning assembly, detested the eyes of the bosses boring through him like those of thought police.

Vice-Principal Mori had a secretary switch on the video monitors. Three women in modest leotards with skirts modeled a set of gentle exercises while a piano played through some repetitive themes. The drills were being replicated in schools and companies around the country. Everyone was thoroughly familiar with these piano pieces and physical exercises: gentle rotations of the head and shoulders, swinging of the arms, shallow squats. More than contributing to our fitness, the session tuned us in to our identity in the company context and, in turn, to the rhythm of society: scores of millions of us swinging our arms, doing our bends together each morning.

Responsible, right-minded types and, of course, the managers gave the exercises their best effort, swinging their arms precisely and performing deep, crisp squats, reflecting their dedication to duty. A sleepy, almost painful look on his face, Amachi made the most token of gestures. Each morning someone different had a turn at leading the exercises, standing beneath a monitor and facing the group, but those in charge never extended the honor to Amachi, knowing he would reduce the exercise to a mockery. His desultory behavior expressed more than just his aversion to exercise; it was a brazen show of insubordination. In harsher historical times had he behaved like this to his superiors, he might have found himself without a head.

Yet for some reason he was trapped here. The bosses were as aware of his attitudes as everyone else, and Vice-Principal Mori in particular relished any opportunity to belittle him. During the annual working bee, we had to spend the day scrubbing, scouring and polishing our building. Mori stood over Amachi and stared at him as he toiled away, glass-papering the rust from the iron lattice roller-doors that secured the basement parking.

"Everyone says I look like a *tanuki*," Amachi said laughing one day. "That's the statue that stands outside some restaurants, inviting you in. Unfortunately, I do have a belly like the tanuki, from drinking the saké." Indeed, he was the image of that cute animal, a racoon-dog, they call it, like a badger—round face, kind eyes and sensitive chin. Those who made the observation meant him no disrespect: the tanuki was, like a fox, a magical animal, but lovable and jolly as well as mischievous. Amachi was a gentle soul, bighearted, humble and intelligent, like the tanuki. His pride suffered at work, and I felt for him. (Incidentally, and irrelevant to this comparison with Amachi, the male tanuki is also renowned for possessing gigantic, magical testicles, which he can transform into a range of useful objects limited only by the folk imagination.)

One weekend we were driving somewhere in his plush sedan, when I noticed a button on his dashboard with the word "Economy" printed on it.

"What does that do?" I asked.

"I don't know," he said, with his classic self-deprecatory chuckle, "I have never pressed it"—which, I felt, well exemplified his unique and generous nature.

As we drove, he related a story from his student years in Tokyo.

"One day I went to the racetrack and won a lot of money—about nine *man* yen. What would that be? Around nine hundred dollars American. I was very happy—that was more money than I ever had. But you know what? I remembered something my grandfather used to tell me. He said, 'If you ever have good fortune, you should share it with your friends'; so I asked my pals out with me to the Roppongi entertainment district to treat them to a good time. I took them to a high-class restaurant for a dinner party, and we kept on celebrating until dawn. Then when the waiter brought me the check, I nearly fell over. Nearly three thousand dollars! I had nothing like that sort of money, so for the rest of the year I had to work part-time at the restaurant to pay it off."

COLLEGE ASSEMBLIES were held weekly in the Engineering building across the road, Building 3. We herded the students over there, up and around the stairwell and into a gymnasium on the top level. They sat cross-legged, crowded together on the floor, with the instructors moving around among their charges to ensure they kept silent and awake, by means such as bopping them on the head with a rolled up newspaper. Some groups of students stayed in classrooms in the other buildings, where they could watch the assemblies televised on big video screens. When Principal Ikeda came on stage to commence the assembly, all the students rose and bowed, including those watching by television, who bowed to the principal's image on the screen.

Principal Ikeda, Division-chief Watanabe and other senior figures gave tedious addresses to the hundreds of students gathered. Excruciating onslaught of Japanese for the endless duration of the assembly. At first I concluded that the mind-numbing effect must be because I lacked the ability to abstract sense from the words. But then, the more language I acquired, the more I came to realize the trivial nature of the content—how students should comport themselves, dress and keep their namecards straight—and the harder it became to endure the harangues. When suffering after a late night at the Fantastic Shop, I feared I might pass out. I used mental exercises to get through the assemblies, first visualizing the ninety-six *hiragana* and *katakana* syllables in the phonetic writing system one by one, then moving on to the kanji I was studying.

Watanabe's discourses were particularly loud and aggressive. Once while he was delivering one, the behavior of a male student standing at the very back of the hall caught his eye. After finishing his talk, Watanabe strode through the body of students, marched up to the offending student and ordered him to remove his glasses. The student complied, and Watanabe slapped him sharply in the face and strode out the door.

This was the most dismal example of the culture of corporal punishment that I had so far observed. Prior to this, in addition to the aforementioned head-bopping, I had witnessed some minor acts of physical intimidation and a punishment in which students were made to kneel in a position called *seiza*—sitting back on their heels, a posture used in *zazen* (Zen meditation)—for an uncomfortably long period.

"I couldn't believe my eyes," I said to Amachi after the assembly. "I'm surprised the student didn't go immediately to the police station."

"The police would not do anything about it," he said, "and the student would only get kicked out of school. And you know, the parents themselves think these students need to be treated strictly."

A month later in our own office, the principal himself lost his temper and slapped at a female student who showed him attitude when he criticized her for the way she was dressed. The ugly incident took place in our office, and though his clout failed to connect, the intent was clear. Soon after, a legal case involving corporal punishment at a high school in Nagoya received widespread coverage in the media. At the next assembly, Principal Ikeda gave a speech about what a shocking practice it was and how the ethical standards of our academy would never allow such a thing to occur—and face slapping ceased as though it had never been.

A GROUP of prospective students and their parents were to visit, so we instructors were set to work waxing and polishing.

"When I first came here for my interview," Amachi said as three of us walked through the lobby with our buckets, "I was impressed by the beautiful shiny glass and silver railings." My own initial impressions ran through my mind. "Then, when the day came for the high school students to visit," he said, "I understood *how* they get them so clean and shiny."

"Yes," said Onoé, "he found out that it is we teachers who have to make them so clean and shiny."

For a demonstration class, I decided to introduce the visiting students to some drama and movement exercises, improvisation and acting games in English—an application of "whole-body learning" I hoped would help coax them out of their shyness. At one point, the surveillance camera started gyrating conspicuously. Later, Amachi told me that, back at headquarters, the "unbusinesslike" activities underway in the classroom caused some agitation among the managers as they watched the monitor. They charged Fujita with getting me into line, but their tune changed when the student questionnaires ranked my class as the one they would most like to attend.

The whole staff assembled on the front steps to bid

our guests sayonara. Our superiors, all pearly grins and obsequious bows, unfurled a flag in front of them to display to the departing visitors, while Principal Ikeda made a speech. The flag was divided diagonally into four triangles: yellow, red, blue and black.

"That is a famous flag that our navy flew when they attacked the Russian navy in 1905," Onoé said. I had heard of that historical event, the Battle of Tsushima in the Russo-Japanese war, when Japan accomplished what was then the unbelievable feat of winning a battle against a Western country. "It is called the *zetki* — 'Z flag' — because it is the international semaphore signal for the letter Z," Onoé said. "That means, 'there is nothing after this'; so the Japanese commander gave it the meaning 'The fate of Japan hinges on this ultimate battle. Everyone must do their best.' It raised the spirit of the sailors so they could win the fight. And we must aim for the same goal now: strive to do our very best."

"I hope it doesn't mean we are going to go down with the ship," I said.

My young colleague Ikari looked at me askance. Recently he had given me the feeling he disapproved of the quips I occasionally let drop these days, as I became more and more disenchanted with the organization. Or else he had decided he just plain didn't like me.

We arrived at our office worktable.

"How can you work in a place like . . . like *this*?" Ikari hissed contemptuously, looking across at me. I wasn't sure who or what was the object of his venom, the college, me or both.

"I don't know — it's okay. I feel I have an obligation to the students."

"I think you are . . . crafty," he said malevolently.

"Thank you."

He regarded me with a disappointed look and took out his dictionary. "*Warugashikoi*," he sneered. "If you take it as a compliment, then I do not use the right word. 'Sly . . . cunning . . .'"

I smiled and shrugged. "Sheesh," I thought, wondering about the source of his growing spitefulness, which I was never able to identify satisfactorily.

"Do you know why America dropped the atomic bomb on Japan but not on Germany?" he asked out of the blue one day.

"No, I don't."

"It is because we Japanese are . . . a yellow skinned people." A dark, unblinking look.

"I can't work out why they call Japanese skin yellow," I said, playing dumb in an effort to defuse him. "It looks like more of a brownish color to me; but anyway, I can hardly see any difference between your skin and mine."

On payday, the staff crowded together in a meeting room in Building 2. The arrogant, muscular Sogabé, the thin, dark, evil-looking Vice-Principal Mori, and the short-legged, delicate-handed Principal Ikeda stood before us. Sogabé called out the names of all the employees from the highest ranked to the lowest, and we stepped forward one by one. Mori passed a pay packet to Ikeda, who held it in both hands and with a ceremonial air presented it to each employee, one after the other, who took it in both hands. Ikeda and the employee would face each other squarely, thank each other and bow, the employee withdraw. Over and over, until everyone had received an envelope and the entire hierarchy been acted out, and thereby reinforced. We shared the ritual with yakuza organizations, which bespoke its effectiveness as a socializing device.

"We get our bonus today," Onoé grinned at me wryly as we strolled together to our office. "But it's about as big as a sparrow's tear."

I, on the contrary, was happy to weigh the fat envelope of cash in my hand, and fond of the gentle, muffled, percussive sound it gave from the inner breast pocket of my jacket, when I patted the hidden wad every once in a while to make certain it was still there. I made my farewells more buoyantly than usual.

"*Osaki ni, shitsurei shimasu!*" ("Excuse me, I'm off before you!")

"*Otsukaresama!*" ("You must be tired!")

"*Gokurosama desu!*" ("You've worked hard!")

Stretched out on the tatami in my apartment, I counted through the *ichiman-en* (ten thousand yen— then approximately one hundred dollars American) bills in the envelope like Scrooge McDuck, then combined them with my growing hoard, which I took down from its hiding place behind a board in the top of the *oshiire* closet. I spread the bills out on the tatami and sat to take in the spectacle of that carpet of cash that was *all mine.*

I opened up a glassful of cheap One-Cup saké. I had another and then another, feeling the alcohol spreading through my veins and softening up my brain as I reviewed its recent contents. On the inner surface of the label attached to the glass was a color photograph of a Japanese bikini girl, which one looked at through the liquid. More than the physical attributes of the girl, I appreciated the masterstrokes of visual and psychological marketing design. The convex glass worked in concert with the liquid contents to magnify and distort the girl's image, giving her a remarkably enveloping, floating, dreamlike quality, since you viewed the image from very close up, between sips. Most intriguing, I reckoned, was the design's ability to co-opt the mental haze induced by the alcohol itself, producing an effect of dreamlike magnification that compounded the visual illusion. As one became intoxicated, the scene was ever more surreal, as though the bikini girl in the saké cup came to life, wielding a mermaid's power to captivate the male gaze. Truly, in their conception, the One-Cup saké girls rivaled the inspired illusions of kabuki theatricians, making into art this sordid scenario: a man boozing on the cheapest available saké, ogling a photo of a bikini model.

You have to be careful of the saké, though, or it will catch up with you—the drink is a powerful soporific. On midwinter evenings, one came across salarymen lying prone and paralytic on the snow-covered steps to a railway station, briefcase still in hand, their condition due to the warmth and bodily paralysis imparted by the liquor. A cautionary tale of my own: the first time I overdid the saké. One night—one very much like this, except with work in store the next day—I sat leaning against the wall and downed several One-Cups while studying my Japanese language text. At some point I must have closed my eyes, and when I opened them again daylight filled the room, I looked at my wristwatch to discover with horror it was nine the next morning. I was propped in the same position, fully dressed, book in my lap, and already an hour late for work—a serious offense for which I was made to apologize formally to the principal.

* * *

THE DAY before graduation, we prepared seating for the parents and guests. The ceremony was to take place in the gymnasium in Building 3 where we held the assemblies. We trooped over and pulled hundreds of chairs out from where they were stored; they were foldable metal chairs joined together six per row. Then the procedure began for placing them end to end to form *absolutely* straight lines, each row parallel and equidistant from the next, to the millimeter, a feat accomplished using an ingenious measuring device constructed from pieces of wood and lengths of string. Higher-ranking managers bellowed directions while groups of staff working like teams of ants shook and clattered the chairs into precisely calculated positions with cries of *"Hai! Hai!"* given in response to each order. Language reduced to reflex, an automatic valve to regulate the group mechanism of command and action.

In their perfect alignment, the rows upon rows assumed a certain beauty all their own, like the aura of care that suffuses a Zen garden, touching each branch, each individual leaf.

"These have got to be the straightest chairs in Japan," I said, staggered by the glow of perfection that radiated from the straight rows, the parallel lines and the precise relations among the hundreds of chair-seats and backs, the thousands of tubular metal angles and struts.

The purpose behind our working on Saturday mornings was to augment the management's control over us. We were finished preparing for classes and had little to do—certainly nothing we couldn't have achieved during the week. Thus one day, a senior instructor from the Travel Department was delegated to take the English teaching staff (barring Fujita-kacho) up to clean the rooftop. He was intelligent looking, with round, thin-rimmed glasses. Seemed loath to carry out this job, embarrassed to have to supervise us in such a foolish and demeaning task for an instructor or lecturer—particularly as he must have had a fair idea of our attitude. We carried some brooms up to the roof of the eight-story building, where we each took turns noncommittally sweeping dust to and fro, while the others stood about gazing at the urban view, hands in pockets, chatting.

Our overseer summoned us together for a briefing, in which he drew our attention to an architectural detail. The windows jutted out at an angle on every floor, producing a triangular platform above each window; some dust might possibly settle on those, he pointed out. He finished talking, climbed over the safety barrier that ran around the roof, and made a wide step over onto one of the narrow triangular window-cappings. If an earth tremor happened to strike at that moment—and they did occur every now and then—he might easily be shaken off and fall to his death.

I couldn't watch. I turned away with a twinge of nausea and a hollow sensation in my stomach. The man climbed back over the barrier, walked over to us and held out a handful of dust that he had retrieved from the concrete platform. His way of saying, "I won't expect you to demonstrate my level of dedication, but please do make an effort and don't be so arrogant about all this."

* * *

SOGABÉ DEPUTIZED me to help him write an essay for his Master's course—on the thought of Mahatma Gandhi, of all things. In return, I had the title Academic Consultant appended to my *meishi* (business card). We finished a session on the project, sitting at the English Department's table.

"Harada-sensei wants me to move to a position at the university soon," he said, reclining on his chair, "and when I go, I would like you to move there too."

He was referring to the university within Harada's own private academy. By no means did I fancy becoming Sogabé's academic serf, the role he evidently had in mind for me; nevertheless, the suggestion carried a scent of hope. Fed up with the college, I had begun to look around for part-time teaching spots at universities such as the fine Nagoya and Nanzan Universities and was offered something modest, but my bosses denied me permission.

"Anyway, why would they want Guest to work for them?" I overheard one say derisively. *Gesuto*—no *Gesuto-sensei*, thanks very much. I commenced in earnest searching for another full-time job and tried to build up my publications so I could apply to some universities. Harada's school of law and economics, another professional college, published an article of mine about Japanese and Australian relations, researched from books I borrowed by mail from the Australian Embassy Library in Tokyo. I was in a bind: getting valuable teaching experience, but in a limited sphere, lacking in prospects.

* * *

ISABELLA FLEW over to visit me. Her first trip to Japan, so we caught the Shinkansen to Tokyo to stay a few days. I had picked up a newly published guidebook in Maruzen bookshop—American writer Rick Kennedy's *Little Adventures in Tokyo*—and thought it could be a good project to write a newspaper feature article along the lines of "doing Tokyo by book," which the literary editor of the *Weekend Australian* agreed to commission. I planned to go on some of the outings recommended in the book: the quaint old downtown area, the vast Tokyo fish markets, the frenetic electronics district of Akihabara, and in Yokohama, the world's biggest department store and Ferris wheel (an exciting attraction in a region so earthquake prone—at least a thousand per year strong enough to feel, and about one per year of magnitude seven on the Japanese seismic intensity scale of one to seven).

Exhilarating to ride on the Shinkansen through its most iconic postcard location. Elevated above the rice paddies, we hurtled at two hundred and seventy kilometers per hour past the southern face of snow-capped Mount Fuji, which gave the illusion it floated majestically in the sky. The Tokaido-Sanyo Shinkansen serves the five-hundred kilometer line between Tokyo and Osaka, Japan's most vital economic artery. Businessmen in the carriage with us lounged in the luxurious seats; some had slipped off their shoes for greater comfort, and their feet rested on cushioned footrests. They were so accustomed to seeing Mount Fuji that they did not bother to look up from their newspapers. For me, another vivid moment of quintessential Japaneseness.

Tokyo's fish markets, the biggest in the world and a popular Tokyo tourist attraction, were located in the suburb of Tsukiji. Unfortunately, we approached them from a bad direction and I could not find our way through the maze of roads and warehouses that made up the transport hub. Refrigerated semitrailers roared by in every direction. After about half an hour of frustration and breathing in exhaust fumes, we gave up on the markets and retraced our steps toward Tokyo Station.

We found a seafood restaurant along the way, where I ordered a sashimi dish called *ikizukuri*. After the fish market fiasco, I was showing off my developing Japanese skills to Isabella by reading from the menu, though I couldn't tell precisely what kind of sashimi the word *ikizukuri* signified. The chef, in his blue apron and headscarf, asked me to select two fish from some doomed specimens about eight inches long, peacefully circling in a glass walled tank, and in no time he had them carved up and arranged uncooked on platters before us. The head and tail of each fish were still attached to its spine and impaled on a slender bamboo skewer, forming a D-shape tipped forward: the skewer was the upright of the D and the fish's spine the curve. The flesh lay neatly filleted on the plate, along with some uncooked shrimp, octopus and a garnish of seaweed. Suddenly a series of minute shudders gripped the remains of my fish; then it twitched in a slightly more violent spasm. Oh, I get it, *ikizukuri* . . . "prepared alive."

"A new one on me—the fish is still alive . . ." I said, staring at the emotionless black eye, which seemed to contemplate its own flesh lain out before it. I grasped a fillet with the tips of my hashi and swallowed the moist pink flesh, the most delicious sashimi. "It seems a bit macabre," I said. "Are you okay about eating it?"

"The fish is dead, really—it's been filleted. That twitching is caused by autonomic reflexes, that's all. But I do wish it had been killed more humanely—it couldn't have been a painless death." She put a piece in her mouth. "The sashimi is good," she said, and then, trying an uncooked shrimp, "I don't much like these though."

The black eye seemed to grow larger and expand into an infinite void. A most existential dish: reflecting on life, I continued with the meal, its twitches and shudders diminishing as I ate.

I recalled an earlier culinary oddity.

"At that restaurant under my apartment, I ordered some fish the chef was cooking. About an inch long— maybe they were whitebait. Anyway, he would grab a fistful of the wriggling fish, swirl them in some tempura batter and toss them into the deep fry still alive—*pfft*— like that. He let them cook for a matter of seconds before serving them up. They were the most scrumptious deep-fried fish I ever tasted. A customer was washing down some species of live shrimp or fish with saké. He was clowning around, pulling faces, making out the shrimp gave him a weird sensation as it went down his throat.

"Generally, I like to try whatever is going. I ate *fugu* (blowfish) once, which can be fatally poisonous unless a specially qualified chef prepares it and removes the toxic organs. But I've drawn the line with dolphin and whale, though I've had the opportunity—it's simply not necessary. Anyhow . . . this variety of sashimi has a philosophical edge for me," I said, mesmerized again by the fish's round black eye.

Late in the afternoon we made our way to the Jinbocho section of the Kanda district and browsed through some bookshops, before searching out the nearby "Balalaika" Russian restaurant. We descended a narrow brick stairwell into the dark interior of the restaurant. The place was empty, and we were about to turn around and leave when a slim, slick-haired waiter materialized in formal dress. In theatrical style, he showed us to a table, flourished menus, lit candles and brought in water and oshibori towels. We started with vodka and salted herring, a favorite dish of Isabella's.

How surprised we were to hear the tremolo of a balalaika drift in through the service door. Then a troupe of six musicians, all young Japanese, entered in single file and stood in a semicircle before our table, playing their guitars, balalaika and fiddle. They wore long, satin, luridly colored Cossack-style shirts embroidered in crimson and gold, with sashes tied around the waist. Quite an unconventional ensemble, but Isabella applauded them warmly and gave them compliments in Russian, which one of them, a Russian language student, gleefully interpreted for the others.

In the candlelight, we dined on minute, Japanese-sized portions of borscht, piroshki dumplings and lamb shashlik, while the waiter hovered over us and the musicians earnestly performed their repertoire of folk tunes, tickled pink with their authentic Russian listener. Isabella set them at ease with her native sociability and nostalgia. She became moist-eyed and sang along quietly when they played "Stenka Razin," a stirring folk-song on the themes of camaraderie and sacrifice.

"This is excruciating," she whispered lightheartedly. I sipped on my borscht, taking immense pleasure in both her company and the ersatz spectacle before us.

WE CELEBRATED the rice harvest with Sogabé's extended family, participating with them in their traditional custom of pounding hot steamed rice into a thick, glutinous paste called *mochi*. The rice was pounded using a wooden mortar the size of a small barrel and a heavy wooden mallet swung from the shoulder. One person swung the mallet, and on their backstroke, another folded the rice paste over in the mortar. The better the synchronization, the less the chance of a crushed hand. The women shaped the mochi into cakes, which they filled with sweet bean paste. Every year, media reports cited the numbers of elderly who died choking on the sticky treat.

Sogabé took me for a visit to Harada's university. A cut above my present college—set in wooded grounds, with a domed gymnasium instead of an unused rooftop driving range. He informed me of how a certain foreign lecturer was being "uncooperative" and would soon have to leave, thus creating an opening for me. Sogabé and I were becoming buddies. He invited Isabella and me home to meet his wife and children and even had me "work out" with him in a gymnasium so that he could astound me with feats of strength. His machinations were in full sway. Then all at once they were over: the dangling carrot, the possibility of transfer, came to nothing.

"Principal Ikeda and Mori-sensei are happy with your work. They do not want to lose you, so they have decided not to permit you to transfer."

I searched through the positions vacant pages in the

Japan Times and submitted some applications. My current contract was nearing its end, and I no longer wished to renew it. The bosses had the attitude they could do whatever they wanted with me, and I resented the idea that the effort I put in had in fact hindered my advancement. We were playing to different sets of ethical principles. I had come to realize how culturally relative my own ethics were—no better than theirs, just different. Frequently, when the need arose, if it seemed the rational course of action required I sacrifice my values, then I would. Even Sogabé was surprised when I accepted Principal Ikeda's proposal that he and I co-author an English language article for a journal published by Harada's university. On top of his role as college principal, Ikeda also ranked as a professor at the university.

"Maybe you don't understand," Sogabé said. "He is inviting you to include his name as co-author on an article you write. He doesn't understand any English at all."

"I have the very article in mind," I said. "It's already completed"—the essay on *Apocalypse Now*, which I had written a year before, intending to submit it to an academic journal on film and literature, but put on the back burner while I settled in here. I no longer found it surprising that someone would propose attaching their name to an article they had not written, in a language they could not comprehend. If his name graced it, the paper would be published, if not, not. Logical enough, and a practice that I was sure Ikeda had not invented himself.

Then Sogabé turned on me. Fujita had convened our daily end-of-work English Department meeting and was reviewing the itinerary for our annual company trip, the departure scheduled for next morning. The trip was compulsory, he reminded us, but we would have to pay for the coach and hotel bills ourselves. When he finished, he cleared his throat and switched his speech to English.

"Sogabé-sensei has advised me that Guest-sensei does not seem to be doing enough work in between classes," he said in a measured tone.

"What?!" I burst out. "When I'm not teaching, all I do is read, prepare for classes or sit at this computer cataloging books for the library."

That was not entirely true. In fact, I had been taking advantage of the new departmental Apple Mac to work on my resume and compose application letters. I had noticed Sogabé cast me a brief sidelong look while snooping around over here a day or two earlier. Had my efforts been uncovered? I was not turning paranoid without good reason: often my mail would arrive at my desk already opened. Such petty surveillance was integral to the insidious control strategy. I put up with it in silence, knowing that to balk would elicit increased pressure, along the principle of the Chinese bamboo finger trap. But enough was enough. I got up.

"Well, I'm going to see about this," I said grimly. My colleagues watched me stride out resolutely.

I greeted Sogabé curtly at his desk, where he sat at the head of his own group of direct subordinates in our sister building.

"Fujita-sensei told me you complained that I haven't been working hard enough," I said. "I wonder whether you would mind explaining to me what you mean by that?"

His face registered the rapid computations of his brain.

"No," he said, stiffening. "No, I didn't say anything like that."

"You didn't?"

"No, not at all."

"Well, he says you did, so let's go over and get to the bottom of it."

In ten minutes I had them seated together at Fujita's desk. The others had gone.

"You told me a little while ago that Sogabé-sensei said I wasn't working hard enough," I said to Fujita. "Is that correct?"

"Yes, that's right."

I turned to Sogabé.

"But when I asked you about it a little while ago, you assured me you didn't. Is that right?"

"Yes."

"You didn't say it?"

"No."

"Well, this is interesting," I said. "Fujita-sensei says that Sogabé-sensei told him I was slacking, but Sogabé-sensei says he didn't say any such thing. Is that correct?"

They both nodded at me in silence. I considered stating the logical conclusion that someone must be lying—but thought better of it. Looking back, that was a sound intuition and one that most likely saved my stay in Japan from being terminated forthwith.

"Well then," I said politely, "I'm glad we've worked that out."

We bowed and parted amicably, as though having reached a consensus, and nothing more was ever said about the issue.

Next morning, we piled into two luxurious tour coaches and set off southward for the city of Isé in Mié

Prefecture. As Amachi and I climbed up into our assigned coach, a hostess wearing a puce pink uniform, matching toque and white gloves welcomed us in. Occasionally during the trip, she took up her position, braced against a handrail, to announce some tourist information to us through a microphone or input requests into the karaoke machine. Our destination was the incomparable Isé Jingu (shrine), established in the third century. The trip took most of the day, after refreshment stops, a restaurant lunch and a sightseeing tour of the pearl beds at Ago Bay, where Mikimoto Kokichi created the world's first cultured pearls. Numerous group photographs at noteworthy sites, where there was often a tiered stand in situ for that purpose.

Isé Shrine maidens, in their white kimono-jackets and loose red pants, followed us in to an inner tatami chamber, where we sat down cross-legged. Three dancers, wearing white robes and animal masks and carrying leafy sprigs, entered and began to chant and dance hypnotically. A priest intoned the name of our college several times as they bestowed their blessing on our enterprise.

After another, much longer trip back north then east, we stayed at an inn in the mountains, and the next day a further trip took us to a seaside resort on the Izu Peninsula, where we would spend the night. We dressed in comfortable yukata, partied and wandered around getting tipsy. We played ping-pong, bathed in the hot spring and dined sumptuously. When night fell and some of our junior contingent were drunk enough, they took to chasing our younger OLs ("office ladies")—also in yukata—who fled from them squealing.

On the final leg of the coach trip home, we pulled up outside a big *omiyage* (souvenir) shop. I was in the seat next to Amachi, who had chosen a strategic spot near the front, close to the refrigerated box that held the liquor.

"I believe I will stay here and drink beer," he informed me. He sounded jaded—tired, hungover and overdosed on company cheer.

"Get me one, too," I said, feeling something the same way—though at least for me the experience had an element of novelty.

We cracked open our cans and sipped from them, saying nothing. We watched everyone troop to the shop in the highest of spirits, absolutely in their element. They emerged laughing together half an hour later, clutching the handles of paper carry-bags full of omiyage—cakes, sweets, tea, a potpourri of local specialties. I noticed Principal Ikeda beaming smiles at everyone and no one in particular, looking as pleased as Punch—the picture of how he must have looked in his schooldays on outings just like this.

8

Night Train

B ut now my days of being an instructor in a senmon gakko professional college were behind me. I had no regrets about my time in Nagoya, having learned much about teaching, about this wonderful country and, indeed, about myself. But now the Seven Gods of Happiness had smiled and I'd become a national university academic, though I had little idea of what that might entail. I saved the omikuji the fortune-telling automaton of Shizuoka Station dispensed to me, inserting the paper slip somewhere between the pages of an old copy of the ancient Chinese text of philosophy and divination, the *I Ching*. Unlike the Japanese (as according to Sogabé), I didn't pray that the prediction would come true if it held good fortune, nor pray it wouldn't if it didn't. I didn't bother to translate what it said but left it untouched in its proper home, enfolded in the potentiality of change and chance. Sometimes I remembered it secreted away in that "book of changes" and indulged a warm glow about my good luck. Nevertheless, I had to check myself. Perhaps it hadn't yet fully discharged its prophecy; or maybe all it said was . . . so far so good.

MICHAEL BANCROFT was the Brit who had sat on my interview panel. Now in his early thirties, he had lived in Shizuoka for eleven years and become a darling of the Japanese and a local legend among the established foreigners, none of whom had lived here as long or was so well-adapted and well-accepted by the community. Invariably, he impressed any Japanese he met with his flawless speech and impeccable manners. He possessed a prodigious ability for learning languages and had mastered several. His best foreign language was French, and this he spoke perfectly, as Jean-Claude Jugon, a French psychologist teaching in the Liberal Arts Faculty, informed me. Bancroft delighted in the social dimension of language.

"I'm not interested in studying Japanese to get some qualification or other," he said. "It's important to me as a way to get to know the people here." A social animal, he was attracted to the tastes and intricacies of Japanese society. He loved the Shizuokan natives and they him.

He was of a slim build and, standing at six feet, an inch or so taller than me. He was pleasant looking, with curly brown hair and a squarish face, and favored an open-necked, casual style of clothing, unlike me in those days in my silk ties and sports coats. His considerable personal charm bestowed on him a wide circle of admirers. National universities permitted their full-time academics to take on extra part-time work, which many did. Bancroft took advantage of the privilege, teaching

English part-time at the prefectural university, working in local television and radio and giving private language lessons, exclusively to the most beautiful women in the city.

"A private student of mine booked a ticket on a luxury cruise to the Arctic Circle," he was telling me. "She out-fitted herself in furs and ball gowns for the trip. The travel company sent her a pamphlet containing safety instructions, including a warning not to get between the penguins and the sea, and she was terrified. She pictured herself standing on a plateau of ice in her high heels and mink coat, with hundreds of penguins attacking her. She nearly canceled her trip."

This extraordinary type of Japanese woman is a delicate flower, insulated from our coarser reality. Suspended in her floating world, she is intoxicated by beauty—above all, her own. She thrives on wealth, fashion and European holidays.

Bancroft appeared to be totally acculturated into the society. He was his own man, raised in Western ways of seeing and being, but distanced from them, and equally as competent operating within a Japanese worldview, as though each culture afforded him a perspective on the other. Perhaps to live suspended between two polarized cultures was a possible recipe for self-actualization. I wondered whether I might not have the right stuff, too, for such a process to take hold, fancying I had been a loner and outsider in my own country. This trait may serve me well for life here, I felt, where you are by definition a gaijin, and hence truly an outsider. Yet I knew I had a very different personality: over-analytical and lacking both the energy and personal magnetism that allowed him to make so many diverse inroads into the community. Frankly, it would drive me mad to spend as much time with people as he seemed to.

We entered easily into something resembling a mentoring relationship, a helpful state of affairs for me, for I was a novice at Japanese life, and the professional experience I'd acquired, although intensive, was in an atypical, excessively authoritarian setting. I could hardly believe that the roomy office a secretary showed me to was now my own working space—my very own *kenkyushitsu* (research room). Moreover, I didn't have to slave in an office all day every day but could work at home if I wished, as long as I was punctual for classes and meetings. No clocking on! I felt like a freed slave who needs time to throw off his mindset of subjugation even after the physical chains are gone.

Bancroft gave me a pep talk when I first visited him in his office. He took a sheaf of photocopied pages from out of a filing cabinet and leafed through to find an article from the famous British periodical *Nature*, with the title "Japanese universities are slow to welcome foreign faculty." "You may find this interesting," he said. "It shows the number of foreigners who hold permanent full-time faculty positions like ours in national universities. It seldom happens—nearly all foreigners are on fixed term contracts. This publication ran a survey last year, so I'm included in their figures." He indicated an entry that showed his name beside "Shizuoka" in a list of nine out of all ninety-eight national universities. The total number of permanent foreign nationals was only seventeen: next to none among a population of thirty-seven thousand faculty.

"No Australians," I observed.

"No, that's right, you aren't following in anybody's

footsteps. We selected you from fifty applicants here and in the US. You have a good opportunity to accomplish something worthwhile, because you don't have to worry about a contract running out."

I was to find out over the next couple of years that the low number of tenured foreign faculty was a sore point among expatriate academics, causing some high-profile industrial disputes between universities and contracted foreigners.

Disaffected expatriates labeled the situation "academic apartheid," alleging that racist attitudes underpinned the disparity. The same people made bitter criticisms concerning not this issue alone, but all aspects of the university system different from the Western model: teaching styles, examination methods, administrative approaches. They couldn't tolerate any departure from the educational models they were trained in and insistent on imposing; they became frustrated and furious when the academic establishment simply ignored them and their recommendations. The "debate" came up within English language forums such as the Japanese Association of Language Teachers (JALT), where foreign critics joined the cause periodically, vehemently attacking the system. When I wrote in a JALT forum that cultural issues were a factor and the Japanese should be allowed to do things the way they considered best for them, they hooted me down as a "cultural relativist," evidently a low form of life in their eyes.

In any case, whatever the underlying causes, the fact was that very few permanent foreigners worked within the national university system. I thanked my lucky stars for the rare privilege of an insider's frame of reference, at least in this one important respect.

"You're free to do just about whatever you like," Bancroft continued. "But keep in mind one cardinal rule: no sex with students. That will get you thrown out. There was once a scandal here involving a professor whom a secretary discovered with a student, when she heard suspicious noises coming from his office. He was fired, of course. In another case, a lecturer married his former student soon after she graduated, but they had to relocate to another city, since it now came out they'd been having a relationship when she was still enrolled."

As HEAD of my selection committee, Professor Tokui now assumed the duties of making sure I was registered with the immigration bureau and city council, and finding me accommodation. I noted how he introduced himself to local government and immigration officials, which was more assertive than the style I'd borrowed from Amachi in Nagoya. "*Shizuoka daigaku no Tokui desu*," he said ("I'm Tokui of Shizuoka University"), and I subsequently adopted this as a fail-safe way to ensure a hearing. Faculty members of national universities enjoyed an elite status, and government agencies in particular held us in high regard, for we had the status of being "national officers."

He soon corrected me on the too formal way I addressed him.

"You know, there's no need to call me 'sensei.' You are just the same status as me."

The practice of always referring to every other teacher as "sensei," which my authoritarian college had upheld strictly, was more typical of schools than universities.

I entered at a time when the university was nearing

the end of a laid-back era. Before long, the government would introduce a five-year contractual system for previously tenured academics both Japanese and non-Japanese, and several national universities, including mine, would become semi-privatized as national corporations. Such changes meant an increasing level of accountability for staff; however, the paradigm shift was yet to occur. Nor did college life hold any particular sense of urgency for students. Universities had exceedingly high student pass rates—an indication of how undemanding the courses were. The most difficult period for a student in high school was that known as "examination hell," leading up to the university entrance examinations, for the students' futures depended on which of the hierarchy of universities accepted them. University life was considered an unofficial holiday between their high school years, when most spent extra hours studying in after-school *juku* (cram schools), and their professional life, when a proportion would work themselves to death.

One day, Professor Munakata and I were discussing one thing and another.

"In Japan, universities are known as 'the night train,'" he said with a gleam in his eye.

"Why is that?"

"Because, just as in the night train, here you sleep until you arrive at your destination," he chuckled.

One may well have commiserated, therefore, with the critics of the system; but bear in mind that Japan boasted the world's highest rates of literacy and numeracy, so someone must have been doing something right.

Liberal Arts was the least demanding faculty in which to work. The idea behind the liberal arts system was to provide students with a comprehensive education, rather than one geared to a purely employment-oriented specialization. A student studying mainly in the Engineering faculty, for example, had to take a certain number of subjects in liberal arts—an assortment from the arts, sciences and physical education—though these may be irrelevant to the field in which the student planned to specialize. The same was true for a humanities major, who included in their studies non-humanities subjects listed in the liberal arts. My faculty thus catered to students from all the other faculties but offered subjects only at first and second year levels, before they took up their specialized studies. Most of us did not need to teach third and fourth year students, let alone postgraduates. It would not be long, however, before the liberal arts system was abolished in conformance with the national program of restructuring.

The faculty climate was much in keeping with the notion of a cultivated lifestyle. The equivalent term to "liberal arts faculty" was *kyoyobu*, implying the sense of "being cultured"—and being cultured precluded being too much of a workaholic. The seniority-based system and the relaxed and "cultured" atmosphere harmonized quite well together, generating hardly any sense of competitiveness or accountability. The ethos was definitely old school. Tenured academics were assailable only by Father Time himself, with the scene in some ways resembling an idyllic ancient arbor of learning. One professor strikingly resembled an ancient Chinese sage—a thin, tanned man with a long, white, bifurcated beard. Personal appearance and dress generally inclined toward the casual. Long hair was in vogue among those who had hair, and academics sported more mustaches and beards than would be found in a random sample on the street. Most salarymen stuck to businesslike suits and coiffure. Only a high-ranking businessman would grow a beard or mustache — possibly a company director.

Here on campus, no such restrictions held. Suits were not popular, but there were some. Young staff wore jeans and t-shirts as they saw fit, or trousers and sports coats; the occasional stand-up collared, long-sleeved shirt lent an Eastern touch. Jackets and blazers were common, but the physical education instructors were rarely out of their tracksuits. About a hundred members were present at my first faculty meeting, faces looking intelligent and open, folding fans aflutter to combat the humidity. They were mostly men, with a small minority of women interspersed among them: equal employment opportunity had far to go. Anyway, the look of collective intelligence was an improvement. I was used to a tired, toughened and browbeaten assortment in business suits.

The university's main specialization was agriculture, and as a result, the grounds were graced with a rich variety of meticulously tended plants and trees. In springtime the exquisite pink and white of *sakura* (cherry blossom trees) graced the campus, the breeze stirring their transient blossoms into flurries. From our elevated position, a view of the coastal plain stretched to Suruga Bay, the deepest bay around the archipelago and among the deepest in the world. From the windows on the other face of the building we could see the Southern Alps in the distance, snow-covered in wintertime; and then too, breathtakingly close, snow-capped Fujisan stood out crystal clear against the sky. She was *our* Mount Fuji and, as the official university symbol, figured prominently on our crest.

The Foreign Language Department common room was on the fourth and highest floor of a Liberal Arts building, close to my research room. Housing the pigeonholes for our mail and an administrative bay where two female secretaries worked, the common room was the venue for many of our meetings and informal gatherings. Regulation low tables, comfortable low chairs, and an electric thermos, a constant source of hot green tea. In one corner were stacked some sets of the Chinese game of *go*: wooden boards marked with grids and small wooden bowls filled with polished black and white *go* stones. According to Munakata, a group of colleagues used to play *go* every day during lunchtime, but they got out of hand on occasion and continued late into the afternoon. He had to put a stop to it by confronting the offenders and telling them they shouldn't be idling about playing games all day, particularly as they made too much of a racket for him to concentrate on his work. Occasionally during a sushi party, the *go* buffs would take a board out and start a game, amid raised voices, billowing cigarette smoke and flowing saké.

Years later, I happened to be discussing chess with one of the culprits, now a senior professor himself, who repeated the lunchtime *go* incident to me. "We used to play in the common room," he said, "but an *important* professor complained."

"Really?" Betraying no sign, of course, that I had heard the story before.

"Oh yes," he said, dripping with sarcasm, "a *most eminent* professor."

They had knuckled down because of Munakata's seniority, but resented it ever after. The incident revealed something of Munakata as well:

"He sure knows how to turn on the charm," Bancroft said one day with a laugh. "He knows how to turn it off, too."

Around the same level of seniority as Munakata was Professor Soga, who was faculty dean and a member of the English Department. A handsome, lean, white haired man with a broad smile and canny expression. During my first week on the job, I was standing chatting in the common room when Bancroft introduced me to him. Flashing me one of his wide grins, Soga shook my hand and greeted me cordially in quite well-articulated English, with a trace of impediment in distinguishing the l's and r's. Then he made a remark to me in Japanese, the meaning of which I didn't quite pick up. He gave the group of onlookers a round-eyed look of disbelief.

"Doesn't he speak Japanese?" he said and abruptly walked out.

"Don't worry about that," Bancroft reassured me. "When I was new to the faculty, he took me aside one day and said, 'Don't think you are going to walk around here without bowing your head when you meet someone. You'll bow your head the same as everyone else.'"

I next spoke with Soga about a month later, early one afternoon. I needed help with the procedure for buying books on my research allowance. The department seemed deserted, semester having not yet begun, but the door to his office was ajar. I knocked and pushed the door further open; the venetian blinds were drawn, so the room was quite dark. He was lying on his convertible couch decked out in whites. Suddenly aware of me standing there, he opened his eyes with a start and raised himself stiffly to his feet.

"Sorry to disturb you," I said.

"Oh, Guest-san, hello," he said, flashing his toothy smile and blinking his eyes.

He came over to me, hobbling a little. I explained my problem and he helped me fill out an order form from the booklet I was holding.

"Have you been playing tennis?" I asked. The campus had excellent sports facilities: a row of six beautiful synthetic grass courts and two hard courts, along with an Olympic swimming pool, gymnasium, playing fields and stables.

"Yes, a group of us often get together." Something occurred to him. "Do you play, by any chance?" he asked. "There have been many Australian champions, haven't there? Rod Laver, Ken Rosewall . . ."

"I used to," I said, "but I've had only one chance since coming to Japan."

"Oh, then you must come and join us," he said keenly.

That was the beginning of several friendships with the tennis players among my colleagues. Subsequently, when I fitted out my research rooms, I made sure that the first thing I put in was a convertible couch, to ease my tired bones after social matches and have somewhere to sleep after working late at night on research projects.

Soga was every bit as formidable a character as Munakata. Whereas his colleague turned his energies to his pet loves of noh and Shakespeare, however, he had hitched his wagon to administration and social networking, spheres in which his charisma and sharpness of wit and tongue held sway. He was always at the center of a group if the group was worth being in at all, and his voice was always the dominant one.

For me, every day was a learning experience, always presenting something new and remarkable to come to terms with. It was like falling into the middle of a foreign film, and though there were times I would have appreciated subtitles, I was making progress with the language. But as well, I was wary of languishing in what I found to be the extremely pleasurable processes of cultural immersion. Having had to scramble to get work published, I appreciated the value of being in print. I needed to busy myself in research, despite being isolated from the Western university system — the Internet being then in its bare infancy. The faculty's in-house publication, known generically as a *kiyo* (bulletin), appeared twice yearly, so I prepared a paper to publish in each issue, on topics from my doctoral dissertation. Kiyo were not then peer reviewed publications, as some of them have become, but universities distributed them to universities and research institutes across the nation, as a standard method of disseminating research findings. After the first year, I received a heartening mention in an annual national review of literary research and eventually had some papers accepted by refereed journals.

Tokui found a convenient apartment for me, on the second floor of a building with the grand name of Yamamura Heights, a three-story concrete eyesore with a rusted out metal stairway at one end and covered stairwell at the other. A vigorous twenty-minute walk away from campus. One of his honorary duties as selection head was to sign off as my guarantor for the apartment, a necessary requirement for a foreign resident.

We sat cross-legged in my freshly appointed tatami room, negotiating the details with a real estate agent and completing the documents. Tokui remarked on a comment of the agent's.

"She says you may not give private classes here — it is

your residence, not a classroom," he interpreted. "How stupid. Of course he has no intention of doing that," he said to her dismissively. "Ridiculous."

"Nice view," I said, gesturing out the glass door and over the rear balcony. Close by, a compact, turquoise-colored excavator had been left parked by a mound of earth on an empty block. Beyond that, a quiet country neighborhood. "They're not going to build anything on that block are they?" Silly question.

"No, no," the agent reassured me, "not build there." Not long after, a sullen block of flats materialized, effectively blocking the view.

I'd had a *hanko* (personal seal) made for signing my official documents, a short bamboo stick engraved on one end to spell out my name vertically in three katakana symbols corresponding to Ge-su-to. I pressed it onto the agent's red ink-pad and stamped the lease in the appropriate places.

A 2DK, the apartment was similar in size and layout to the one in Nagoya, but completely fitted out with brand new appointments: a bath-shower unit with a traditional style sit-up bath, a pristine tatami room, and state of the art remote controlled air conditioners.

My friends Amachi, Onoé and Yanagi had driven me up from Nagoya in two of their cars, with the possessions I'd accumulated crammed into a tiny Suzuki van. I showed them around my new place and they crowded into the bathroom to appraise the late model Western style toilet (the traditional toilet is the squat style), with its electronic console to control the temperature of the seat and various other functions. An innovative convenience then, even in Japan.

"This is for . . . *bideo* (video)?" said Yanagi, wide eyed

with surprise, misreading the katakana label on one of the buttons.

"No, not bideo,'" said Amachi. "It says bidé."

"Bidé?" said Yanagi, still acting the clown — "What is bidé?"

He pressed the button and, as we stared down into the lavatory bowl, the toilet emitted a thin electrical whine, and a plastic pipe that looked like a thick drinking straw extended itself from the rear of the bowl, stopped moving and squirted a stream of water up at our faces.

Shortly after I moved in, I met a neighbor, who lived in the apartment directly underneath mine. I was walking home from the campus and he getting out of his car, a dark green Range Rover. A burly young man with swarthy skin and a pleasant round face framed with wavy hair and a beard, he wore a checked shirt and jeans.

He spoke in fluent English flavored with a British accent.

"My name is Matsuki but my friends call me Kuma," he said smiling. "That means 'bear.' You see, I am bigger and look a bit different from most Japanese."

He owned his own English language cram school in the nearby city of Shimizu.

"My wife and I plan to drive down to the Southern Alps with our friends this weekend to enjoy the red and yellow leaves. Won't you join us?"

A quaint aspect of Japanese culture is this sweet attitude to nature, as exemplified in diversions such as moon viewing, snow viewing and flower viewing. *Hanami*, the custom of flower viewing, is the most popular one and has come down through the ages from as early as the Heian period (794–1185), as has *momijigari*, the viewing of autumn leaves. In spring, the media chart the progress of the blossoming cherry trees, as the front of warmer weather moves northward; everyone holds outdoor hanami parties for a week or so when the cherry blossoms reach full bloom in their town. My workmates in Nagoya had taken me along to one, which I found amusing, flower viewing not being among my embedded conceptions of what blokes did together. But great fun partying on a tarpaulin spread out underneath the cherry trees in a public area set aside for the activity, not discussing sport, news or work, but musing on the delicacy and transcience of the cascading blossoms.

The next weekend, Kuma and I bundled into his Range Rover with his wife, Noriko, and drove off to the mountains for a spot of autumn leaf viewing, linking up with some of his friends, a Mr. Ojima and his family, along the way. They had brought along a confident and robust young Australian English teacher named Sharon, who turned out to be well known on the local expat scene for her ability to hold her tequila. Ojima was a keen camper and trout fisherman. After dallying in the mountains to view the leaves, we followed him to a remote spot and parked the vehicles. He took us through woods and over boulders to an expansive, dry, rocky riverbed, where we spread out tarpaulins and set up portable outdoor furniture. He lit a fire inside a pottery charcoal-cooker called a *shichirin* and used it to feed all ten of us a tasty barbecue consisting of slices of meat with vegetables. The pint-sized cooker was wonderfully economical and elegant. They have a two hundred year history, and once upon a time every household owned one.

Some weeks later, Mr. Ojima invited Kuma and me to his house to share a drink or two with him in the traditional fisherman's style. He grilled a fish and immersed it in a big bowl of hot saké. We dipped our cups into the bowl, filling them up with the now salty, smoky, richly fish-flavored brew. Later on, he threw away the fish, as all the flavor had been drawn out. We drank from traditional square cups, little wooden boxes called *masu*. After the prepared saké was gone, he opened a fresh bottle and placed a pinch of salt on the rim of each of our masu.

"Japanese people have never liked to drink alcohol by itself without eating," Kuma explained to me. "In olden times, people who were too poor to have anything to eat with their saké would drink it this way, to give them at least the feeling they were eating."

The saké started to do its thing. So comfortable reclining on the tatami I dozed off. My mind loosened its grasp on Mr. Ojima's speech, so his story of the mountains and days of yore lost sense for me, and his voice continued as a low gravelly murmur, punctuated with quiet chuckles and mellow growls.

9

Main Street Middle Japan

At Shizuoka Station you descended steps and escalators from the Shinkansen platform and went through automatic ticket gates to a spacious covered plaza, which connected to local lines, taxis and bus terminals and housed an array of restaurants and food stalls. You could shop in a multistory department store that had entrances from the plaza. The sparkling complex bustled with consumers and commuters so well-dressed you felt almost privileged to enter. The central stations in big cities like Nagoya and, of course, Tokyo, were like towns in themselves—not to mention Kyoto station, with Hiroshi Hara's soaring, futuristic architecture. Shizuoka Station had an atmosphere of efficiency and class, but without malls and passages heading off every whichway like the big city stations and without the hectic rush. Wide exits at opposite ends of the plaza opened to the outside world.

Bancroft and I arranged to meet at a fountain by the northern exit, so he could show me around the city. Sun showers had threatened that morning, so I carried my umbrella — an oversized dark green one with a wooden handle. I heard a male laugh close behind me and turned to see Bancroft approaching, his own more modest umbrella raised above his head.

"I knew it was you as soon as I saw that umbrella. I thought, 'It definitely must be a foreigner,'" he said.

"Not bad, is it? It must have cost me a hundred bucks." I brandished the sturdy wooden handle. I had never owned such a good umbrella, and I felt rather British with it, tapping the metal end on the concrete as I strutted along with it furled, toying with it like a walking stick. Umbrellas were available everywhere, including cheap plastic ones that you could get at a convenience store for little more than a hundred yen, but I had bought mine at Isetan, an upmarket department store.

"They are an amazingly accurate predictor of rain in Japan," I said. "It may be the brightest day, but if you notice one or two people carrying one, you should take yours out with you too."

"I'd be careful with that one or it might go missing," he said. "Everyone is honest, and no-one would ever dream of stealing something because it is so dishonorable — except when it comes to umbrellas. Many Japanese don't seem to consider it theft to pick up a stray if they're surprised by rain, which is, of course, the usual circumstance. One time on campus, a student complained that an American exchange student attacked him after he had walked off with the American's umbrella. The American was pushing him, calling him 'son-of-a-bitch' and all that." He laughed and I chortled at his pantomime.

Lean and broad shouldered with a wide forehead,

heavily lidded eyes and a strong, cleft chin, he had a gracious, British manner and the trace of a northern accent. When I looked at him, I couldn't help imagining him dressed for battle in a chain-mail vest and coif like a latter day Prince Hal—perhaps with a dash of Peter Sellers.

Bancroft was right about the umbrella. One day it disappeared from the umbrella stand in front of a convenience store. It had stood conspicuously taller than all the others, so perhaps someone's hand strayed upon it absentmindedly, I thought, giving the anonymous culprit the benefit of the doubt. Then, somebody stole the next umbrella I bought—another good quality one, too—from where I'd left it in a stand in the carpeted stairwell of a nightclub. An annoying thing about this second incident, compounding the basic annoyance of having something thieved, was that it was pouring with rain and I got soaked, unable to bring myself to make off with someone else's. A further aggravation was that, both times, my good quality article was chosen from among a range of shoddier ones; thus the miscreant was not purely motivated to avoid a soaking, but they guessed they might as well do it in style. In future, I refused to leave my umbrella in a designated receptacle unless I could keep an eye on it. This weakness for picking up umbrellas not their own was indeed an aberration in an otherwise exceedingly honest population.

We went down some stairs to a busy underground mall, from where a broad passage took us underneath the highway adjacent to the railway line. Young buskers played guitars, sitting in a circle on the ground. Along the passageway, youthful pedlars—Westerners and Middle Easterners as well as locals—sat on mats with jewelry and other imported odds and ends lain out in front of them. A Buddhist monk standing straight and motionless, his back to the tiled wall of the passageway, cupped a wooden begging bowl in his hands. He wore the traditional *kasa* of the traveling monk, a head covering like a broad inverted bowl woven from rice straw, concealing the upper half of his face: the act of giving and receiving should be an anonymous exchange. I dropped some coins into his bowl, and he tinkled a little brass bell for me.

We walked along Gofukucho-dori, a leafy street lined with flowerbeds, from the station to the downtown shopping area, through what was called "the Scramble," the main intersection in the center of town. Here traffic lights would stop all the vehicles simultaneously, allowing pedestrians to cross in any direction, straight across or diagonally from corner to corner. As usual, everyone was polite and well presented. No sense of rush; everyone went about their business with the minimum fuss and noise. The Scramble seemed to hold the potential for chaos, yet there were no raised voices or aggressive behavior, no collisions, no blaring car horns.

Japanese are often averse to creating any kind of public fuss. Once at a railway station, I saw a woman accidentally bang her head against a concrete column so hard she nearly collapsed, blood running down her face, but she just held her head and laughed it off as a joke. At a department store in Nagoya, a man suffered an epileptic fit on an escalator near me and was dragged to the bottom, where he lay convulsing, while the other shoppers gave him as wide a berth as they possibly could. People coming down the escalator were forced to step right over him, but no one stopped. I was the only one who went to his aid; then, when he came to his senses, his eyes widened at the sight of a foreigner bending over him, and he jumped up and hurried away without a word.

We turned into Aoba Shimboru Rodo (Symbol Road) and headed along a wide central pedestrian strip featuring novel sculptures and fountains, stopping to contemplate a conceptual fountain entitled "Zen." An open barrel occupied the center of a set of intersecting rails that allowed it to tumble in any direction. Jets of water arcing into the barrel gradually filled it up. On becoming full, it would suddenly topple without warning, empty its contents, wobble on its base and finally right itself; and the process started over again. Compulsive viewing.

The dynamic fountain was reminiscent of Daruma, the Japanese name for the wandering Indian monk Bodhidharma. The legendary founder of Zen Buddhism in sixth century China, having brought teachings of the meditative Mahayana tradition from India, Daruma lost the use of his arms and legs from sitting meditating in a cave for nine years. Papier-mâché daruma dolls have been popular since the sixteenth century. The red, gold and black, barrel shaped dolls — body and head but no arms or legs — are painted with Bodhidharma's mustache and bushy eyebrows and two white spaces where the eyes should be. The dolls are for good luck; you paint in one eye when you decide on something you want and the other when your wish comes true. Campaigning politicians are forever painting eyes on giant darumas for the television cameras. A common talisman and children's toy sometimes made in the form of Daruma is called an *okiagari koboshi*

123

("little monk who gets back up"), being weighted in such a way that it rights itself whenever it is knocked over. A famous saying extols Daruma's qualities of unrelenting perseverance, dedication and determination: *nanakorobi yaoki*, meaning "Daruma fell down seven times and got up eight times." (He was also credited with founding the martial art of kung fu, at the Shaolin Temple in China.) The fountain must, I reflected, engender in passers-by the very Zen-like meditative state it symbolizes, one inevitably bound in an eternal cycle of quest and failure, life and rebirth. "Becoming full," it whispers, "empties."

We crossed an intersection and entered a park whose centerpiece was a hideously tacky fountain and clock. We were just in time. The hour struck and the fountain burst into action, water spurting and spraying everywhere, choreographed to gay electronic music. Perhaps for the enjoyment of the children, perhaps not. Adults, too, displayed a capacity for delight that often appeared to jaded Western eyes as childlike, if not childish.

Bancroft wanted to show me his favorite soba restaurant. Soba (buckwheat) noodles are about the healthiest food you can eat. They often come in a hearty soup, such as the popular *gomoku soba*, with five kinds of primary ingredient including an egg and meat; I liked this alongside a bowl of rice garnished with a slice of pickled daikon radish. My favorite, though, and the better to enjoy on a more sociable occasion such as now, was *tenzaru soba*. The *ten* is from *tenpura* (pronounced "tempura"), one-half of the meal: tempura battered vegetables and seafood; a *zaru* is a bamboo mat used to serve the freshly cooked, cooled soba, so as to allow any residual water to drain off. You break a quail's egg into a cup of cold *tsuyu*, a deliciously salty sauce, and stir in wasabi root and finely chopped chives, before using your hashi to dip morsels of food into the sauce.

"Wait until you see the plates they use here," Bancroft said after I ordered my meal.

A waiter struggled up the narrow staircase carrying a rough textured, artistically formed pottery platter, to where we sat shoeless and cross-legged at our table. The platter was as big as a birdbath, its size completely out of proportion to its function, my meal occupying a small space in the middle.

"They are proud of the quality of pottery they use to serve their meals," Bancroft explained. "These giant dishes are their gimmick. The restaurant is a popular spot for famous sumo wrestlers, too, so the food has to be good." He pointed to a row of framed and signed photographs of wrestlers that hung from the far wall.

The showers were lifting and the sun glimmered though the clouds. The district was unpretentious to the point of drabness, contrasting the tinsel modernity of downtown Shizuoka. Bancroft rented a house nearby, a freestanding two-story dwelling built from wood and corrugated iron, modest but quaint and comfortable.

"This is a brilliant neighborhood," he said, getting a bottle of saké from his refrigerator and pouring us a glass. "The locals used to be master swordsmiths but there's not much call for that any more." Held the bottle up to the light. "Someone gave me the saké as a gift. See the flecks of gold leaf floating in it? Drinking it is supposed to bring you health and prosperity."

He struck me as a model of successful assimilation: a kind of existential project, exploring the possibilities of oneself uniquely discoverable here, due to the melange of various elements specific to the culture. There was no single best way. Watching him and examining my own experience, I gained an inkling of how there was an aesthetic to the process and how each act of adaptation was a growth node.

We finished our saké and went outside. He slapped the seat of an old black bicycle propped against the wall of his house.

"I've got a new one, so I don't need this anymore," he said. "You can have it if you like."

We continued on our outing, first ambling through Sumpu Park. Bancroft told me that the shogun Tokugawa Ieyasu built Sumpu Castle in 1585, but it was flattened during the Second World War. A gate and turret had been reconstructed next to the original moat and walls. Within the park stood an orange tree planted by Ieyasu himself, and a bronze statue of him with a falcon perched on his forearm. Ieyasu was raised in Shizuoka a hostage of Imagawa Yoshimoto, rival of Nobunaga's. He grew so fond of the area that he retired here in 1605. Sumpu Castle ranks with Osaka Castle as Ieyasu's grandest fortification outside of his capital of Edo (present-day Tokyo).

Another stroll brought us to the Shizuoka Sengen Shrine, nestled at the foot of a wooded hill, one of more than thirteen hundred shrines of a Shinto cult that honors Mount Fuji as sacred. We looked around the buildings of the shrine with their magnificent sweeping roofs, and Bancroft took me along a trail that ran up the hill. As we climbed, the city spread out beneath us. At the summit was a clearing containing a granite monument, a rectangular pillar about seven feet tall, with an inscription including the characters B-29.

"In 1945 an American air raid in Shizuoka killed seventeen hundred men, women and children in a sea of fire," he explained, resting his hand against the monument. "Waves of B-29 bombers flew from Guam and fire-bombed the city.

"Two bombers collided during the raid. One exploded and the other crashed, killing most of the crew. The local citizens were furious about the raid and attacked the crewmen's corpses with rocks and sticks. A monk rescued the only two survivors, but they later died from their injuries. Well, that's the official version . . . it's commonly thought they might have been helped along.

"Despite the antagonism of the townsfolk, the monk buried them and set up a cross. After the war, he had this cenotaph erected for the American fliers. The statue there is Kannon, the goddess of mercy. It's a monument to all the victims of the war.

"Every year now, representatives come from the American military and hold a ceremony in which they pour a flask of bourbon whiskey over the memorial. There's a saying to the effect that 'there are no friends or enemies in death': the memorial symbolizes the wish of the Japanese people for world peace and harmony."

The next year, I met a Shizuokan physician, Sugano Hiroya, who survived the air raid. Since 1972, he had taken it on as a personal duty to preserve the B-29 memorial. Dr. Sugano also belonged to the Zero Fighter Admirer's Club and had developed a relationship with the Americans. He and other Japanese representatives were now planning reciprocal ceremonial visits to Pearl Harbor to honor the fallen of both countries.

* * *

I RODE shakily in the direction of my apartment, trying out various methods to carry the umbrella, none of them entirely satisfactory. I hadn't ridden a bike since I was twelve years old. The rain held off, so I didn't have to try to emulate the locals, who could cruise along effortlessly even in heavy rain, with one hand on the handlebar and the other holding an umbrella aloft—a trick I never mastered. An *"obasan* bike" (a so-called "aunty's" model) with no horizontal bar and on the too small side, with swept up handlebars and a rusty chain that made a racket inside the metal cover. I sat on the broad saddle, my knees pumping up far higher than was ergonomically sound and the umbrella jammed behind the wire basket attached to the handlebars. I rang the bell for fun and exulted in sensations of freedom and flight forgotten since childhood.

Bancroft had said that the only road rule for bicycles was that there were none: I may ride on either side of the road or on the sidewalk, and everyone else had to get out of the way. Whether he was serious or not, I was content to stick to the sidewalk, because the road was the principal route between the city center and the outlying university suburb, and the traffic was heavy. Following his directions it took me half an hour to arrive at the shopping area nearest my place, a street called Oshika Shotengai. Oshika was a working class suburb, its main street as dull and dusty as an old sepia photograph. But it seemed to have all the necessities: a grocery, pharmacy, liquor shop and other modest concerns.

Rattling along, I noticed a little barbershop in a lane that ran off from the main street. I'd been thinking I needed a haircut, so I stopped, spun my noisy mount around and wheeled it down the lane.

My experience in Nagoya taught me that a session with a hairdresser was a complicated affair. They would insist on washing and conditioning my hair before cutting it, while I lay back with my head suspended above a basin and a towel covering my face. Then the hairdresser wrapped the towel around my head like a turban and showed me to the chair for the cut. He or she would pummel my shoulders, neck and crown—they were skilled at giving a massage, so this part was relatively relaxing given the stressful nature of the procedure as a whole. While other customers relished the pampering, I didn't at all, and would have preferred to have it done as quickly as possible.

Japanese males seemed quite hair-conscious. There was a nascent fad among city youths to want to alter their naturally straight black hair, and some had it hennaed or colored. A particular style of middle-aged man, often observed in loud sports shirts gracing bars and pachinko parlors, favored a tightly curled look. To see someone receiving this treatment, his hair sticking out in tufts through perforations in a plastic shower cap, was quite amusing. Several people were intrigued by my curly hair and asked me in all earnestness whether I had it permed.

A bell screwed to the door tinkled as I opened it and went in. One of two primitive barber chairs was taken by a balding customer covered up in a yellowed sheet, being worked on by a small bent woman as advanced in years as he. They saw me standing there and froze. A small gent in a short-sleeved shirt and gray slacks was seated on a stool. He rose unsteadily and greeted me with the customary shopkeeper's welcome, *"Irasshai-mase!"* He was clearly the proprietor and the old woman his wife. As our eyes met through his thick lenses, he did his best to control his embarrassment at my foreign-ness.

I asked him for a cut, please, fairly short. With af-fected nonchalance, he placed me in the empty chair, shook a sheet out over me and tied it up behind my neck. Facing the mirror, I noticed the woman and her client gaping at me. They were frozen in a tableau, her arms fixed in their raised position, holding a comb and scissors to his head. Before me, on a shelf beside the mirror, a wire cage, in which an ancient, balding, green and yellow budgerigar perched motionless on a swing, its head inclined, an eye piercing through me.

I inspected my gaijin reflection and wondered what was in store for it. Most likely this haircut was going to be more intensely unpleasant than the one I was used to in Nagoya. The barber looked studiously at my long-ish curly hair and decided it needed a special measure. He came at me not with scissors but with a single edged razor blade enclosed in a toothed plastic holder, a relic from a cheap do-it-yourself haircut kit of the kind ad-vertised on TV twenty years earlier (the infamous "K-tel Hair Magician"). He scraped the thing across my skull with a hacking action, while I closed my eyes and breathed, knowing that any objections or suggestions would escalate his anxiety. I dismissed too the option of escape. There would be a fuss, the man have his feelings hurt and the incident become a topic of discussion in the district for ever after, evoked by my every appearance. No, I had gotten myself into this fix and all I could do now was bear up stoically.

The blade chopping at me sent shivers down the spine. Hearing some activity going on beside me I opened my eyes. The other customer was thanking the woman for his trim. She brushed him down and took off his sheet, and he paid her, made a droll comment to the old man working on me about what an inter-national establishment it was becoming, and left with a slam-jingle. The budgerigar kept peering at me sus-piciously—could it tell I was non-Japanese? I saw from the mirror that the hacking-implement was having the effect not so much of shortening my hair as scissors would do, but of thinning it out. The sides were shorter but the top still much the same. I sat there benumbed as the man rubbed a gob of grease between his palms and applied it vigorously into my scalp, before combing my glistening locks directly back from my forehead in the pompadour style of amateur Elvis Presley imper-sonators. Of course. The King—*za kingu*. An exemplary fashion and a compliment indeed, this recognition of my movie-star looks. Having resolved not to intervene, I was overcome by a strangely masochistic feeling as I underwent my transformation. Finally, beaming, posi-tively chuffed, the barber whipped off my sheet, pow-dered and brushed me down. Free at last. I paid him the price displayed in marker pen on a cardboard sign near the budgerigar's cage and thanked him enthusias-tically, as though the hairdo was exactly what I wanted. The bird was flapping around and using its beak to scale up the bars of the cage. It spun upside-down and screeched, setting loose some tiny feathers, which floated down around it.

Arriving home, I went to the bathroom and examined my hair in the mirror, recoiling at its hideousness. A melody rang perversely in my brain. *Well, that's alright, mama, that's alright for you.* The goo the barber put through my hair had a vile, sweet smell. *That's alright, mama, any way you do-hoo* . . . I showered and washed my hair, thinking that my appearance might improve with conditioner, which it didn't. No choice but to make an emergency trip into the city the next morning in search of a more bourgeois salon.

10

Sempai and *Kohai*

S tudents respectful and co-operative as reputed, but not so shy and reserved as to cause any diffi- culties, either. Outside the classroom, it was entertaining to watch them play out the daily rituals of university life, which served as important a function as the knowledge they acquired in class in conditioning them into society, by reinforcing the same conventions that governed their earlier education.

A student's sensei was at the top of their social hierar- chy, next came their *sempai* (senior), then their *dohai* (peer) and then their own *kohai* (junior). The terms re- ferred to one's standing or ability in a group or activity, with the emphasis on whether one was involved "before" or "after." Thus, the sempai-kohai system was based on seniority, incorporating an idea of guidance and a men- tor-protégé type of relationship between colleagues or fellows. Student "circles" (*sakuru*)—a wide range of ex- tracurricular clubs for activities such as karate, judo, tennis, soccer, American football, charity work, and classical or jazz orchestra—were governed by this system, such that the entire university life of a student could be structured by the groups and hierarchies to which they belonged.

I was playing tennis regularly with Professor Soga and ten or so colleagues and some of their wives. Social tennis was more structured than in Australia, with everyone doing stretches and squats at the beginning of a session. Friendly contests were held throughout the year, involving speeches, trophies and après tennis parties with beer, more speeches and obento. In an annual challenge, a team of physicians traveled from various parts of the country to play against us academics. Most players wore spotless whites and owned the finest racquets, shoes and accoutrements, down to designer drink bottles. I bought a good racquet and shoes, but stopped short of dressing up for midweek hits, beyond baggy khaki shorts, t-shirt and floppy hat. In the searing midsummer heat, I brought water in a liter soft-drink bottle, and cooled myself off by filling my hat up before putting it on, so it splashed over my head and shoulders. The others were at first appalled, then amused: my foreignness, together with my enthusiasm for the game, licensed this degree of idiosyncrasy.

My friend Tsuji-san, a colleague from the English Department whom I encouraged to take part in the tennis group, was another who abstained from wearing whites. He had been a keen "soft tennis" player in his high school days. The Japanese developed this variation on tennis in the late eighteen hundreds, when they appropriated the Western sport but lacked the technology to manufacture proper tennis balls. The sport uses soft, smooth rubber balls, lighter racquets and slightly different rules. It has become popular in other parts of Asia—Korea in particular—and represents something like forty per cent of the tennis played in Japan, because so many high schools adopted it. Devotees continue to play at university; ours, for one, had a soft tennis club for students. The flight of the ball is slower and more lobbed than in standard tennis—many people prefer soft tennis because the rallies are longer and not dominated by heavy shots. Anyway, Tsuji-san adapted remarkably well and inherited good topspin ground-strokes, which are a staple of the Japanese sport.

English proverbs were a research interest of his—a good topic for us to discuss, for there was always something relevant. We would be on the losing end of a set:

"Don't worry"—I would call to him and give a pointed glance—"it ain't over till the fat lady says so."

"What saying did you use then?" he would say as we changed ends with our opponents—Soga-san and Amagishi-san, who was soon to be elected president of Shizuoka University. "I believe that 'it isn't over till the fat lady sings' is an opera metaphor, isn't it? The fat lady is the soprano."

"Yes, I guess it's an ironic, mocking reference to the opera—but suggests comically that the person speaking knows nothing about opera . . ."

"Of course, opera has an upper class connotation—"

"That's right, that's part of it—so the saying reacts against that snobbish connotation . . . makes a very basic statement of the obvious—'Things haven't run their course: it's not over *yet*, so don't give up hope.' It's like a self-parody, or rather, reverse snobbery. The saying became clichéd, so someone came up with 'It ain't over till the fat lady says so'—and also, 'It ain't over till it's over.' An American baseball legend named Yogi Berra coined that one, so-called 'master of malaproprisms.' I think maybe Yogi Bear is named after him. You know, the cartoon bear?"

"Hmm . . ." A reflective pause, then back on the job of serving to stay in the set.

Members of the student tennis circles often practiced on the synthetic grass courts. They played proper sets for a portion of the time, but much of their activity consisted of structured workouts and training sessions, with a sempai telling the kohai what to do. Two extra concrete courts were reserved primarily for staff. Married couples from outside our party turned up sometimes but chose to play by themselves rather than join us, a perfectly acceptable arrangement. Instead of having a hit-up or playing a sociable set, however, the man would often treat his wife to a coaching session, standing near the net with a bucket of balls at his feet, hitting them to her one after the other and demonstrating how she should swing her racquet. These women were, in fact, usually at least as good as the men, because they played together most days while their husbands were at work, but they always deferentially assumed the role of pupil.

The *kendo* (traditional bamboo sword fighting) circle trained in a gymnasium on higher ground, overlooking the staff courts. Heavy thumps and blood curdling screams echoed from the gymnasium as pairs of fighters tangled with each other. Wearing protective masks, helmets, breastplates, gauntlets, hip-protectors and thick, quilted tunics, they rushed at their opponent, gripping their bamboo *shinai* (kendo sticks) vertically in both hands, aiming for the head. Kendo is, like judo and *kyudo* (archery), one of the arts of *budo* (the "martial way") that aims to instill Confucian and Buddhist values through the rigors of physical training. (The better-known term *bushido* refers to the "way of the warrior"—the ethical or chivalric code of the samurai.)

Student life seemed less differentiated from high school than in the Western system. Very few mature-aged students attended university; and the institution held a responsibility of care in more than purely academic matters. Freshmen joined academic guidance groups; particular academics were made responsible for orientating each group to their studies and helping with any difficulties encountered in student life.

In their third year, students joined a professor's or associate professor's laboratory or research room to pursue a specialized study toward their fourth year graduation thesis (all degree courses were of four years duration). While they wrote their thesis, they also tackled *shushoku* (job hunting) activities in their fourth year. The academic whose laboratory they joined had a responsibility to support them in their job hunting; and the universities collaborated with business enterprises in facilitating job-hunting, in an elaborate national support system. Academics and their advanced charges generally built up strong bonds during the phases of graduation and job hunting, and many academics saw it as their role to encourage morale and the students' sense of belonging by hosting parties for them in their research room or at a restaurant.

Most of us in Liberal Arts did not have the responsibility of teaching graduating students, but some staff chose to involve students in their own extra-curricular or research activities, with the purpose of enriching their education. Professor Munakata encouraged interested students to participate in productions of noh drama and treated his noh and Shakespeare followers to lunch in the university restaurant. Another colleague, Shibutani-san, an accomplished kendo exponent and newspaper columnist on the sport, coached the kendo circle. Attention to this extra-curricular dimension of caring for one's students and setting an example for them at close quarters contributed to one's professional fulfillment and to the legacy of a good sensei.

Here was the Confucian ethic in action, such as has infused Japanese thinking since the fifth century. Confucius proposed that leaders of a society should lead by moral example rather than by setting rules and laws. Thus one's duty is to strive through study and application to become what the *I Ching*, a classic Confucian text, refers to as the "superior man." Known as *Ekikyo* in Japan, the *I Ching* arrived here during the sixth century at the latest and had a profound intellectual influence during the Edo period of 1603-1868. The cornerstone of Confucian morality is filial piety, meaning a child's obedience and duty to their parents (in the tradition, specifically the father). The virtue of filial piety teaches one to honor one's ancestors, father and teacher, who in their turn, reciprocate with benevolence and altruism.

WE WERE indeed like one big happy family in some ways. The university owned off-campus apartment buildings to accommodate staff at a cheap rent. They were not available to me, because staff with families had the first option. Even if I could, however, I would not have taken advantage of the apartments, preferring to keep more distance between my private life and work.

On the date of our annual physical, we were organized in groups to meet with medical staff on a designated day, each of us waiting for our turn, sitting together in our underwear. We drank barium meal to illuminate our digestive tracts for the x-ray machine housed in a big medical van that stayed for the week.

All traces of personal vanity evaporated inside that vehicle. First, the x-ray attendant had me imbibe a milky potion. Not realizing how strongly effervescent the stuff was, I involuntarily discharged a noisy belch. He explained carefully that the idea was to hold the gas in so it could inflate my digestive pipes and tubes for the barium meal to irradiate them. He then had me mount a contraption consisting of a cushioned plank attached to a mechanism of rods and gears. I was initially in a standing position, until he took hold of his control switches and levers, and mechanically moved and rotated me in every attitude and direction, while I held on grimly to a metal bar to stop myself falling off. The attendant barked out orders for me to roll over and turn this way and that, but the situation was so abnormal and his orders so rapid-fire that I became confused, and he had to stop from time to time, come over and physically move my body into the required position.

Finally I was given a dose of laxative and told to hurry to my office and not stray far from a lavatory. When the potion kicked in, the effect was so sudden and violent that everyone in earshot knew that the procedure had reached its conclusion.

The annual housecleaning day was in December.

End of year housecleaning was a traditional activity, a way of greeting the deity of the New Year; our faculty subscribed to the custom, as did most organizations and companies.

A noteworthy feature of the campus, in addition to the splendid setting and pleasant, utilitarian architecture was the general grubbiness of the buildings, inside and out.

"Private universities need to be clean and modern-looking to entice students," my colleague Kishino-san explained as housecleaning day approached. He was an upstanding young man, a Wordsworth scholar and Anglophile. "Being a national university we attract them anyway, so we do not need to have cleaners to keep our buildings quite so immaculate."

Apprehensive about what the day would entail, I had been describing the furious activity that took place on cleaning day at my old college, when we had to scour the building from top to bottom; it had been our grueling job to polish every stair and landing of all eight floors.

Kishino-san gave a quizzical little smile.

"Don't worry too much," he said. "Dirty buildings are an emblem of our elite status, I assure you."

Housecleaning day arrived, and about a dozen of us assembled in the common room, where the head of department took charge, delegating duties and distributing mops, polishers, gloves, brand new terry toweling cloths, and plastic bottles of detergent and window cleaner.

Exclamations of *"Yosh! Yosh!"* resounded in the corridor as we got to work, noisily signifying our zeal. The department head put me in charge of a section of floor and asked me to give it a once-over with a mop. When I completed the job, he assigned me a dozen windows in the common room to clean, and after I finished doing them, the windows in my research room. This was a matter of spraying on window cleaner and wiping it off with a cloth and must have taken fifteen or twenty minutes. By then everyone else had finished too.

The call went up for refreshments and good cheer abounded as we set the low tables with glasses and hauled bottles of beer and saké out of the refrigerator, where someone had placed them earlier in preparation for the post-cleaning festivities. Before long the *sushiya*-san (sushi man) arrived carrying big covered platters laden with freshly made sushi: somebody had discreetly ordered by telephone, and everything happened with precision timing born of years of experience. We joked, laughed, made toasts—*Kampai!*—scoffed down the delicious sushi, and everyone contributed money to cover the expense—and then supplementary cash to send someone out for more liquor.

"This is my type of working bee." I took a piece of sushi without using hashi but with my thumb and two fingers—acceptable sushi etiquette in friendly company—turned it over and wiped it through a saucer of soy sauce to coat the ruddy raw tuna, then popped it whole into my mouth. The room was getting loud and festive, and I laughed along with an exuberant rapid-fire conversation that I did not fully understand.

Tsuji-san drew up a chair and gestured to pour me a saké. I held up my little pottery *choko* (saké cup) for him to fill, then I returned the favor. Uncivilized to pour your own, so sometimes you have to alert your companion that you're empty by topping up his or hers first.

"Guest-san, how do you understand the proverb, 'A rolling stone gathers no moss'?"

"I think it means it's best to keep on moving and not get bogged down in the one spot."

"That would be a good thing then, not to gather moss?"

"I guess so . . . lacking material belongings, responsibilities, cares . . . I think it's saying that people who keep moving are freer and don't get stuck. I mean, moss is something additional, soft, rough and organic—not like the smooth surface of a rolling stone . . ."

"But you know, Japanese people consider moss beautiful and providential, and we often try to cultivate it in gardens. It symbolizes antiquity, harmony, tradition, tranquility, life itself . . ."

"I suppose that's right," I said. "I always presumed the moss was meant to be taken as negative, but now I see you can interpret it either way, depending on how you look at it . . ."

Our choko were nearly empty, so I made to pour him another.

"No thanks, I should get going," he said, and threw in a cautionary, "Careful not to drink too much . . . we must remember: all things in moderation."

"All things in moderation!" I raised my cup in a mock toast, laughing. "That's good."

PROFESSOR MUNAKATA and I were developing a bond—likely in the mold of sempai-kohai, though my conviction in my own individualism may have caused me to disdain such a suggestion. Thanks to my past association with Sogabé and Ikeda, I was shrewd about both the potential value of symbiotic relationships and the ethical nuances that might attend them.

Munakata was a former Fulbright scholar and professor. His business card introduced him with the title "Leader of the Noh Shakespeare Company of Japan," which was not so much a conventional repertoire company as a conceptual entity consisting of the projects that its leader had conducted over many years. These, indeed, included several formidable achievements: acting in international solo presentations of extracts from Shakespeare plays that he had adapted into the noh form, and directing full productions, such as *Noh Hamlet* and *Noh Macbeth*, by first-rate professional actors. Although other slickly marketed companies specializing in noh Shakespeare sprang up during later years, he was a real pioneer of the genre.

Before long I was proofreading and improving his English language essays on noh Shakespeare for international journals, a task I was more than willing to do for the insights it afforded into the forms and techniques of noh, yet a further window onto Japanese tradition. Occasionally after work we would catch the bus into town and have supper at a sushi restaurant while he waited for his Shinkansen. We spent an hour or so sitting on stools at a superbly carpentered pinewood bar, on top of which was integrated a long, low refrigerated glass cabinet displaying prime fish fillets and other varieties of uncooked seafood (squid, octopus, anemone, tuna roe, shrimp, eel, etc.).

Munakata was well acquainted with sushi chefs in the city and entertained them with his wit and banter. They were appropriately deferential, laughing and chiming in as they expertly rolled pieces of sushi, patting on the topping and plopping them down for us: *"Ja, dozo! Dozo!"* ("Go ahead, enjoy!"). Most chefs were in their own right as accomplished raconteurs as he, but they knew, too, on which side their bread was buttered, so to speak, and when it was their turn to play the admirer.

Every so often, Munakata would come out with a pronouncement or quotation in English, engaging me and astonishing the chef with a masterly display of bilingualism.

"Zeami writes that Zen is the soul of noh." He turned his head to look at me with an enigmatic smile, the corners of his eyes crinkling, as the gem of wisdom fell from his lips. Stuck for a reply, I arched my eyebrows and put on a thoughtful face.

Zeami (1363–1443) was the most illustrious noh writer and actor in history. He raised the drama from being a folk form to a classical theater art, and his critical treatises have defined the art even to the present. Noh expresses the absorbing, exquisite aesthetics of Zen and embodies the Buddhist worldview. The central character, or *shité*, enters the stage over a pathway from the darkness as though materializing into the world, and at the closing of the play, exits over the same symbolic pathway into the darkness once again, freed of karma. Zeami himself became a Zen monk when he retired from the theater aged seventy, ten years before his death.

"That is why, in my *Noh Hamlet*," Munakata continued, spreading the fingers on both hands and touching the opposing fingertips together, forming the framework of an invisible pyramid or jewel, "I have changed Hamlet's line 'To be or not to be, that is the question' to 'To be or not to be, is *no longer* the question . . .'"

"You mean, because he is in a space beyond rational oppositions, a Zen-like space?" I remembered reading an article that an artistic director of the Royal Shakespeare Company had written after watching a performance by the Noh Shakespeare Company of Japan; he commented fairly that "it gives us more of an insight into noh than into Shakespeare."

Munakata arched one eyebrow cagily, shrugged his shoulders and gave a laugh. I was unsure whether he did not know what I was talking about or vice versa—perhaps the very state of mind he intended for me. He adopted the stance of Zen sage, leaving just one role available for me—that of the thick-headed pupil:

A pupil comes to Suiwo, disciple of the Zen master Hakuin, seeking to become enlightened. Suiwo says to him, "You must hear the sound of one hand clapping. Go away for ten years and meditate." The pupil meditates for ten years and returns despondent. "I could not hear the sound of one hand clapping." "Then meditate for another five years. You must hear the sound of one hand clapping." The pupil meditates for another five years and returns more downcast. "I still could not hear the sound of one hand clapping." "Then try for another year." The pupil returns after a further year even more dejected. "Yet I could not hear the sound." "In that case," says Suiwo most gravely, "you should persevere for another three days. If after that time you still cannot hear the sound of one hand clapping, then you should kill yourself." On the second day, the pupil finds enlightenment.

Munakata displayed no fervent interest in much that I said, and he possessed the ability to switch off his hearing at will. This is a skill not reserved for Buddhist adepts, who are immune to distraction, but those with healthy egos can also be good at it. In Japan, it is appropriate for the teacher to speak and the student to listen in silence; in the West, the student is supposed to be encouraged to communicate on equal terms. I didn't mind his attitude, knowing I had much to learn from him. If to a degree he valued me in terms of how I may be of use, then that was a fair enough quid pro quo.

After we'd eaten our fill and Munakata caught his train, I'd drop in at a pub or nightclub before taking a cab home. Shizuoka offered an ample nightlife, its glitter and mild decadence centering on a district known informally as "Sleaze Street." Bancroft told me that the city had more nightspots per capita than anywhere else in the country.

MUNAKATA INVITED me to work on a translation of a tourist booklet about Shizuoka's neighboring city of Shimizu, an international seaport with a population of two hundred and forty thousand. I was already familiar with some of Shimizu's attractions, since it had become a weekend recreation of mine to cycle along a track that ran by the edge of Suruga Bay to Shimizu Harbor. The ride was rich in natural and cultural interest, as well as in the entertainment provided by unwitting Japanese engaged in sundry pastimes of their own. Mount Fuji was straight ahead as I rode along the seaside track. The highest mountain in Japan, Fuji is glorious in winter but barely visible in summer due to atmospheric haze.

Abutting Fuji, Suruga Bay has the deepest troughs to be found anywhere in the archipelago. Between these highest and lowest geological points so precipitously juxtaposed, one tectonic plate inches its way from east to west forcing itself beneath an opposing plate. Both bend under the strain of incalculable tons of pressure, the colossal stores of destructive energy producing a fault-line, an ominous crack in the ocean floor.

You see, Japan does not actually rest atop an infinite pile of turtles, but on a giant carp that flicks its tail sometimes. Scientists have placed measuring devices in the fault in Suruga Bay that show how every year the tectonic plate moves a further 8.9 centimeters in its fateful course. The scientists know that the carp is going to flick its tail soon, but on their geographical timescale, "soon" means perhaps tomorrow or perhaps in a hundred years. They have already named the awaited catastrophe: the Great Tokai Earthquake.

I visualized a tsunami thundering in, a split second after the earthquake had rocked the bay as if it were a basin, the entire body of water shifting in a mass. Many Japanese would not come near the area. At work we drilled for "earthquake preparedness"—the administrators hurrying around in earnest, most academics with no direct responsibility in the matter going through the motions fatalistically and bored, the same way they submitted to bureaucratic procedures in general.

To inhibit erosion, millions of tons of concrete blocks were piled up in the water close to shore, creating a polygonal breakwater all along the coast. Once I saw a gathering of men fishing from a heap of these huge blocks. One stood hand on hip, arching his back as he guzzled from a can; he then tossed the empty can out to sea, though the highway neared the bay at this point and he was in clear sight of the stream of cars motoring by. A disappointingly apathetic attitude to behold in a country that so exalts nature. Another feat of engineering had transformed the section of the Ohya River that I rode beside from Yamamura Heights to the bay, converting it into a concrete canal. They were fortunate concrete and construction companies that had won the tenders for such massive developments.

The highway ran alongside the bicycle track for a distance before branching off inland. The track meandered over diverse terrains, promenades and paths: some asphalt-covered, some bare concrete or dirt; wide in places, thin in others; crossing high above a stream or drain at one or two points. Comfortable, level riding for pushbikes. Across the highway, set back into the hillside, were hundreds of glasshouses used to cultivate strawberries, a product Shizuoka was "famous" for (everyone's hometown, no matter how humble, has something to be "famous" for), along with green tea, wasabi root and mandarin oranges. In spring, growers opened up stalls beside the highway and sold strawberries to the passing tourists. Young women wearing pink in imitation of their merchandise stood by the highway to encourage drivers to stop. They held in their hands balloon-sized inflatable plastic strawberries attached to string, which they would twirl around in front of them to catch the drivers' attention.

The gentle hillside reared up into a tall, sheer sided mount named Kunozan. Sometimes I left my bike chained to a post and climbed the wide stone stairway that zigzagged to the top—according to the Shimizu tourist booklet I was working on, there were eleven hundred and fifty-nine stairs. I paused halfway up to take in the panorama of Suruga Bay with its fractured coastline. At the summit was an ornate Shinto shrine dedicated to Tokugawa Ieyasu, founder of the Tokugawa shogunate (also called the Edo period). Named Toshogu shrines, there are over a hundred of these around Japan, the foremost situated in the city of Nikko, in Tochigi Prefecture, central Honshu. A proverb goes, "Don't say *kekko* until you've seen Nikko," which is to say, "You haven't seen everything until you've visited Nikko," referring to the beauty of its Toshogu Shrine; but the shrine at Kunozan is said to rival it. When Ieyasu died in 1616, his remains were kept at the Kunozan shrine and taken to Nikko the next year. There they deified him as a *gongen*, a spiritual avatar of the Buddha, and named him Tosho Daigongen ("Exalted Gongen Illuminating the East").

The Toshogu shrines are a throwback to an era when Buddhism and Shinto amalgamated. In Ieyasu's time, all Shinto and Buddhist deities were believed to be manifestations of Amaterasu Omikami, the Great Divinity Illuminating Heaven.

From the peak of Kunozan, you could ride on a ropeway over to Nihondaira, an elevated plateau. There I entertained myself with people-watching, lunched on zaru soba or udon noodles and wandered about absorbing the spellbinding scenery and panoramic view of Mount Fuji, starkly etched against the steely sky.

Other times, I rode on past the foot of Kunozan. After the highway veered off, it took twenty minutes on a desolate seaside track to reach Miho-no-Matsubara, an ancient pine grove on Miho Peninsula in Shimizu and a UNESCO World Heritage Site since 2013. Over tracts of time, the onshore winds have bent the pine trees over to the west; undernourished by the sandy soil, many are twisted and stunted. Thus it is said that at this sacred mythical location even the pines bow over to honor Mount Fuji.

Here the track turned at a right-angle away from the seashore, and I steered into the pine grove, where all was hushed and solemn and the wheels of my bicycle glided over a carpet of pine needles. The ground turned sandy at the far edge of the grove and I had to walk my bicycle up an incline and out of the trees.

Overlooking the beach was a clearing with a long shed divided into a souvenir shop and three or four stalls that sold noodles and *oden*, treats consisting of hard-boiled eggs, firm tofu, daikon radish, *konnyaku* (konjac or Devil's Tongue) — a jelly-like derivative of a bulbous plant — and skewered pig's intestines (*horumon*). The snacks were kept separately in the compartments of a rectangular metal container, covered in simmering broth. One ate the oden from a bowl with broth, hot mustard, and a sweet brown miso (bean paste) sauce.

"Irasshaimase! Dozo!" The smiling women called from their stalls, beckoning me to sit down at one of their tables. Red and white plastic streamers and vertical gold colored banners with images advertising beer decorated the shops, and tarpaulins shielded the customers sitting outside from the breeze.

I wheeled my bike past the souvenir shop, a treasure trove of cheap, portable items: local craft and produce; dolls, green buddhas and red darumas; plastic shinkansens; toy samurai swords, and novelty samurai wigs with the shave-pated *chonmage* cut originally meant to make wearing a warrior's helmet more comfortable. I passed by to a shop at the far end that sold light meals in addition to souvenirs. After I had visited a few times, the attendants in the competing shops stopped trying to attract my attention, and the proprietor of "my" shop would welcome me courteously. I sat and ate my oden gazing at the beach, lulled by the music of ripples faintly lapping on the shore, the streamers and banners flapping in the breeze.

"The pure white sands of Miho-no-Matsubara . . ." the tourist booklet announced. One problem: the sand was black. Was it an instance of mass delusion, the conventional image of a beautiful white sandy beach having subverted the reality, like the magical rat of the Fantastic Shop? Even if long ago the tide had washed away the once pure white sand—the same currents that the coastal breakwaters were erected to counteract—one thing was certain: the beach had not been pure white for a long time prior to the publication of the booklet. I was unwilling to perpetuate the fallacy that black was white, but "the black sands of Miho-no-Matsubara" didn't scan too well, so I changed it to "the volcanic sands," alluding to the proximity of Mount Fuji. Geologists could refute it if they liked.

Tourist groups would appear from a grove of pines on the northwestern side, having climbed a steep path up from the parking area where their tour buses were parked. They ambled down to the sand conversing and laughing insouciantly and, without removing their shoes, wandered to the shoreline. Well-dressed women adorned with jewelry and men sporting gold chains and watches. All ages and types, a cross section of society. Taking their own good time, everyone stopped at two particular places: a sacred pine and a small Shinto shrine. They carried out their devotions before the shrine—many tourist outings incorporate an act of pilgrimage, lending spiritual significance to the trip and the sense of place. The tourists assembled for photographs, making peace signs at the camera, Mount Fuji rising up behind them.

Miho was a poetic and mystical place, the actual site where the Hagoromo ("feather robe") story occurred, a legend known throughout Japan. A nymph descended from heaven at this spot where the pines bow in deference to the mountain. She took off her feather robe and left it draped over a branch when she went to bathe in the waters of the bay. A local fisherman discovered her robe and refused to return it, so she had to marry him and bear his child. Eventually she managed to recover the garment and fly to heaven.

A noh play inspired by the legend was performed every year at the very same site at Miho-no-Matsubara where the nymph descended to earth, right by the tree where she left her robe.

The play is slightly different and even more poetic than the original Hagoromo legend. In the play, the fisherman picks up the feather robe to admire it, and as he makes off, the nymph returns and begs him piteously to return it.

"How can I fly back up to heaven without it?" she cries. "Please, please! Give it back to me, and I shall perform a celestial dance for you."

"But if I give it to you," says the fisherman, "how do I know you will dance for me and not fly away immediately?"

The nymph shakes her head sadly.

"That is how things are done here on earth, not in heaven . . ."

Hearing this, the fisherman relents and gives her the

robe, and the nymph enthralls him with her sublime dance, until, trembling on high, she mingles into the heavenly mists that shroud Fuji.

11

Old Ego Dies Hard

*The old ego dies hard. Such as it was, a minister of
dullness, it was also an agent of security . . . It
disappears—with wailing and gnashing of teeth.*

—Samuel Beckett, "Proust"

Never during the time I'd spent in Japan had I
once been bored. I still experienced the cultural frisson, that momentary thrill. Every day
brought new experiences and lessons. But I felt too the
pangs of a solitary existence, at their sharpest when I
was away from my work—home alone, cycling or out
and about town. Fewer foreigners were to be seen here
than in Nagoya, but one or two of them unsettled me
with their haunted look. I might smile and nod but get
no response. Everyday pressures intensified feelings of
isolation and foreignness with visible effects that you
read in someone's face or behavior.

Bancroft and I were standing side by side in an elevator at the university. It stopped on the ground floor, the door slid open, and we came face to face with a pair of male students. Their faces froze in surprise at the two gaijin confronting them. *"Bikkuri shita!"* ("What a shock!") one remarked to the other as we walked out past them, and we heard them dissolve into laughter behind us—a certain high-pitched laugh of youth was most irritating and resembled the hoot of a lunatic.

An understanding and patient individual, Bancroft looked at me and laughed at the reaction of the students. I grinned wryly in return but would have had to admit I was masking an id-impulse to take them by the throat and shake them. If, as I theorized, living here may help you to expand certain higher aspects of your nature, freed as you were to an extent from the formative forces of your own culture, it also magnified your neuroses. But outside, in the clear, elevated space of the hillside campus, I breathed in the fresh air, looked over at the distant coast, and once again my heart was fit to soar.

Late one crisp morning I went into the departmental common room to check for my mail. I glanced out through the windows, to see the vast pale blue sky and, on the distant horizon, the peaks of the Southern Alps glimmering with the first snow.

Occupying two low armchairs were Bancroft and David Cutler, a lanky Canadian who taught English part-time in the faculty and was a long-term Shizuoka resident, though not for as long as Bancroft. They were chatting over coffee, facing each other across a long, low meeting table; newspapers, journals and sample textbooks were scattered over the tabletop. Cutler reclined in his chair, one leg crossed over the other. They looked up and welcomed me. I glanced in my pigeonhole and went over to get some tea from the electric *potto* (thermos), which stood on a bench by the refrigerator.

"Did you hear the news about Jameson?" Bancroft asked me. "Had you met him?"

"I don't know anyone by that name."

"An American studying here as a postgraduate in the Education Faculty," he said, "and he taught English for us part-time."

A haunted face appeared to my mind's eye. I'd nodded a greeting to him once or twice, which he didn't return, but instead, passed me by with a deadpan look. He would have been about my age; I hadn't known his name until now.

"I think I might know who you mean."

"He committed suicide last night," Bancroft continued. "He was found hanging from a bridge in Ohya early this morning."

"Good god."

"He put on a backpack filled with barbells before he jumped," Cutler commented in his resonant voice. "His neck was stretched close to six inches."

The description staggered me, and the man's face flashed before me again, imprinted on a hanging corpse. I sipped my tea. Tealeaves danced on the bottom of my handle-less little cup.

"I believe I saw him once or twice, and he was quite . . . distant." No one had introduced us, and he made it clear as we passed by each other that he wanted nothing to do with me.

"He'd lived here a while, and I guess he felt he wasn't

getting anywhere," Cutler said. "He applied for your job and was pissed he didn't get it," he said in my direction.

"Horrible for the people who found him," said Bancroft. "Not good form."

Cutler made a more disparaging comment. I was appalled at the unsympathetic attitude. I thought of the isolation and despair that Jameson must have endured, but I said nothing. It was as though they believed that Jameson's action reflected badly on them (although some might have considered suicide a Japanese sort of thing to do, given a rate roughly sixty percent higher than the world average).

"He left a note and last will and testament on a floppy disk," Bancroft said. "Hashimoto-san is responsible for taking care of it all."

I recalled that I'd seen this man Jameson with Professor Hashimoto in the common room once when he came into the faculty to do his teaching. Indeed, Hashimoto was the only one I'd seen him speak to.

A week later at the regular faculty meeting, Hashimoto stood up and reported on the unhappy incident. The distinguished looking man went over the details, punctuating his talk with sighs and silences. All the academics listened somberly; they sat along both sides of five rows of tables, the dean and his administrative staff occupying desks set at a right angle across the room. Hashimoto was plainly upset. He spoke sadly but clearly, running a hand over his head, his bald crown fringed with fine white hair, his head sinking forward onto his chest when he needed to refer to the documents he had placed on the table before him.

* * *

ISABELLA CAME over to visit twice a year. I had no reason to return to Australia yet and I loved being abroad, exploring my identity away from its native elements. Whatever political events were happening in Australia, what Australians thought and felt had become marginal and meaningless. My identity was forming itself around my expatriate life, the need to fend for myself, and my sense of pride in my personal independence, which grew as I met the demands of life away from home.

I was improving at communicating and getting around, and I showed off to her, introducing us to experiences that were possible owing to my fortunate insider's position. I reveled in my new-found mobility even at the everyday level: reading signs, conversing with strangers, finding my way through the subway system in Tokyo, knowing what and how to order at a restaurant or izakaya. Looking out from a train carriage, I would spot a foreigner on a platform, weaving through the crowd, at a loss which turn to take and unable to merge with the flows and eddies of the Japanese, who would part and stream around him like a river around a lumbering bear. A developing Japanese bodily sense got me from A to B without difficulty and rendered me relatively inconspicuous while doing so. I caught in myself a warped feeling of amusement at the expense of foreigners less acculturated than I, who appeared clumsy and foolish—exactly as I had, of course, not so very long ago. Was it a strange prejudice that was affecting me as I unconsciously metamorphosed? Comic loons in television shows caricatured Westerners as ludicrous bumblers—roughly similar to what I did to those

innocent strangers at whom I unreasonably, if involuntarily, silently scoffed. A comedian would fall down
on the studio floor in fits of laughter at the antics of a
straight man done up as a gaijin, an oaf with a ridicu-
lously big nose and reddish brown wig. And here was I
with my delusion of belonging to the homogeneous society—inwardly disdaining those who seemed more
foreign than I was.

Xenophobia is a subtle and pervasive element, deeply
rooted in history. A policy of National Seclusion
(Sakoku Edict of 1635) was enforced for over two hundred years, until the American Commodore Mathew
Perry sailed his black ships into Tokyo Bay (known then
as Edo Bay) in July 1853 and opened Japan up to the
West for trade. A deep ambivalence toward foreigners
persisted and Western prejudices would aggravate it.
The Japanese resented the West treating them as second-
class citizens. After all, they had their direct link to the
kami . . .

I read volumes of Lafcadio Hearn's complete works,
having retrieved them from the dusty library stacks. The
peripatetic American reporter (born Anglo-Irish and
Greek, raised in Dublin) spent the last fourteen years
of his life in Japan. This was near the close of the Meiji
era (1868–1912), when the country slid into modernity.
Hearn worked as a professor of literature at Tokyo
Imperial University and kept a holiday house at Yaizu,
a seaside town and Shizuoka's neighbor on the other
side from Shimizu. He married Koizumi Setsu, the
daughter of a prominent samurai, assumed her family
name and became a naturalized citizen, Koizumi
Yakumo. He was an archetype for the foreigner who aspired to "turn Japanese." A Japanese wife may be a

significant asset in that ambition, then and now. Hearn would listen entranced to the traditional tales his wife, Setsu, related to him. He was the first to record much of this material, she making an indispensable contribution as his ethnographic informant.

Even in my day, gaijin life in relatively homogeneous Japan had a tiresome side. Everyday incidents that occurred even in a large city, such as standing at an intersection waiting for a traffic light to change and suddenly noticing that every face in every car and bus window was turned in your direction, provoked stress. Imagine how it must have been for Hearn at a time when foreigners were as curious as a circus attraction. He wrote about staying at a small hotel in the countryside: he got up in the morning and threw open his windows, to be confronted with local children and bumpkins everywhere, even on the rooftops of the neighboring houses, straining their necks to get a glimpse of him.

A Setsu would have proven invaluable in teasing out for him the impenetrable webs of cultural norms, the intricate regulations and attitudes that ordered the society, a mechanism for compressing an endless variety of phenomena into a closed space. Like Chinese boxes: you open one box to find another one inside, open that to find another, then another, intriguingly—but frustratingly—to infinity. The culture expands in an inward rather than outward direction, and the outsider finds this an odd thing, infinity opening up in a closed box. Social anthropologist Joy Hendry refers to Japan as the "wrapping culture," and every day one sees why. A rice cracker is initially wrapped in *nori* (dried seaweed), then in an individual plastic wrapper; next it is placed in a plastic bag, then in a box with its companions. When you buy the box at a department store, the sales assistant wraps it for you professionally in gift-paper and stows the package in a decorated paper bag.

Inward expansion comes about paradoxically, as a process of miniaturization, through perfectionism, the Zen of perfectly spaced chairs, rigorous discipline and the sacralization of space and order. Every iota of available space used, divided and sub-divided upon itself; so too, the forms of daily life serve to order, differentiate, compartmentalize—a mode of cultural production that moves ever inward, dividing upon itself. Roland Barthes aptly called Japan "the empire of signs"—already a model for virtual reality, the compression of the mundane world into a dimension of signification, meaning and perhaps ultimately spirit—the ghost in the machine.

The cultural codes take patience, application and a key to unlock them. Webs of signification, like the degrees of politeness inscribed into the very language, serve to enrich and preserve the life *within,* sealing it against invasion. In the West we say that all roads lead to Rome. In Japan, it is not so easy to find the way. You can see the castle but the tangle of surrounding streets tries to ensnare you and each turning wants to push you further away. You enter the gates, and tall stone walls block your way again, turning you to the left or the right, into killing zones designed centuries ago to greet the invading army.

A GOOD place for me to be, here in central Japan, an hour to Tokyo by Shinkansen and with room to breathe and have a life. I could go for a day or a night out in

Tokyo and come home to real people. History underpins the place here, moreso than a condition of quasi-hyper-reality. Furthermore, this is "middle Japan" in a demographic as well as geographical sense: the population typifies the values and mores of the entire country. For that reason, market researchers and political pollsters conduct their surveys in this region, in order to inform their ideas about nationwide opinions and trends. Kyoto, the ancient capital, is eighty minutes by the Tokaido Shinkansen line if you take the Hikari, the fastest available express. Cultural polarities of the Tokaido Highway—ancient and modern, traditional and superficial—embody historical currents and the Buddhist precept that it is the journey that matters, not the destination.

Rising to power in the fourth century in the present city of Nara, the Yamato court, the first central government, established the Tokaido ("Road to the East Sea"). In the twelfth century, the shogun Minamoto no Yoritomo set up his command in Kamakura, a city located to the south of Edo (in that era a fishing village). The highway became a critical link between the shogun's military capital and the imperial capital, the emperor's court in Kyoto since 794.

In 1600 the unifier of Japan, Tokugawa Ieyasu, established his capital in the city of Edo. The shogun wielded control over daimyo throughout the country by having them set up secondary residences in Edo, allowing him to keep a close eye on them, while inflicting a constant drain on their resources. They were permitted to return home every other year but had to leave their families and officials behind as hostages.

Each daimyo traveled to and from Edo in a procession, creating as grand a spectacle as he could. He rode along in a palanquin carried on the shoulders of his men, heading a retinue that may number in thousands, depending upon his importance: officials, servants, vassals, porters and banner carriers, pikemen, swordsmen and samurai. The Tokaido was one among five key highways that converged on the capital like spokes on the hub of a wheel; the transport system throughout central Japan was at the same time a system of social regulation, communications and surveillance.

Remarkably, this feudalistic system of motion and regulation, developing from a unique constellation of historical factors, evolved into a form perfectly adaptable to the modern world. Japan's primary transportation and economic passage, the Tokaido-Sanyo Shinkansen (incorporating a line that extends beyond Kyoto to Osaka and further west to Hakata, on the island of Kyushu) now conducts the pulsing energy of the economic dynamo.

The line runs alongside the historical route of the Tokaido highway. A little way out of Shizuoka city, the train streaks past crops of tea tucked into impossible nooks among the hills, before the terrain levels out and you pass by rice paddies and through alternating rural and urban scenes. This route defines the industrial and socioeconomic hub of the country. Approximately two thirds of the population live in the five hundred kilometer zone between Tokyo and Osaka, a zone that occupies only fifteen per cent of the land area but produces eighty-five per cent of the GDP: the "Tokaido megalopolis." This belt is the world's most populous merging of the urban space of multiple cities, home to some eighty million people—significantly more than the forty-four million living in the next largest such conurbation, the Northeast megalopolis of the United States (Boston–New York–Philadelphia–Washington).

Riding on the Shinkansen does not impart a breathtaking impression of speed unless you try to focus your eyes on objects close to the train, such as the posts and wires flickering past, as on a speeded-up film. Since the tracks are elevated high above the ground, the Shinkansen rides so smooth it seems to be moving at a leisurely pace, cruising at 270 kilometers per hour. The scenery floats by dreamily, then the rice paddies dwindle—you see one tucked in here and there among the houses . . . and then, suddenly, you are in a real city.

Entering the outskirts of Kyoto, the train decelerates through some gentle shudders, downshifts that slow it to a crawl. The first-time visitor's expectations may be disappointed. From the train, the cityscape is understated: a typical dusty confusion of buildings, noticeably low-rise. Surely this can't be the dazzling Kyoto you've read about, this nondescript place? But over there . . . you can discern an ancient temple on a hilltop, and from the other side of the carriage, a pagoda rising imperious above the shops and houses. The city continues to reveal itself to you in this way long after you leave the train: a subtly blossoming grandeur, its roots in the everyday and ordinary.

On our first trip to Kyoto, the severe heat of the day, combined with the walking tour I had planned, had a bad effect on Isabella's feet, which started to swell up as the day wore on; the extreme midsummer temperature brought on an attack of heat rash. I dragged her about relentlessly: my feet were fine . . . and hell, *This is Kyoto*. She didn't appreciate my superior (I considered) knowledge of Japan; even worse, she was starting to remind me of that albatross I had come to abhor and strove to escape: my shadow figure, the lumbering gaijin.

We left our bags at the *ryokan* (traditional inn) I had booked for our stay and set off looking for somewhere to lunch back near the station. But I got us lost. Busy streets and cement sidewalks everywhere—no shops or restaurants, just people on their way to someplace else. I was becoming quite frazzled. Then eventually, thank god, we discovered some steps that went down to an opulent underground mall, which bustled with consumers swathed in chic Kyoto poise, including elegant women in kimono. A myriad shining display lights, sparkling glass and spotless stainless steel illuminated, reflected and re-reflected the latest fashions, an infinite kaleidoscope of color and motion. A delicious aroma of heated green-tealeaves hung in the air.

"Let's find somewhere down here," I said.

"Oh, that *would* be nice." A sarcastic edge, so back up we climbed to the concrete expanse and the humid midsummer day.

"I thought your feet were sore."

"Not *that* sore. I don't want to sit underground. Did you say there is a river around here?"

"Let's get our bearings first."

Another block, we turned a corner and came across a fairly nondescript assortment of restaurants.

"Let's try this one," I said.

"I can't stand these places where the first thing you see is a row of credit card logos stuck on the front door."

"It doesn't necessarily mean they're expensive."

"That's not the point; it's depressing and vulgar."

"Well for goodness sake, that's the way they do it, just like every other place in the world, and I really want to eat. What about this one? How about that place over there?"

We kept walking. I'd become unused to tolerating someone else's foibles and obsessions. Being in a relationship with a willful partner had the advantage of saving you the bother of making decisions; but then again, one benefit of my solitude here was that I now did precisely what I wanted, when I wanted.

Suffering from wear and tear, our relationship was becoming charged with resentment. We had never discussed the possibility of Isabella coming over permanently and it did not occur to me that she had any wish to do so. I couldn't see a future for us. I was emotionally split. On the one hand, during the months between her visits, I was a free agent. Set adrift, I was enlivened by the process of discovery—both the novel experiences and encounters that each new day offered up and the gradual assumption of mastery over my new existence with its challenging language and customs. Yet at the middle of this new personality was an aching, empty core, a longing for a truth that existed exclusively in my connection with her—my absent other—and the life with her that I'd cast off.

The old ego dies hard . . . superb line of Beckett's. The cold thought struck me that as difficult as it may be—or may not be—the relationship might have to be sacrificed in order to fulfill the promise of—would it have been more truthful to say, "capitalize upon"?— the possibilities crystallizing for me. Then the pendulum would swing again and strike with loneliness and heartache, as I pored over photographs I took during her previous visits. She stood astride a bicycle, smiling trustingly at the camera, wearing a white blouse, shorts and a broad-brimmed Panama hat. In the background were the coastal cement blocks of Suruga Bay, along the path to Shimizu. The images sliced through my present self and laid it open as a charade.

Her letters arrived and I soaked up her news and inner thoughts, her tender expressions. Time assumed the single function of erasing this pain of separation. For months, she would be coming and I planning where I would take her, the things we would do together. Then she would be here—

"What do they call this, again?" She tapped her hashi on the rim of her plate.

"*Yakisoba*—fried soba noodles." She had chosen it from among the wax models of various dishes on display in the front window—something I would never be seen dead doing any more, because anyone watching would take it to mean I couldn't read the menu.

"Well, now I know why they call it 'yucky' soba," she said. Not particularly amusing, not up to her usual standard, though my wit was beginning to flag as well.

"You ordered it."

"That model looks nothing like this tastes. Those noodles look crisp, not soggy and greasy like the real ones."

"It's good for you. It has cabbage and egg with the soba. It should have a nice spicy soy-and-ginger flavor." I attacked my bowl of ramen with spoon and hashi. "Actually," I admitted, "I was surprised you chose it. I didn't think you would go for fried noodles."

"Thanks for saying something."

I sucked in a mouthful of the hot wet noodles noisily into my mouth, chewed and swallowed. That's the proper way to eat them, expressing your appreciation of the noodles by the noise you make slurping them up. Hope it doesn't irritate her.

I shrugged. "I wouldn't want to presume to tell you anything."

The music of cheery, polite Japanese conversation played on around us, and outside the pedestrians bustled past. A pall had descended on us alone. Alone together. I was keenly aware of our foreignness, these fractious communications of ours effectively magnifying it. We were alienated even from each other and thus doubly excluded from the Japanese, whose tacit rules of social intercourse prohibited any hint of disharmony.

We sat on like this, alone together. I looked down at us from high above, from a distant, receding viewpoint: two featureless, microscopic figures, barely touching, surrounded by an exterior void, and a gulf broadening between us, within us.

Isabella broke our silence.

"You would be happier with a Japanese woman," she said in a brittle tone affecting gaiety. "Then you could try to become a present-day Lafcadio Hearn with his Japanese wife. You could have a Japanese family and learn everything there is to learn. Surely you've considered it?"

"That's ridiculous—never crossed my mind. But if you insist, I'll have to give it a shot"—trying to dismiss the element of truth in what she said.

She permitted herself a short, quiet laugh, its hint of bitterness masking her fragility—and this stung me the more.

"It would help you perfect your Japanese."
Was I truly so cynical and self-serving?

NIJOJO (NIJO CASTLE) stands at the south side of the city, not far from Kyoto Station. We strolled in the immaculate gardens, once the setting for socializing in the Tokugawa court, now UNESCO World Heritage sites. Some vistas straight out of ancient scrolls: haphazard conglomeration of pond, arched stone bridge, trees and jagged boulders conceived in an other-worldly aesthetic. Women wearing bonnets, long sleeves and gloves were on their knees tending the flowerbeds. We took off our shoes before entering Ninomaru Palace, erected within an inner zone of the castle grounds. Family groups padded alongside and overtook us in the broad, timber-floored corridor, commenting in hushed but happy tones. The children were quiet, not in the least boisterous, though some shuffled past more speedily. Their giggles and quiet chatter echoed gently, and the subtle fragrance of the dark polished timber pervaded the atmosphere.

I was aware of a faint chirping sound and, suddenly realizing the cause, made a sign to Isabella to stop. We watched the backs of a group of schoolgirls recede down the corridor.

"These are the famous 'nightingale floors.' The floorboards are anchored in a special way, so they emit squeaks calculated to imitate a nightingale singing, alerting you if someone is trying to sneak in. Tokugawa possessed the military might not to have to fear the threat of an army breaking in, but someone might still attempt to assassinate him or hire ninja for the job."

"It's cunning," she said.

"Incredibly. If you don't understand the trick, it's hard to realize you're causing the sound."

The corridor emptied, apart from us. I contrived to thwart the device, shifting my body weight minutely, raising my left foot and placing it down again as lightly as possible. Doing that much made no sound, so I put all my weight down on the left and moved my right foot forward; when I'd shifted half my weight, a chirp emanated sweetly from some indeterminate place along the corridor. Tried to take another, stealthier step, but sure enough—a lilting whistle from behind us. Simply impossible to negotiate these corridors without them raising the alarm; the sounds came so capriciously that the illusion of birdsong fooled you even when you understood the mechanism behind it.

The corridor turned sharp to the right, and a little way along, the ornately painted paper sliding screens were all open, to reveal a tatami-floored room containing a waxwork tableau. Shogun Tokugawa sat serenely on a dais, in front of an ornately painted screen depicting a leafy pine. He held court, folding fan in hand, attired in august wide-sleeved black robes. Along both sides of the space before him knelt his court officials, the upper part of their costume an inverted triangle, with the shoulders protruding, a little suggestive of wings. Beyond the officials, ten supplicant samurai prostrated themselves.

"It adds life—gives you a good sense of the era," Isabella remarked. A wave of relief passed over me. I was certain she was about to disapprove of the tableau. Counterfeit and kitsch . . . spoils the beauty of the interior . . .

From Nijojo we took a twenty-minute bus ride through first busy then leafier streets to Kinkakuji temple, located in the northwestern hills on an aristocratic estate with stunning gardens. Kinkakuji's golden pavilion, a breathtaking three-story timber structure, overlooks a deep, wide pond, in a luxuriant setting. Gold leaf covers the walls of the top two levels of the pavilion, and a shingled roof caps each level, curving up gracefully at the corners. The top level is smaller and more ornate, and at the apex of its diminished roof perches a feisty bronze phoenix.

There is an irony appropriate to the statue, for the golden pavilion did indeed rise from its ashes. We knew this from Yukio Mishima's *Temple of the Golden Pavilion*, a novel that recreates the mentality of a psychotic acolyte of the temple, who set fire to the pavilion in 1950 after becoming obsessed with its beauty.

In the heat, the pavilion towered above its golden image, which was mirrored on the still surface of the pond, the real appearing no more or less substantial than the reflection. Both floated at the center of a hollow, sky blue sphere, the blue of the sky also reflected in the water. An astonishing effect: reality and reflection, nature and artifice, fused in a perfect gem suspended in the observer's perception. The pavilion appeared to be, moreover, a manifestation of the insight and potency of Zen. Lifetimes of dedication and rigor produced this symbolic experience of transient perfection and enlightenment.

12

Dry Garden of Ryoanji

The ancient pond:
A frog jumps in . . .
Sound of the water!

—Basho

We strolled south from Kinkakuji along a route I had highlighted on a map. A short walk downhill along a tree-lined road was Ryoanji ("Temple of the Dragon at Peace"). Isabella's ailing feet were bearing up and I was thankful to have her for a companion.

"I can't believe you're with me again," she said softly, as we walked along side by side.

A woman in kimono stood stationed at the entrance handing out eggcup-sized paper cups of green tea for visitors to taste her wares. We accepted her samples and sipped the tea standing beside a refreshment annex full of carefree Japanese pilgrims. The atmosphere was relaxed and the drink delicious and invigorating, with the sour-salty tang of dried *umeboshi* plum. I complimented the woman on her tea and purchased some from her, in an ornate paper package flat enough to fit nicely in a pocket. She beamed at us and bowed repeatedly in thanks.

We sat among some other visitors on the long steps of the wooden viewing platform. Ryoanji Temple's ultra-famous *karesansui* ("dry landscape" garden) occupies an enclosure a little smaller than a tennis court, formed by three mud walls and the temple itself. Each wall has a peaked roof covered in cedar shingles to shield it from the elements. Structural divisions in the walls, the effects of weathering, and oil seeping from the mixture of mud and oil used to build the walls, have combined to form broad rust-brown patches and long streaks of cream and gray across the rough surfaces, which look like abstract expressionist canvases. Tall trees standing beyond the far wall exulted in Kyoto's blazing summer sun.

Fifteen rocks of assorted sizes and shapes rest in the courtyard, arranged in groups on five low moss-covered mounds: five rocks, two, three, two and three. In their simplicity, the stones express a certain grandeur. At their base, the mounds sink into a layer of coarse white sand covering the ground. Zen monks painstakingly rake the sand, creating a series of grooves around the margins. Concentric furrows encircle the groups of rocks themselves. Where the straight lines and curves pass through each other, they create a shimmer of interference, canceling each other out for a moment, before resuming their perfect courses.

The circular grooves are stylized waves surrounding islands in the sea; but that image might flicker and the rocks become mountaintops breaking through a canopy of cloud. One traditional interpretation says the rocks represent a tigress leading her cubs across a river. A contrived idea, as though a narrative or allegory is necessary to produce any significance—yet maybe that can hold true too in a sense, so long as one doesn't stay fixated on any single particular reading. I couldn't avoid glimpses of the tigress and cubs once I'd heard of that scenario; but my perception would skip from the tigers to an imaginary scene of mountaintops above cloud, islands in the sea, or mere rocks and pebbles. As though the garden was showing me those possibilities in order to say, "I'm not this metaphor nor that." Like the immortal Zen master Nansen on the nature of dharma, cosmic law: *not mind, not Buddha, not things.*

To our left, two monks in black robes tiptoed along the tiled border, careful not to tread on the sand bed. One carried a wooden rake. Something must have disturbed the patterns, though we discerned no irregularity. One monk gripped the other's arm and acted as a counterweight as his colleague leaned out and used the rake to make a precise adjustment to the grooves in the sand.

We must have sat together without speaking for half an hour, before Isabella quietly got up and went off to explore other parts of the temple. I stayed put, intent on extracting all I could from my brief time here, trying to burn the experience into my memory, with the idea of taking this garden with me in a corner of my mind, a portable refuge, whose potency I would reinforce with future visits—pilgrimages, so to speak. My eyes roamed the space absently and I became quite absorbed, so much so that I had an impression I may have lost my sense of ego for a fraction of time a moment earlier.

How can I put this? It seemed to me I stumbled on myself in the instant of losing myself.

People came and went, their stockinged feet producing soft, innocent sounds on the wooden platform behind me, a muffled thump when someone sat down on the steps. Occasionally somebody commented or queried in a hushed tone, in consideration for those meditating on the garden and perhaps in deference. The white sand shone in the midday sun. Light shimmered over the surfaces, and the forms and colors leaped out, surreally tangible. A consciousness inhabited the garden — or an illusion of one . . . but what is consciousness but an illusion?

A consciousness machine, the garden mirrors our mental projections. A psychical echo chamber, its surreal glow is an effect of an ancient intelligence, a long and imperceptibly slow vibration that emits a shimmer as it intersects with present time.

People assembled in dribs and drabs, and the viewing platform became quite crowded. Perhaps another tour bus had arrived. Our communal awareness reflected against the silence and blindness of the rocks, echoed among the canyon walls and above the gleaming white ocean. Time was frozen within this universe — as still as the sculptured waves in the microcosmic ocean. We were at the still center, while around us spun a chaos of phenomenal input. Human reality.

Some young Japanese tourists near me were enjoying an animated conversation about the garden. I got the gist of their comments.

"It is a 'nothing garden,'" one young man scoffed, affecting a dismissive growl and cynical attitude, punning on the karesansui's nickname of "the garden of

175

nothingness," in reference to the foundation of its design in Zen Buddhism. "It has no meaning." His girlfriend tittered admiringly, and his other friends chimed in. The garden was supposed to facilitate a perception of nothingness, he said. No matter where you stood on the viewing platform, you were unable to see all the stones at the same time: at least one would be hidden by at least one other. When you achieved enlightenment, you would be able to visualize in your mind's eye all fifteen stones.

"I read that in the olden days this was an ordinary garden with plants and flowers, but they died off," said the first young man—more manifestations of nothingness in this suggestion that the psychological power of the garden was bogus, a placebo effect.

I stirred myself and went inside to a room where monks were selling souvenirs and religious trinkets from behind a counter. I walked past and found Isabella coming in through a door from outside.

"Come and look out here, Michael," she said gaily, and I followed her out and down some steps. "Do you know you've been sitting there for two hours?" It seemed that about twenty minutes had passed since she stood up. Time had evaporated in the dry garden.

"Listen to the frogs," she laughed. We stood still on the steps. At irregular intervals, from some concealed spot within the greenery came a deep hollow croak—then a sudden splash. "It's the haiku of Basho's about the frog jumping into the pond!"

A solid, squat cylindrical stone is set on end in a leafy corner. A basin for ritual hand-washing: water is contained in a square carved depression in the top, fed by a bamboo pipe. The basin's top face resembles a five-yen coin, patterned on old coins that have a square hole pressed through, originally so they could be kept strung on a cord. The roundness of the coin stands for heaven (yang), the square hole the earth (yin)—thus the earth penetrates the sphere of heaven. Like such old coins, the face is engraved with big Chinese characters, one at each cardinal point of the basin.

Isabella leafed through the temple's information brochure. "The water basin is called a *tsukubai*. Each of the characters around the rim combines with the square hole—representing the character *kuchi* or "mouth"—to form a whole character. Taken together, they make up the saying *Ware tada shiru taru:* 'I know only contentment.'"

We went back inside and spent a while browsing through various artifacts displayed in wide glass cabinets standing next to the counter. I asked the young attendant monk for some postcards and a piece of calligraphy that caught my eye: energetic brushstrokes had rendered the circle of the tsukubai and its paradoxical Zen phrase.

"And this looks like a model of the tsukubai, is it? *Ware tada shiru taru?*" I pointed to a metallic object about the size of my fist, with the square hole in the middle and the Chinese characters embossed around the rim.

Chuckling, the monk took the object from the display case, brought it over and handed it to me to feel its weight: heavy, like a paperweight. I handed it back, and he held it in one hand and tapped it against the palm of the other.

"A very interesting thing," he said, "and it will bring you contentment just like tsukubai says. It is '*sennuki*' *desu ne*. I do not know the English word."

"I think it may be 'talisman,'" I said. "Or 'good luck charm.'"

"You put like this, on top of *bin biiru* (bottled beer)," he explained, using his left thumb to demonstrate how the top of the bottle should be inserted into the square *kuchi* hole and—*ffuhp!*" He tilted the object up and made a single implosive pop with his lips.

"Bottle opener," I laughed.

"*Botoruwopenaa*," he repeated. "Yes!"

13

Kindred Souls

Shibutani-san raised an eyebrow during a chat we had about his sport of kendo, and before long I was transcribing interviews he had recorded with foreign participants in the international kendo championships, for publication in a specialist magazine. He was planning to translate traditional texts on kendo into English but made little progress, so I was off the hook. I performed this and that piece of proofreading and rewriting for one colleague after another, commentary on disparate topics I had little scholarly interest in—Hearn, Russian history, Thoreau, D.H. Lawrence, Wordsworth, ancient Welsh myths—so the activity could become a chore. Moreover, I felt distinctly that certain of my colleagues were none too interested in my comments on the content of their writings, comments I offered with the, yes, perhaps presumptuous idea of encouraging them and helping improve their English writing skills. They seemed to have to endure my remarks purely to get the thing done. In some I

detected a trace of smugness about having me as a convenience—but for god's sake, couldn't I please keep
quiet and get the checking over and done with quicker?

Quite often I exceeded the territory of the proofreader
and became more a collaborator or ghostwriter, redeem-
ing incoherent passages and infusing the article with a
more erudite tone. The published pieces often carried
an acknowledgment for my assistance in having
checked the English, either a candid gesture of gratitude
or a carrot calculated to elicit ongoing cooperation.
Once I asked an author to delete a note of thanks from
his manuscript, preferring not to have the published
piece advertise my services.

Pleasant on the surface as some were, they could also
be quite pushy and passive-aggressive. They seemed to
interpret my cooperative manner as a sign of weakness,
which they had no qualms about exploiting. To accede
unquestioningly to every request would mean entering
into a form of intellectual slavery—unspeakably small-
minded and mean though I would have appeared had
I expressed that opinion.

One or two made repeated demands but gave no indication of reciprocity on any level. Yet I continued to
give them a hand, doing my bit to enhance their academic profile, counting this a gesture of "giving
back"—I was able to make this contribution to the faculty in general as a native English-speaking academic.
Others, however, were happy to help me out when I
had translation problems, and I formed valuable personal and collegial friendships. Tsuji and I kept up our
tennis, occasionally went out for a drink together and
helped each other out with various research projects.
Our friendship put me in mind of the camaraderie that

Amachi, Onoé, Yanagi and I had shared in Nagoya, the difference being that at Shizuoka University we enjoyed an enviable degree of autonomy, with no one to pummel us into a state of mutual dependence.

At my desk early one afternoon, when the telephone rang. A young associate professor from the Education Faculty, whom I had met socially and helped out with proofreading.

"Gesuto-sensei, would you please check an English thesis I must finish soon?"

"I'm busy with my work right now. I should have time during the next day or two."

"I am sure it will be very easy for you. It will take you just a short while."

"No, I'm sorry, I can't help you today. I think I can manage to make time tomorrow or the day after."

"It is isn't long and there are not many errors; it is almost perfect."

"Yes, I'm so looking forward to reading it tomorrow. Would you call in at my office at one o'clock, please?"

An agitated mutter came from the other end, which I read as agreement, having left no avenue for any other appropriate response. "Goodbye," I said, replaced the receiver and returned to my work.

A matter of minutes later, there was a tentative knock at the door, which was slightly ajar, and the same associate professor let himself in, smiling and bowing an effusive greeting, holding a printout of his essay in his hand. I pivoted in my chair and indicated an empty place at a table by my desk; he sat down and presented me with his document.

"You are very busy, Gesuto-san!" He laughed as if at a hilarious joke—it was a common custom to complain

with an exasperated laugh about how overworked one
was.

"Yes, I have so much preparation to do for my classes,"
I laughed. "Whew." I shook my head.

"In a national university we have too many classes to
teach," he complained, shaking his head frantically, dra-
matically wide-eyed, overwrought at our desperate lot.

"Oh well," I said quietly, "it can't be helped . . ."

He moved his chair closer and rifled through his pages,
scratching his head demonstratively. He donned his
reading glasses and bent over the paper, lightly tracing
the tip of a red ballpoint pen under his lines as he read
them aloud. I watched his profile in silent disbelief as
he persevered, not looking up at me, intentionally
swamping my space with the sound of his voice in a bla-
tant imposition of his will, assuming I would be too polite
or too weak to resist.

"Sounds good," I said when he stopped, flabbergasted
by his performance.

"The part after here I cannot get right with my poor
English." He laughed self-deprecatingly, with a touch
of hysteria, and looked up. "I am sure it will be easy for
you."

"As I said on the telephone, I can't do it now," I said,
summoning a firm resolve, to which he appeared obliv-
ious. He took my hand, which was resting on the table,
physically inserted the red pen into my fingers, clasping
them around it, and then placed my hand, together with
the pen it now held, on top of the paper. Again he looked
fixedly at his thesis as though willing the pen to start
moving, his straight black hair falling over his forehead.
He was as alert as a dog waiting for a cornered rabbit to
come bursting out of a bush. I could see him visualizing

the red corrections flowing out like automatic writing, imagining the drone of my voice with its pointless semantic and grammatical explanations. But nothing happened—my hand remained stubbornly inert.

"I'm afraid I'm busy with something else now and can't help you with it today, but I'll be happy to as soon as I have time."

"It will take just a little while for you."

I put down the pen.

"I am unable to do this right away," I said in as unambiguous a tone as I could muster without twitching.

Our meeting ended as politely as could be, given the impossible constraints he had imposed upon it. Gathering up his sheaf of papers, he left briskly with a precise bow and *"shitsurei shimasu"* ("Excuse me")— the standard phrase for excusing oneself when taking one's leave.

The associate professor redeemed his lost face weeks later, when we found ourselves together at a luncheon party hosted by a friend of his who owned a small art gallery. He introduced a young woman standing nearby as his graduate student. He had her produce an essay of hers from out of her handbag, and asked me whether I would be so kind as check it for her on the spot. The social dynamic was so much in his favor that I was obliged to sit down at a table in the corner and go through her essay with her. Thus, he restored the universe to its proper balance by demonstrating to me my place and function in it.

DURING HIS university years, Munakata's English lecturer was the celebrated Englishman Reginald Horace

Blyth, who lived for ten years in Korea before moving to Japan in 1936 and residing there until his death in 1964, aged sixty-six. Something of a would-be Lafcadio Hearn—but dismissive of Hearn in his writings in a pompous and rather defensive way, as if envious of his fame—Blyth authored books on topics related to traditional literature and Zen Buddhism. He was known best for his four-volume work on haiku, one of which I had purchased from Maruzen bookshop in Nagoya, without paying any attention to the author's name. After Munakata spoke to me about Blyth I located it again in my bookshelves.

Munakata was genuinely devoted to Blyth's memory, as though Blyth were his spiritual father. He was his mentor in Zen as well as English literature and had been a friend and student of the renowned Zen master Daisetsu T. Suzuki, who introduced Zen to the modern Western world. As Munakata pointed out, Blyth did the same thing with haiku in the early 1950s—or at least, continued the task begun in 1904 by the poet Yone Noguchi (father of the sculptor Isamu Noguchi): Blyth's books inspired the San Francisco Beat poets Jack Kerouac and Gary Snyder to start writing haiku themselves. Suzuki described Blyth as "one of the most eminent exponents of Japanese culture."

Munakata introduced me to a sushi bar where the chef prepared plates and put them on a conveyer belt that circled the top of a self-service island bar.

"We don't need to take those," he said smiling wisely, after I selected one. "It's better to ask him to make them up fresh." He ordered for us, and the chef hand-shaped portions of vinegared rice and loaded them with delicious cuts of raw fish—tuna, bonito, sardine, sea bream—and treats such as sea urchin, thinly sliced octopus, shrimp and glistening orange salmon roe. Variously colored saucers piled up in front of us comprising the record of what we had eaten. When we finished, the chef used them to tally up the cost. We always paid *betsu betsu*, separately, a convention widely known here, too, as "going Dutch."

"Do you know," said Munakata, topping up my glass of cold, good quality saké, "I was Blyth's student for longer than anybody else except Emperor Akihito and Empress Michiko, the present emperor and his wife. Blyth was their private English tutor for several years."

"Really?" I smiled and raised my glass. "To Their Imperial Majesties."

"When the war began, he endeavored to adopt Japanese nationality," he continued. "But he was not permitted. He was placed in an internment camp in Kobe for the duration. He didn't mind too much, however, for he was allowed to study, and he finished his first book there, *Zen in English Literature and Oriental Classics.*"

"It may have been Mahatma Gandhi, too, who found his time in prison very productive. I believe he wrote most of his autobiography there."

Munakata made an ambiguous "Hmm," either in approval of the level of impressiveness conferred by the comparison or suspicious that the Mahatma was stealing Blyth's thunder.

"After the Japanese surrender," he went on, "he acted as a go-between in the Showa Emperor's (Hirohito's) negotiations with General Douglas MacArthur, the Supreme Commander of the Allied occupation. It was actually Blyth who had the idea for the Emperor to renounce his divine status and announce publicly he was a human being. He convinced the Emperor to do that, realizing it was the one way to satisfy the Americans and yet allow the Emperor to remain as ceremonial head of state."

After our dinner Munakata caught his train and I went my own way, leaving behind our loftier reflections, to explore the nightlife. The entertainment district glittered and crowds of merrymakers thronged the sidewalks. Trendy young women shrieked and giggled in groups; flashy touters slipped me pamphlets advertising hostess bars and girlie shows; students trooped tipsily to their celebrations; restaurants, ramen shops, izakaya and shot bars plied a thriving trade, a lively throng of patrons pouring in and out of them. It was worlds from the Australian drinking culture, with its attendant elements of vulgar machismo and alcoholic belligerence.

Here the scene was all harmless merriment. People were approachable and approached me easily if for some reason I took their fancy. I roamed the streets, explored the inexhaustible supply of nightspots. Yet I felt a bit like Herman Hesse's Steppenwolf: hunted and driven, somehow perverse, my foreignness on display, my increasing sense of loneliness confined within, haunted by my own nagging, solitary discourse. I hankered for female company, and I supposed it a natural thing to surrender myself to the same drives that governed these streams of giggling and shrieking humanity.

SOMETIMES AT night I found myself in a quiet corner of town, footsteps scuffing the asphalt sidewalk, vision absorbed in the glass reflections and neon signs. Hit with a sense of the emptiness of life and the realization that underneath the dazzling appearances of electric light and incandescent, crabwise-dancing kanji, there was nothing but cold, hard, lifeless matter, the asphalt, concrete and steel.

One chilly eve I was walking, some distance from my apartment, by the canal-like Ohya River toward the suburb of Oshika. A wind kicked up and suddenly it began to rain. Detouring down a side street in search of shelter, I stumbled upon a *sunakku* ("snack") on the next corner—a seedy sort of drinking establishment that exudes superficial luxury, resembling a private club, often with hostesses serving cheap brandy and whisky expensively and stroking the egos of predominantly male clientele. I might have been able to make it home without getting soaked, but the lights of the sunakku gave it the look of a cheerful refuge. A Sufi saying crossed my mind: "Go through this door, for there is no other door." Here again, the tavern of ruin.

A friendly Mama-san welcomed me in. A lone woman was sitting on a stool at the bar; petite and demure, neither outstandingly attractive nor plain. Her name was Yumiko. She spoke no English apart from isolated words and expressions from the universal store. I was by now used to socializing solely in Japanese and had fun doing it. Our conversation was not overtly flirtatious, but we came closer together by degrees as the bar filled up with regulars. She did not appear to know them, so we engaged in our own conversation, until a merry group of strangers drew us in with their entertaining banter.

She was engaging and attentive, and for the first time

in many weeks my craving after human closeness was allayed. Late in the night, when couples started to dance to the karaoke, I was intoxicated enough to suggest we join in. We moved tentatively in the shadow and dim flickering light until the impromptu party broke up. I became involved in a sequence of loud, disorderly farewells with the other acquaintances I had made during the night. All of a sudden I realized she had gone.

I ordered a final whisky and sipped it, sitting beside another late stayer, who entertained Mama-san and me with maudlin, off-key karaoke. I was calling to mind the pleasant time I'd had with the woman when a telephone rang behind the bar, and Mama-san handed me the receiver. It was she.

"You remember you said you had to go to the Immigration Office at Port Shimizu tomorrow? If you want, I can drive you there." I had told her I needed to go the next day to apply for a visa for re-entry into Japan, because I planned to visit Australia come New Year's break.

"Thanks very much," I said, "I'd appreciate that." The memory of the pleasurable interlude lingered, numbing my underlying feeling of emptiness.

"Telephone me tomorrow after eleven if you still want to go with me," Yumiko said.

"I will."

"Be sure it is after eleven." She had told me she was married to a businessman but I saw no immediate reason why that should prevent us getting together for a platonic outing—I should have known better. I even convinced myself it was perhaps fortunate she was married, for that would surely stop anything from developing.

Next day we met outside the sunakku, and she drove

me to Shimizu Harbor in her big cream-colored Honda. On arriving, I pointed out the way to the tongue-twisting *nyukokukanrikyoku* — or *nyukan* for short: the immigration office. Everything went as smoothly as usual. I was now well aware of the benefits of being a "national officer," including a magical power to pass through official channels. My details were fastidiously documented and my visa now read "Status: Professor." But what earned me a complete tacit acknowledgment as a peer in officialdom — what really got the wheels turning — was being asked to show them my contract with a university, in which case I would reply that I was not employed on a contract. My record was adroitly checked, my unusual, permanently tenured status confirmed, and I was guided along with the innate, understated efficiency of the Japanese government bureaucrat.

As we drove away from the immigration office, I asked Yumiko about what looked like a birthmark, slightly visible above the neck scarf she wore. She took the scarf away in an almost provocative gesture, to reveal severe scarring on her throat.

"Do you know what a *kotatsu* is?" she asked.

"Of course — it's a low table with an electric heater attached underneath. A futon is spread over the frame but under the tabletop, to keep your legs warm in the winter."

"When I was three years old I was underneath the kotatsu and a kettle of boiling water was knocked over on me. The pain was terrible and I passed out. My parents took me to the hospital, where I nearly died. Anyway, I'm used to my scars — they don't mean anything to me."

I visualized her as the poor infant and felt a rush of sympathy and admiration. A real blessing here for a girl to be pretty. The culture—particularly the youth culture—invested the attribute of *kawaiisa* (cuteness) with a transcendent value. A group of young women would break into a high pitched, bell-like unison of *"Kawaiiii!"* at the sight of a puppy, a pretty child or film star, or a friend modeling a new outfit. To be disabled or disfigured was a cruel lot—to have one's new outfit met with silence or a half-hearted, condescending *"Kawaii ne"* ("Don't you look cute?") with a sad overtone. Scarring like hers branded her an outsider in her own way. I was attracted and felt protective because of this fleeting connection between us two species of outsider.

We arrived at Yamamura Heights and I invited her to come up for tea. She declined and I got out. She reversed to leave, but then changed her mind and pulled back into my parking space. We climbed the noisy metal staircase together, went inside and shared tea in my tatami room, resuming the thread of our earlier conversation. An innocent enough tête-à-tête, but a precarious line of transgression was drawn through all the actions that led up to it.

14

Heaven to Hell

Professor Munakata proposed I edit a book with him, a selection of his mentor Blyth's writings. The Tokyo publishing company Hokuseido agreed to publish it, and he contacted a Shimizu printer, Tamura Press; it would be our job as well to oversee the book's English language printing. Munakata was old friends with Mrs. Tamura, the widow of the company's founder, and her son, who was now company director. They were an old established Shimizu family, so our meetings with them took us to some exclusive clubs and restaurants in Shimizu and Shizuoka cities. Mrs. Tamura never allowed us to pay for anything, no matter how much I insisted. I told Munakata that I'd prefer to contribute in future, but he waved my concern aside with his inimitable enigmatic smile and a shake of his head.

The Tamuras referred to Munakata as "Sensei" and were quite deferential. I was plain "Gesuto-san" and content to play the role of his sidekick as we drifted from one stylish venue to the next, he drawing copiously on his bountiful reserves of wit and bonhomie. It became apparent before long that he had employed the Tamuras' services in past entrepreneurial and academic projects and would continue to bring them business in future. This may have explained Mrs. Tamura's generous hospitality to some extent; but I would not like to reduce her motives for sponsoring our outings to such mundane concerns. Munakata and the Tamuras thoroughly enjoyed each other's company and the opportunities for gracious conversation and civilized diversions that our project created.

Mrs. Tamura was petite, with a face of pixie-like youthfulness. She wore fashionable rimless eyeglasses and tied her hair in a bun at the back. She dressed discreetly, in conservative outfits of the finest quality and sometimes appeared in kimono, depending on the occasion. Mr. Tamura junior was bespectacled too, short and pampered, with the ample spread of a devoted gastronome. His other special pleasure was music. He played timpani in the Shimizu City Symphony Orchestra and once asked me to a production of *The Marriage of Figaro* in which he was to perform. Unfortunately, I had a severe toothache that evening and grimaced in pain throughout the opera, and I feared he could see my face from his position on the stage. Although the performance was not exactly virtuosic, it was far less painful than my expression would have indicated.

But anyway, Mr. Tamura didn't seem to take offense. Shortly after, he invited me to a traditional festivity held early one morning at Miho-no-Matsubara, where we joined in with a crowd of local families who were casting out a big fishing net from the beach. Four sushi chefs waited lined up behind a table to prepare a sashimi breakfast for the excited gathering. A quaint scene and oddly biblical. We dragged up and emptied the net, but it had hardly snared enough fish to cover the bottom of a single plastic bucket. A boat was rowed out a little farther offshore, where it bobbed in the swell for a while, until the fishermen drew the net up chock-a-block, so everyone enjoyed a breakfast of ocean-fresh sashimi after all. For the rest of the morning, the adults sat around under the bent pines socializing while the children played.

We had our first meeting with the Tamuras to discuss the details of the book in a ritzy Chinese restaurant overlooking Shimizu Harbor. Mrs. Tamura was in her element, with waiters in black suit and bow tie attending on us. We sat equidistant around a broad round wooden table and rotated the lazy Susan to share around the delicacies; the highlight was Peking duck, with pieces of crispy duck skin enfolded in plump little pancakes and seasoned with a spoonful of miso paste. A lantern hung over the table threw dancing shadows across Mrs. Tamura's face as she demonstrated some special paper that the company recently obtained for use in some bizarre contract they had won from the government.

"This notepaper dissolves in water," she said, "so a secret agent can eat it after reading a message written on it." She asked the waiter to bring a saucer of water and dropped a slip of paper into it. The four of us gazed at the slip floating there, sodden but refusing to disintegrate. "That is odd," she said, breaking the silence. "I must have brought the wrong paper."

"I hope the secret agents don't try to eat this," I joked, but my attempt at levity stimulated an uneasy reflection.

"Hmm . . ." she murmured, raising an eyebrow and tilting her head to one side, her eyes fixed on the stubborn slip of paper.

Another time, she took us out to an *unagi* (eel) restaurant, the best in Shizuoka Prefecture, she assured us. The chef came out to our table to pay his respects, and when I lost track of the animated conversation that passed between him and my three companions, Munakata came to my aid.

"He has to examine the face of each customer," he chuckled gleefully, "before selecting the eel that will be most appropriate for them."

Afterward, we accompanied Mrs. Tamura to her exclusive club, where we occupied a private tatami room. Two geisha entertained us, one of whom, it emerged, happened to be a graduate of our university. They prepared our drinks, amused us with sparkling conversation, made flattering comments to Munakata and me, and performed some humorous little songs and dances, each ending in bashful giggles.

"Not upper class geisha of the sort you find in Kyoto," Munakata confided to me when we left. But they were entertaining and compelling to watch. Their thick white makeup ended at the nape in a swallowtail that drew the eye irresistibly to the naked flesh of the neck and shoulder, beneath the jet-black hair of their wigs. The pale makeup around their eyes and covering their eyelids contrasted with a single dab of red placed at the outer tip of each almond eye; the effect was to emphasize the sanguine inner surface of the skin surrounding the eye and the watery glistening of the orb itself. Ornaments dangling from their hair trembled at their slightest movement, accentuating their studied poise.

Their ornate, vibrant kimono, unyielding with stitched silk and inflexible *obi* (kimono sash or cummerbund), emphasized their own feminine softness. They seemed like living artworks.

SUMMER FESTIVITIES, and Bancroft was introducing me to his extensive circle of younger friends. His neighborhood association was putting a team together to carry their *mikoshi* in the Shizuoka city festival, and he invited me to take part. Mikoshi are elaborately decorated and gilded portable Shinto shrines designed for the local kami to ride in, enabling them to leave their home shrine and parade about the streets during religious festivals. In a boisterous procession with pipes, drums and blaring bugles, teams of mikoshi bearers, dressed in traditional *happi* coats emblazoned with their neighborhood crest, chant and heave the glittering mikoshi up and down. Their kami propelling them this way and that, the mikoshi teams zigzag their way through streets crowded with spectators and revelers, competing with all the other city teams to create the biggest spectacle.

The mikoshi was far heavier than it looked at first glance, particularly when two young women climbed up and planted their feet on the parallel timber beams that supported the structure. They waved their arms and bounced about, blowing on whistles to keep everyone moving in time. The mikoshi must have weighed a ton or more. Two rows of us, about twenty people at a time, carried it over our heads, the weight bearing down through the beam resting hard on one shoulder. Being taller than my fellow bearers was a distinct disadvantage, because it meant I was always carrying the maximum burden. Moreover, I needed to bend over at an awkward angle to make myself equal in height to the others, so after a while, the effort was literally backbreaking. When we started out, fresh bearers would come in under the mikoshi from behind, and the ones in front move forward and out, thus affording everyone a break. But as we progressed, I noticed that the number of those willing to relieve the primary group of carriers—which included me—was diminishing rapidly, and I found myself stuck underneath, my back bent over under the weight and my shoulder suffering unbearable pain. I ascribed my suffering to the spiritual dimension of the parade and hoped the kami aboard was satisfied.

Fortunately, we were allowed to take breaks in our course through the city; we lowered the mikoshi down to rest on wooden blocks and stood or sat around in the street recovering, while partaking of beer and saké, which followed along behind us in a handcart. When the parade was over, we returned to our neighborhood headquarters and partied noisily into the evening.

A celebrity in the anglophile community, Bancroft arranged for me to receive invitations to some functions held by the Japan-British Society. Shimizu's wealthiest businessman, a Mr. Sawano, who owned a shipping and trading company, presided over the local branch. I asked Bancroft if I might invite Yumiko to their Christmas charity ball, and I sought his advice about my involvement with her, which was gaining momentum despite my better judgment. But it was a comfort to receive the care and nurture of a close companionship once again. It eased my awareness of being a lone expatriate, which haunted me like a nagging inner voice, despite my budding social life. I recklessly allowed the friendship to develop.

Yet even as she and I became more entangled and mutually dependent, I felt stirrings of doubt and angst, some moral, others more about self-preservation. For one thing, I was ignorant of how infidelity was viewed, especially when a foreigner was involved. If I were dismissed because of it, I would have no way to maintain myself, let alone a dependent wife if things went that far. Moreover, she had two children at high school—a complication that further plagued me with guilt. At first, when our connection was at a purely companionable stage, the existence of children hadn't seemed relevant.

Bancroft was a professed Christian, but he seemed unconcerned and counseled me from a surprisingly amoral perspective.

"From the university's point of view, your private life is your own. Nobody cares what you do with it, so long as it doesn't involve a student."

"There's absolutely no fear of that."

"I'm sure," he said. "But you know, it's not as uncommon as you may think for a woman here to have a fling. Sometimes she does it to get her husband to notice her. She may even fabricate an imaginary one for the same reason."

Yumiko and I attended the charity ball and met Mr. and Mrs. Sawano, who welcomed me as a new, foreign, and thus desirable, member of the British Society, though they could not disguise their fleeting expressions of disappointment when they learned I was not British but a colonial. Yumiko wore a kimono, and I fancied myself a latter day Lafcadio Hearn—if admittedly a somewhat degenerate, poor man's version—becoming absorbed by degrees into the language and culture. Though my Japanese proficiency was improving rapidly thanks to our frequent assignations, our communication was far from perfect, leaving me in the dark about where things were heading. She convinced me that her marriage was unhappy; she believed her husband was having an affair.

Yumiko asked me for a spare key, in case she wanted to go to my apartment when I was at work.

"It is the one place where I feel calm and at peace," she said sweetly. She dismissed the misgivings I voiced about her being a mother—the children were old enough, she said, hardly children at all, actually. If we married, we could look after the younger one, the son; we would leave Japan and go to Australia to live. Leave Japan! I was appalled at the idea of having to drop my new life, go back to Australia and . . . do what? Impossible at this stage to take up any sort of academic career over there, let alone something with the salary, opportunities and experiences I was blessed with here. Yumiko insisted that she hated living in Japan and would like to get away, and I began to entertain the suspicion that my nationality—specifically, the potential it held for an appealing life in the West—might be one reason for her obsession to preserve our association at any cost, even if it meant sabotaging any source of stability for either of us.

Our intrigue was becoming intolerably complicated the more intense it grew, but I couldn't seem to extricate myself. I tried repeatedly to end it, but relented after telephone calls and meetings where she dissolved into sobs. I deluded myself that things would work themselves out and fumbled along through a blur of emotional events. I was indeed at sea and lacked any grasp or grounding in the social or legal ramifications of what was going on. To make matters worse, most of what I did know—or thought I knew—came from Yumiko herself, exclusively in Japanese. Now she seemed to seek further influence over my personal life. She secretly contacted my friend Amachi in Nagoya and even telephoned Isabella in Australia, with whom I had broken up by this time. Though quietly mortified by her ham-fisted attempts to intervene in my other relationships, somehow I forgave her these actions.

The Japan-British Society held a reception for the British ambassador, to which I took Yumiko. She wore a kimono and I my lucky New Yorker and a bow tie. Bancroft was away on a trip to England. Waiting for the ambassador to enter, I stood nibbling at some hors d'oeuvres, glass of champagne in hand, when a woman sidled up and caught my attention, speaking to me in perfect English.

"Good evening, Michael," she said, a queer expression on her face, serene but with a hint of shrewdness. Another woman was standing beside her, half a step behind. The one in front smiled ambiguously and raised her champagne flute to her mouth.

"Hello," I smiled. "Do I know you?"

"I am Natsumi and this is my friend Sayuri. We have been having a lovely chat with your friend Yumiko and were dying to meet you. You know, until we spoke to her, we were under the impression that you were the British ambassador, you look so dapper."

"I'm sorry to disappoint you, but as you can see now, the real one is far more ambassadorial-looking than I." The dignitary had made his entrance and was moving through the gathering, nodding greetings to the right and left. He was well over six feet tall and manifestly aristocratic in both manner and profile.

"Oh, not at all," the woman said. "We are happy you live so close by and are lecturing at Shizuoka University. Yumiko told us that you and she are going to marry."

She smiled again with a peculiar, studied charm, contemplating me over the rim of her glass as she sipped her champagne. I looked over to where Yumiko was speaking animatedly to another group of women, however, and wondered what on God's earth she could be telling them.

This Natsumi hadn't finished with me.

"Yumiko thinks it might be possible for us to come and visit you in your apartment."

"Um—what for?" I wondered whether my smile, which I felt to be involuntarily grotesque, disguised my incredulity at the idea.

"We can become acquainted and discuss all sorts of things. We will have a wonderful time getting to know each other and becoming friends."

The woman was dead serious in making her extraordinary proposal and when I later questioned Yumiko about her part in brokering my social activities, and why these women would want to spend their time in my apartment with me, she too seemed to consider it the most natural thing.

I RESTED astride my bicycle by the shore of Suruga Bay, not in an official bathing area but a less populated spot, though some cars were parked on the sides of a lane that ran along the beach. People were enjoying the Saturday afternoon sunshine: anglers, cyclists, lovers walking hand in hand, families playing games and barbecuing their lunches over makeshift fireplaces erected among the rocks. My dealings with Yumiko had sunk to renewed depths and I was brooding. From what I could work out, her husband, to whom she had confessed the affair some time ago, was trying his best to ruin my reputation at the university, in the hope that they would boot me out of my job and, preferably, the country. He was prepared to divorce her, she informed me, though he would require a sizable *isharyo*, an amount I would be obliged to pay by way of compensation for his pain and suffering (a form of consolation prize, I gathered). I would need to meet with him soon to work out what we were going to do. She expressed a degree of resentment that made me suspect I may be a pawn in long-standing marital hostilities.

I gazed down listlessly from the asphalt promenade at a kite flier who had linked together a chain of a dozen or so tiny paper kites, each one no bigger than a couple of inches square. They rose up one above the other over his head, creating a miniature magical pagoda that hovered in the stiff breeze. I marveled at the spectacle, but not for long. My mind returned to the vexing question of how I could have fallen from my state of grace into this nightmare. A fortnight previously, my desire to understand the matter of the isharyo triggered a heated dispute with Yumiko. I had no way of knowing, I explained, that the two of them were not trying to defraud me. She was incensed and stormed out of my apartment, but not before hurling that spare key down on my futon.

"You can take this!" she said viciously, and turned her back on me to leave. "If that is what you think of me, I will not need it any more."

My hand closed around the key and I felt the cold, hard object in my fist. A jolt of optimism shot through my leaden heart, fired by the realization that an important fragment of my autonomy had fallen back into my grasp. She had phoned later and persuaded me to meet her. Abandoning her at this pass, she implored me, would amount to sheer treachery. Unbelievably I agreed not to break things off—though I kept the key.

Something moving through the foreground of my gaze startled me to the present: a pair of rough-looking tattooed thugs, unmistakably yakuza gangsters, were walking on the sand, smoking cigarettes and grunting casual utterances to each other, pulling behind them a wheeled contraption—basically a big wooden box attached to a handcart. They had a hulking brown dog, a powerful mastiff, tied to the rear of the handcart, and it padded along behind, its attention riveted on the box. A wire grille door attached to the box was tied open. Inside, tethered by a rope, a small tan rabbit crouched directly facing the dog, inches from its gaping jaws. A horizontal wooden bar was fastened strategically in front of the mastiff's chest to prevent it from reaching the rabbit. The mighty brute plodded on, staring blankly into the eyes of the rabbit, while the rabbit, paralyzed in terror, stared back. This was, I realized, a *tosa inu*, a fighting dog, which these men were evidently taking somewhere to "blood." I identified sickeningly with the rabbit, trapped in circumstances out of its control and beyond its ken, parading submissively, impotently, to a gruesome fate. A nauseating spectacle. This second moment of epiphany, along with the one I had experienced two weeks earlier, as I held in my hand the spare key to Yamamura Heights, finally awakened me to the inevitability of a dismal outcome if I continued to be weak and irresolute.

I TURNED to my friend Professor Munakata for help.

"I have to ask for your advice—I have gotten myself into an awful mess," I said to him on entering his office.

I outlined the situation as he listened gravely; then he questioned me.

"Where have you been meeting?"

"Mostly in my apartment, but we went out in public sometimes: I took her to some Japan-British Society functions; to a restaurant and nightclub; to a Bob Dylan concert at the Nippon Budokan in Tokyo. Once she took me along to a lesson she had with a *shamisen* (Japanese lute) teacher."

"She is learning shamisen? Is she a geisha? Many geisha learn shamisen." He looked quite interested.

"No," I said almost apologetically, "it's just a hobby—something she does to pass the time."

He eyed me closely.

"Have you ever been to her house?"

"Never," I answered truthfully.

"You know, someone in our position has to be careful not to become involved in situations like this."

"Yes, I can see that now."

Munakata proposed to mediate in a meeting between Yumiko, her husband and me. We met at a cafe in a comfortable hotel where the Emperor once stayed, named appropriately, given my situation, the Shizuoka

Terminal Hotel. We sat down at opposite sides of a table, she by her husband, and I by Munakata. Munakata took the lead in the discussion, dealing almost entirely with the man. I confined myself mostly to English and Munakata interpreted, to make sure everyone understood all the details. Yumiko piped up energetically at one point, but Munakata rebuked her, referring to her as *okusan*—wife—and she went into a huff, said little more, but stared straight ahead into space. Her eyes flashed and her mouth was set in a thin line, her high cheekbones knife edged.

"I apologize for any hurt I have caused you and your family," I said to the man. "I did not intend for any of this to happen, but I accept my responsibility in it."

He made a brief statement to Munakata.

"He says he thinks this is her doing," said Munakata, "and he does not hold it against you."

"Did you know that she is not Japanese?" asked the man, giving me a sinister look. "Her parents are Korean."

A disparaging tone: a racial slur. I regarded him expressionlessly.

"As far as I am concerned," the man said to Munakata, "he can have her. No isharyo will be necessary, if he is afraid of that."

"Guest-san wants your wife to stay with you and your family," said Munakata. "He is going to keep away from her and he wants her not to come to his home. He asked her this in the past but she persisted." He paraphrased what I had told him about the relationship and how I had wanted to end it for some time.

"I do not believe he ever cared for her," the man said. "But anyway, I agree to what he says and trust him to keep his word. But I understand that it may be difficult for them to stop meeting at once, so I will not demand that. They have my permission to take some time to sort things out." But as far as I was concerned, it was finished.

The next day, Yumiko arrived at my place and berated me for backing out and leaving her in the lurch. She intended to move into her own apartment, she said; she could not bear to live with her husband any more. She came to call on me a few more times, and I heard her out without responding to any physical overtures. After our final meeting, she slammed the metal door behind her with a crash that seemed to shake the precarious foundations of Yamamura Heights; I hung up on her next telephone call and left the receiver off the hook. A female friend of hers telephoned me, and I put down the receiver immediately I realized she was about to hand the call over to Yumiko.

A few days later, I found an envelope in my mailbox at work and opened it. There was a business card I had given her on our initial meeting at the sunakku, now scribbled over with denunciations and curses: "This man is a snake and a scoundrel. Women should beware of him, or he will destroy your life. He will soon die and then I will be happy" and the like. And a snapshot of me, taken years earlier in Australia, which I had given her as a keepsake, edited for emphasis: she had used a razor blade to slit out my eyes. I thanked the Shinto gods for warning me in time, for sending me the sign of that dog on the beach.

No matter what differences Munakata and I had in the future, I was forever immensely grateful. Shortly after the episode, he and I went to Miho-no-Matsubara together to see the annual performance of the noh play

Hagoromo, "The Feather Robe." A magical, mystical evening. A temporary stage had been built in front of the sacred pine: a square performance area adjoined a long entrance walkway—the heavenly nymph entered across this bridge and into our world. Sheets of brilliantly patterned fabric quivered in the breeze, screening away the offstage area, an unknowable paradise. The audience filled the rows and rows of fold-up metal chairs placed on the sand, facing the sea.

"The noh actor walks as though not walking," Blyth writes. "The mask smiles and weeps without the slightest change of expression. This is Godlike, this is Zen . . . It is but one step from heaven to hell, and each step of a noh actor is such a step . . ."

The musicians were positioned at the side and back of the stage, their flutes, hand drums and hypnotic voices blending with the footfalls and stamping of the actors in a compelling music, mysterious and eternal. Before the performance, Shinto priests in white robes had set a line of bamboo torches afire at the foot of the stage and along the walkway. Flames leaped and crackled. A cargo ship leaving Shimizu Harbor glided behind the stage and slipped out to sea, toward a horizon that was disappearing in darkness.

We sat alongside each other in the expensive seats near center-stage. Munakata placed his hand on my forearm to catch my attention, and I looked around at him. With his raffish, shoulder length gray hair, and in his comfortable suit, eyes twinkling behind rectangular spectacles, he was the image of the cultured scholar. But not merely the image: he was the ultimate noh connoisseur.

"Zeami says that the eyes of the noh actor look ahead and his spirit looks behind," he said. "There we find the flower and the jewel of noh." A sagacious look.

"Fantastic having those Shinto priests light the torches," I whispered.

His eyes gleamed in the dark, reflecting the flicker of the torchlight, and he smiled shrewdly and leaned over to me, cupping his mouth to whisper in my ear.

"Of course, they are not real Shinto priests . . ."

15

Homecoming

M ost expats returned to their home country for a visit every six months or so, but when I could, I preferred to attend an academic conference in a country I hadn't yet visited. I enjoyed experiencing fresh perceptions of Australia after stretches away of three years at a time; so during the first nine years, I visited home three times. On those occasions, things bathed themselves in a new light: the subtle shades of eucalyptus-green, spacious streets, characteristic Australian accents and attitudes, which, filtered through my own nostalgia, assumed a loveliness I'd never noticed before. So much seemed fresh and new: Sydney's colonial architecture and the vibrant atmosphere of the harbor, suburban streets, twee facades of small town shopfronts striving to be up to date. Even something as unremarkable as an asphalt footpath had an indefinable Australian-ness about it (surrounded as it was, you will say, by Australia). Not that Japan lacked asphalt footpaths — just that this one contributed to the urban scene a specific "there-ness," like an aura surfacing from the unconscious. But I knew that, given time, the asphalt would re-assume the impenetrable density of the everyday.

Great just to disappear into the crowd, to cease being a gaijin—back in a country so multicultural the word "foreigner" meant next to nothing. Yet in another way, I was marked out by acquired body language and gestures. Like my habit of bobbing physically as I spoke—in Japan, more than being a distinct formality you perform from time to time, minuscule variants of bowing punctuate face-to-face communication with the frequency of commas. In an Australian public bar, such behavioral idiosyncrasies could attract a suspicious response—and, depending on the type and temperament of drinkers present, hazardously more than that when exhibited by someone who was obviously an Australian. So I was a bit edgy in such places. At the same time, I had been dying to taste a schooner (a lovely big three-quarter pint glass) of Aussie draft beer, to soak up the atmosphere of a real pub. I craved the delights of Australian cuisine, as well, that I'd missed in Japan: lamb chops (most Japanese either dislike the smell or consider lambs too cute to eat), chocolate milkshakes, meat pies, fish and chips, and related delicacies like potato scallops (known in some places as "potato cakes") and deep-fried battered saveloys.

Qantas Airlines offered deals that allowed me to take an extra trip within Australia, while en route to Sydney, at a cheap price. So I went to Darwin, Alice Springs, Uluru (formerly Ayer's Rock), Perth and Broome—locations that distance and cost prohibited me from visiting when I lived in Australia. The landscape was captivating to fly over: sometimes the arid red of the ground was filtered through a thin, translucent green haze, a bare film of vegetation. Mesmerizing, the resemblance of aerial scenes to those traditional aboriginal artworks that, like maps (which in a sense they are), depict forms derived from geographical environments and topographical features, rendering them in the tangible, authentic hues of the earth. Circling to land at Broome was like entering a hallucination, the gorgeous sapphire sea set against a long ribbon of white sand; then red and multicolored earth, white patches of the salt flats, all the brilliant hues and chaotic forms of an abstract canvas.

My insides rebelled against the cuisine, having become accustomed to Japanese food, which is light and comes in small portions. A trip in a commercial tourist mini-van from Alice Springs to Uluru included a stop at a cattle station somewhere along the way, where a hairy-forearmed mine host slapped a mammoth T-bone steak down on the table in front of me. But I could hardly manage an unmanly intake of a few mouthfuls, earning the visible disdain of my Australian traveling companions. Later the same day, I made the error of deciding at Uluru to purchase a long-awaited first meat pie. Remembrance of pies past! A perfect exemplar I'd consumed as a child haunted my daydreams. Ambrosia of the gods: light, flaky pastry, tenderest seasoned beef that melted in the mouth, barest hint of onions. But as awe inspiring as the great red rock was, it was not a habitat for the elusive perfect pie. The one I bought had endured a protracted, cellophane wrapped, sub-zero existence in one freezer after the next along the supply chain before being micro-waved for my benefit. The inedible specimen ended its journey in a bin outside after two mouthfuls and a seared palate.

MY OVERNIGHT stay at a "resort" outside Alice Springs produced a far more unpleasant incident, from which I could derive value only by embracing it as an experience of "reverse culture shock." The establishment consisted of an array of small cabins, spread out over an area of an acre or two. I left my key, passport and airline tickets in the care of the receptionist—as I once read you should do when abroad (likely an erroneous theory). A pleasant young woman put my things in the office safe for me and phoned me a taxi. Be back before ten, she advised. I assured her I would and departed cheerfully to Alice Springs, which was about a fifteen-minute ride. Despite my experience with the cattle station T-bone and the Uluru meat pie, I continued my culinary odyssey, entering a pub bistro and ordering a meal that was designed as a specialty for thrill-seeking tourists: steaks of kangaroo, crocodile, buffalo, emu and camel piled on a plate, with vegetables and chips. Again my digestive tract reacted and I didn't get far through the meal. I caught another taxi back to the resort, arriving at about eight, to find the office already locked up. It was the off-season, and the entire place appeared to be deserted. A sign on the wall read: "Press button if after hours or office unattended." I pressed but nothing happened.

The taxi driver radioed headquarters and asked them to try to raise somebody by phone, but that was to no avail. Evening was falling fast, but I let him go, not wanting to inconvenience him any further. I located my cabin, which was locked, but noticed a light burning in a cabin nearby. When I knocked on that door, however, I was greeted with some furious male voices warning me to make myself scarce. Understandably hostile voices, for in this desolate region, night having fallen, personal security was close to the front of your mind. In fact, I was starting to feel mortally vulnerable, bordering on desperate, in the realization that I was locked out of doors, with no way to contact help and nowhere to go, pretty much in the middle of what is most likely termed Australia's "dead heart" for good reason.

Back to the office and pressed the button again. No reply and by this time dark. The stars are pretty out there, set against that immense, foreboding blackness of the void. Went to the rear of the building, to which a fenced-off timber veranda was attached. Stepped across the fence onto the veranda, knocked at the closed door and called out "Hello!" And again. Sudden commotion within: bumping, heavy footsteps, cursing. The veranda light came on, the wooden door was pulled open from within, and out through the screen door burst an irate, gorilla-like man in his fifties, followed by a golden retriever.

"What the bloody hell's goin' on here? What the frigginell do you want? Whadaya think you're doin', bashin' the door down!" Sweated and growled, lurching across the veranda at me belligerently. Blustered toward me, flexing his muscles and trying to agitate the dog, who leaped about at his side but displayed no sign of viciousness. Jumped and barked once or twice looking utterly good-natured.

A far cry from the superlative service I had become used to. To a Japanese tourist, this treatment would be unendurable. I explained myself tersely, though not rudely or aggressively—but damned if I was going to let him walk over me without at least a show of indignation. Wrong move. The man was clearly drunk and getting more aggressive by the second as I spoke. He lurched at me again, looking as if he might swing a punch any second.

"And who do you think you are?" he bellowed at me. "I don't care who the hell you are, anyway. Thumpin' around the place!"

"I repeat, I'm a guest here. I checked in about two hours ago. Now, if you look in your safe, you'll find my key and passport there."

"Whadaya mean bangin' on the door? I was asleep, for Chrissakes."

"What would you like me to do?—I'm locked out. You've got a sign out front to press the button. I pressed but nothing happens."

"It's switched orf while I'm sleepin' is why. Dipstick."

"Well, I'm not to know that, am I? What am I supposed to do to get into my room?" I muttered. "Now, would you kindly get me my key and passport from your safe?"

"I'm not gunna open the safe for you. You could be a burglar or anyone."

"I don't look like much of one, do I? Do you get many burglars roaming around here in the evening alone, no car, knocking on your door to have a chat with you?"

His physical momentum had run out. He must have realized I was who I said, a paying guest locked out, but he was not about to admit a fault. Not that this was what I was after—I only wanted my key.

"Then you can show me some ID," he said smugly,

trace of a crooked sneer on his face, eyes bleary, swaying as he stood toe to toe with me, hands now on hips, lumpy torso clad in singlet and shorts. His head looked as indestructible as a steel anvil, a formidable effect compounded by short cropped, crinkly gray hair and bristling chin. His strategy morphed from physical intimidation into officiousness.

"I said . . . show me some ID."

"I'll need my passport."

"Not. Without. Identification."

I seethed but knew I needed to contain my language.

"My passport is my identification."

He processed the dilemma.

"Ain't you got a driver's license or nothin'?"

"No, I don't. Now, how about looking in the safe," I said, refraining from any hint of mockery, "opening the passport you find there, looking at the photograph in it and comparing it to my face?" Pointing at my nose, Japanese style. "That will identify who I am."

The aggravation had seeped from my voice like air from a leaky balloon and was replaced by weary frustration. The heat, the heat, and at the mercy of this rude person. (Scraps of eclectic wisdom gleaned from Ryoanji temple, Sufi sages, Zen monks . . . out the window.)

He leered at me in contempt.

"Well, you go around the front there and wait outside," he commanded me grandly.

While I sat on a bench on the front veranda, beside the office door, he took his time going to the safe and finding my passport—twenty minutes. There is a theory about white Australian society. Because of our origins as a prison colony, in the early days a good deal of status was conferred upon the role of the turnkey, whose duty it was to regulate the convicts' passage in and out of their cells. In modern times, the role manifests itself in all manner of jobs that deal with the public, and can breed a haughty, domineering attitude in a certain cut of people whose job invests them with any form of power over their fellow citizens, from selling them a postage stamp or railway ticket to managing them in the work-place. In Japan, the turnkey attitude would not be tolerated. Characteristically, apart from the pride and satisfaction they derive from doing a good job, Japanese workers don't invest their egos in the interactions their job defines for them. Most feel neither aggrandized nor belittled in doing what they're paid to do. In Australia, the turnkey pops up too often.

He summoned me in. On scrutinizing my face sus-piciously against my passport photo, he tossed my documents and key down on top of the counter without another word. Next morning the female receptionist was in the office to check me out. While doing so, she seemed markedly cool compared with the friendly de-meanor she displayed on the previous day, as though words had been exchanged to my disadvantage. Behind her, the man bumbled about and pretended to look for something in a cabinet. I was certain there would be every chance of violence if I mentioned the incident, which I had no inclination to do anyway. I stole a last furtive look at his formidable skull, bid farewell and de-parted unscathed.

ISABELLA AND I married in a small ceremony conducted by a celebrant and attended by a few friends. We shared a love that proved strong enough to withstand the stresses that the time and distance apart—and admittedly, I myself—had inflicted. I was through with my reckless bachelor's life abroad.

An artist friend and his wife invited us to a barbecue at their seaside house, where I met Laurens Tan, a conceptual sculptor with whose work I was familiar from my days as a regional arts columnist. Laurens was born in Holland, of Chinese parents, and moved to Australia at the age of twelve. An accomplished academic who taught visual art at university, he was an engaging individual, cosmopolitan and entrepreneurial; advantageous qualities in the competitive world of art, in which financial resources were scarce as they were crucial. He told us about renovations underway at the historic Capitol Theatre in Sydney, a project planned to incorporate work by contemporary artists: he was creating a video installation for the foyer. We discussed new trends in Australian "public art"—the injection of art into the public environment—and tossed around the possibility of collaborating on a project in Japan, with the idea of introducing Australian public art to a Japanese audience. An exciting possibility: a nice challenge and a constructive way to capitalize on my tenure, attempting to promote Australian art and make a modest contribution to cultural exchange between the two countries. I asked Laurens to send me a portfolio of work by him and a group of conceptual artists with whom he was collaborating.

We met again in Haymarket some days later. Laurens showed Isabella and me around the Capitol Theatre renovations, before introducing us to a member of his artists' group, Simeon Nelson, and as well, a colleague of Laurens's, the dean of creative arts at the University of Western Sydney. Stinking hot day, so we repaired to a nearby public bar to talk. The dean had been working to establish semi-formal agreements with foreign universities, his aim being to foster collaboration and exchange, and I agreed to present the idea to my faculty.

16

Married Life

Wherever you live is the capital

—Old Japanese saying

K uma had stayed at Isabella's home on his first ever trip to Australia, some months before she joined me in Yamamura Heights. Now he and Noriko eagerly organized this and that social outing for us: karaoke, sushi, and a trip to the historical town of Takayama with Ojima-san. Another of Kuma's close friends was Ida-san, a sushi chef and restaurateur with whom he took excursions into the countryside collecting mushrooms. The four of us visited Ida's restaurant, which was flawlessly appointed in pinewood. He crafted his own pottery cups and dishes and micro-managed the ambiance, the recorded song of a solitary cricket playing in the background throughout the evening. In a more ordinary sushi restaurant, one might be treated to a live broadcast of baseball from a television set fixed to the wall. Ida was an incurable romantic and developed an obvious infatuation with Isabella as the night wore on and the *atsukan* (heated saké) flowed.

A coffee shop owned by other friends of Kuma's provided another genteel experience. They were an attractive, perfectly groomed married couple with hennaed hair and beautiful clothes—new-age fabric designs with a vaguely Indian flavor. They had the appearance of having teleported in from the sixties, or else some utopian planet, and served untold varieties of coffee, preparing the beverage reverently, with a kind of doting fastidiousness. Their cafe resembled a contemporary art gallery, featuring several sculptures—machines that disdained utility, their intricate components crafted from wood and wire.

"I felt that we should be serving *them* the coffee," Isabella joked as we left.

Many of Kuma and Noriko's numerous friends were involved in performing arts. Kuma led an a cappella group that performed in some city venues, including the chic coffee shop. He was master of ceremonies at a concert at an auditorium in the city center, which a pianist friend of his gave to a full house. His bearlike frame, easygoing personality and English language fluency contributed to his popular image among the local university students. In addition to my university, Shizuoka boasted a prefectural university and several smaller private universities. He was forever mentoring students and was so good-natured that I found myself agreeing to be a judge for inter-university English speech contests, attending student plays and leading a drama workshop for a university Shakespeare circle at a holiday resort on the Izu Peninsula. Fascinating to observe how such activities fostered cohesion throughout the university and broader community.

Noriko was a gentle soul, petite, cute and plump, a little female buddha. She exuded benevolence and calm, and she idolized Kuma, who dwarfed her physically. She studied the traditional tea ceremony and acted in community theater. The world-renowned dramatist and director Tadashi Suzuki (who was born in Shimizu) had set up his headquarters on Nihondaira plateau, and Noriko auditioned for him. I was aware of Suzuki's brilliance, having seen his SCOT (Suzuki Company of Toga) company's famous production of Euripides' *Trojan Women* when it traveled to Sydney in 1988 for the Australian Bicentennial Expo. Suzuki's dual aim for his new center in Shizuoka was to decentralize highbrow theater away from Tokyo and establish a national and international base for Japanese performing arts. To this objective, he was directing plays involving the regional community, while continuing to develop high-end works for his stable of dedicated professional actors.

We went with our neighbors to the brand new Nihondaira complex of Suzuki's Shizuoka Performing Arts Centre (SPAC) to see his interpretation of Euripides' *Dionysus*. Isozaki Arata, one of Japan's most influential contemporary architects, designed the buildings. A postmodernist, Isozaki was opposed to the commercial and technological tendencies of modern architecture and had already collaborated with Suzuki in the design of the Toga theaters. His stunning Nihondaira complex merged into the landscape, with an effect that, as one walked among the woods and tea fields of the twenty-one hectare grounds, the buildings subtly revealed themselves one by one. The complex consisted of indoor and outdoor performance theaters, rehearsal and teaching studios comprising a total floor space of twelve-hundred square meters, cafeteria, dormitories and an administrative hall.

We met Suzuki at an informal reception before the play started. He was tall, lean and youthful looking, with intelligent eyes and an aura of understated authority. Theatergoers were gathering in the courtyard outside the entrance to the outdoor amphitheater, many, like us four, chatting over a drink at the temporary outdoor bar. Suzuki appeared and began to schmooze his way through the thickening crowd. Kuma introduced Isabella and me to him, and Suzuki made a genial comment. He was accompanied by a shorter, white-haired man, who was the head administrator. When we were introduced, he gave a bow of his head, his eyes looking past me. After the two of them moved on, Kuma excused himself to use the restroom.

At opening time, the white-haired man cued a team of officious ushers, who began lining us up according to our ticket numbers and commenced herding us through the entrance. I found my place in the line.

A female inspected my queue with the aggressiveness of a prison guard.

"A85? Who has ticket number A85? A85?" she demanded.

"I'm A84," said the person in front of me.

"A86," I said.

"Then where is A85? A85!" the usher called out imperiously, shooting an accusing look at us.

"I think it's my friend's number," I said.

"So where are they?" she demanded.

All eyes were upon me. Such a confronting situation

commonly called for a profusion of self-effacing gestures and apologies, but I looked the usher in the eye and declaimed in a firm voice for all to hear: "He is in the toilet!" causing her to vanish instantaneously into a horrified silence.

Kuma came back and we shared a laugh when I told him what happened.

"So everyone here knows what you've been doing," I said, with a nod to the crowd surrounding us. "You know, I don't think Australians would stand for being regimented and bossed around like this."

"I've never thought about it," Kuma said, "but you might be right. We Japanese don't seem to get perturbed when we are told what to do. But I read somewhere that Suzuki-san believes that the spectators should not just have art handed to them on a platter. We have to make an effort, too."

"I suppose that in a sense we take a pilgrimage up here into the mountain to see the drama." Gesturing to encompass the prodigious surrounding vistas.

"That's right," Kuma said, "and as you know, we regard our mountains as sacred places—particularly here, so close to Mount Fuji. Suzuki-san believes that Tokyoites will want to make the pilgrimage here, as will people from all over this prefecture."

"Well, the aggravation makes sense, then," I said dubiously. "Small sacrifice for a transcendent experience."

The venue was an open-air amphitheater called the Udo Theater, unpretentious and functional—stepped concrete and marble auditorium, black benches of smooth wooden planks attached to the concrete, to hold an audience of five hundred and fifty. Behind the acting space the ground descended into tea fields surrounded by forest. Suzuki's actors exhibited the muscular, kinetic physicality of his training methods; noh and kabuki resonated strongly, as well, in their movements, gestures and speech. Yet the diverse elements of the drama synthesized in an austere, realistic style.

Evening was falling when, midway through the play, shadowy figures appeared from among the surrounding trees and made ghostly entrances onto the stage. The mythical, dramatic space seemed to meld together with the natural scene, receding to the horizon, yet extending infinitely beyond. Primal, potent atmosphere a testament to Suzuki's vision and his mastery over the finest detail.

At the end of the performance, the white-haired administrator was standing not far from me to the rear, applauding energetically as a cue for the audience. The measure struck me as crude and condescending, given the high artistic tone that Suzuki wished to engender.

THE 2DK APARTMENT at Yamamura Heights, more than adequate for me living by myself, felt cramped for two. In Australia we had a roomy house on four acres bordering on rainforest, so over the long term, the new situation would take some getting used to. On the plus side, no gardening chores, and minimal cooking and housework. Isabella enrolled in Japanese language courses offered by the city council, which were attended mostly by Thai, Filipina, Korean and Chinese immigrant wives of Japanese men. There she met Nicole, a New Zealander married to an Australian, and the two became friends. Nicole worked as an English teacher for an agency that provided English classes for businessmen and company workers.

Six blonde, blue-eyed and leggy, slightly tatty but gay and extroverted Russian club-hostesses arrived to join the Japanese class, and Isabella chatted with them in Russian. Ballet dancers by profession, they said, submitting skillful pirouettes in evidence. In their new job, they complained, all they had to do was dress scantily, entertain clients and perform the occasional alluring gyration. They were recruited by an agent for the nightclubs. Their Japanese employers held onto their passports and kept the hostesses in a controlled dormitory, not allowing them to go anywhere unless they were escorted by a client. A few weeks later the dancers turned up again at class, much happier, sporting furs and expensive jewelry.

Nicole told Isabella about a part-time job opening at her agency. Isabella held a qualification in physiotherapy but had no teaching experience of any kind. But for English teaching jobs of this sort, a bachelor's degree or equivalent in any subject was deemed enough. Uncharacteristically fazed by the proposition, Isabella didn't feel confident enough to find her way to unknown destinations by train and taxi.

"The signs on the station platforms are in *romaji* — Roman letters," I said, encouraging her to accept the position, knowing I would have to continue to spend long hours on campus.

"I know that," she said, "but I can't even buy a train ticket or give instructions to a taxi driver."

"Most Japanese speak a little English."

"Yes, but if you ask them for help or directions, they become paralyzed with embarrassment. And anyway, I don't have the faintest idea about how to teach English."

"Neither did I at first," I said. "It doesn't matter. Mostly they want to practice with a native speaker. I'll show you some exercises to get you going." Though English was, in fact, her third language after Russian and German, it was impossible to distinguish her from a native.

She got the job and started giving classes at companies here and in neighboring cities, commuting by train and taxi. The work was sometimes a tough slog, though her innate vivacity equipped her amply. Not much fun to stand waiting for a taxi on a windy railway platform at Fuji City on the way to give night classes to workers in an automotive factory, but preparation for teaching provided something to occupy herself with, along with her language study.

After a year, she took on more part-time work teaching classes attended by retirees and well-off women with abundant leisure time. This they filled with shopping, practicing tea-ceremony and ikebana and traveling abroad, hence their motivation to learn English. She was paid according to the number of participants who re-enrolled, so she soon realized the value of dressing as smartly as they did, and developing a polished, professional approach to her classes. When they arrived for the first time, the women looked her up and down. The average part-time English teacher was younger and more casually attired—young expats were decidedly dressed down compared with the Japanese, who were drawn to designer wear. Nor did Japanese women share the Western aversion to wearing furs in the winter but sported fur jackets unabashedly, and a pure black or white fur collar was a common accessory to a kimono.

Moreover, the young teachers were usually on a short stay, often on the Japan Exchange and Teaching (JET) program. Their mature students considered them as somewhat less than their social equals, and rather more akin to waiters or waitresses. Here on the other hand was Isabella, who was cultivated and cosmopolitan. Often she had been to the countries they were planning to visit, commanded a good knowledge of the politics, history and geography, and had at least a smattering of the language. She spoke with authority and wit about any number of issues that confronted and stimulated them, whereas the teaching styles of the younger foreign teachers were geared to interacting with children or young adults. Clients soon regarded their lessons with her as a status symbol, enabling her to corner a niche market, with the city council advertising her classes to mature men and women.

Once a week, Isabella met up with Nicole, her husband Jeff and a few other expatriate language teachers at a café in the station plaza. Jeff had been a professional tennis coach in Australia, until playing tennis started to feel too much like work. Here he taught English and undertook miscellaneous projects in a quest for fast money: acquiring prestigious cars at auction and sending them back home, ostensibly to relatives; doing bit-parts in television dramas if a gaijin was required; and dressing up as a minister and working as a marriage celebrant in an ersatz church—a flimsy building decorated ostentatiously with Christian paraphernalia.

The expats rehashed the trivial hardships and irritations of life in Japan; but it was indeed the minutiae that affected one throughout the process of acculturation, exerting a continual, indefinable pressure. Nicole encountered a more serious cultural issue when her son Sam, who was enrolled at a junior high school, came home one day with a handprint-shaped welt on his face, where his physical education teacher slapped him. Nicole went immediately back to the school with Sam, berated the teacher and warned the headmaster there would be trouble if it ever happened again.

On her free days, Isabella took walks into the hills and tea plantations or stayed in the apartment to practice yoga and stretching exercises on the tatami floor, listening to a radio program of noh music broadcast every morning. She discovered a boxing gym a couple of kilometers from Yamamura Heights and went there to exercise on the machines and weights. Joined a tennis club and rode there on her bicycle, now her primary mode of transport. She submitted to the group training sessions and drills that preceded playing a game, mixed well with both sexes and was welcomed everywhere she went.

The tennis players were dismayed to hear that Japan had attacked Australia during the Second World War, and one woman apologized for it.

"Not your fault," Isabella reassured her.

Many of her students wanted to visit Australia, and while they were acquainted with the media image of the country—kangaroos and koalas, surfing beaches and tropical rainforests—they knew nothing of the wartime bombings of Darwin and Broome. In the interest of promoting discussion, along with accurate ideas about both countries, Isabella introduced thorny (to them) topics like this. Harboring no uncharitable wish to dispel their stereotypes of the Japanese people as being inherently hardworking, kind, meek and mild, she aimed nevertheless to arouse more thoughtful discussions and reflections.

Older students maintained a love of English that stemmed from school studies prior to the start of the war, when speaking any English was banned. Isabella tapped into the values of lifelong education in a unique and significant way, given Japan's aging population and the role that English language study potentially played in promoting cultural exchange and international understanding at this grassroots level. She made some good friends among her students. Shigeko was one: an elegant lady from an established, wealthy family, who as a girl in Kyoto witnessed the flash of the atomic bomb dropped on Hiroshima. She and her schoolmates had been drilled in fighting with bamboo rods in order to combat the Americans if they invaded.

Nevertheless, as supportive as Isabella was and as fond of her as her students became, they sometimes frustrated her efforts to overcome their reserve. When she raised issues with emotional associations, such as the system of capital punishment, or seemingly innocuous topics that turned out to be taboo—interracial marriage, nursing homes for the elderly, or the contraceptive pill—although the students held opinions and possessed ample English proficiency to explain them, they would clam up, look up at the ceiling, suck their teeth and make a vague, conventional utterance calculated to avoid the issue: "*Ehh-to . . .*"—expressing an ambiguous air of either searching for a thought or wishing to defer it indefinitely. But should a socially sanctioned topic arise, such as food or blood types, they chatted on contentedly.

A group returned from an Australian holiday:

"Oh, it was great!" The women laughed and presented her with an *omiyage* (souvenir), a box of chocolate koalas. "We had a . . . *wonderful* time in Safazu Paradaisu."

"Any chance to practice your English?"

"*Ehh-to* . . . We were always with our group, so we did not have an opportunity to speak to foreigners. The only English we spoke was 'please' and 'thank-you.'"

"Did you enjoy the food?"

"Oh yes."

"What did you have?" Expecting an overview of Down Under cuisine.

"We ate only in Japanese restaurants. Tempura, and yakitori and teppanyaki . . . and *ehh-to* . . ."

Conversations with these older adults opened doors to their everyday traditional attitudes and customs, many with which I was unfamiliar.

"Would you be happy if your son or daughter wanted to marry a foreigner?"

"Oh no, never!" the woman gasped, throwing her hands up to her face in horror. "I would never allow it."

Common practice for parents to hide electronic bugs in their children's bedrooms to keep tabs on their activities. When a wedding engagement was imminent, it wasn't unknown for parents to have a private investigator research the family history of the prospective spouse, to ensure they were not a *burakumin* ("hamlet person")— a caste of people lowest on the social order and traditionally discriminated against—nor had family roots in Hiroshima, in which case it was thought they might have defective genes.

Observation and learning occupied the better part of Isabella's day as she established her life. Most housewives here shopped every day or two, being limited to the amount they were able to take home on a bicycle.

In a neighborhood supermarket, goods came in small quantities: miniature jars of Nescafe, cans of beans, packs of breakfast cereal. In Australia, you bought potatoes in ten-kilogram bags; here they were sold four per plastic bag. Everything was so small—you couldn't even buy a whole chicken. Modest fillets of chicken breast, pork or "Aussie beef" were sold pre-packed in a shallow polystyrene container sealed in plastic wrap. Foods were pre-cut to chopstick size. Fish were small varieties she'd never seen before—no snapper, flathead or trout. Suburban supermarkets sold no cheese but processed cheddar, though exotic varieties were available from department stores downtown. Both kinds of outlet stocked products unrecognizable to the neophyte, either because the kanji on the labels were indecipherable or the foodstuff an ingredient in an unknown dish. Until she learned to read the relevant kanji, she couldn't tell salt from small-grained sugar without taking a sample that had permeated through onto the surface of the plastic bag and putting her fingertip to her tongue.

A typical Japanese housewife would don her best pinafore, plop her infant in a dicky-seat on the back of her bicycle and pedal off to the supermarket. She wore her pinafore proudly. Whether plain or elaborately designed and decorated with lace, it was a symbol of her status as a house manager. Indeed, she controlled the household finances: her husband handed over his pay, and she returned him an allowance.

An M-size in Australia, Isabella was an XL in Japan, where people were generally smaller. Stockings or pantyhose were mandatory, and women wore them in midsummer temperatures upward of thirty Celsius. Isabella was five feet two inches, which was quite tall here: "*Se ga takai!*" ("Aren't you tall!") everyone exclaimed. The difference was most pronounced when standing in a department store elevator and able to see across the heads of the other women. Her acquired stature gave her an advantage over the *obasan* ("aunties"), who were characteristically short, stocky, middle-aged ladies, notorious for taking advantage of the customary Japanese reticence in public. Wearing child-size backpacks, they jumped queues waiting for buses and trains, their low center of gravity enabling them to bump everybody else aside as they burrowed like trolls to the front. Isabella could, however, effortlessly block their progress, looking the other way as though they didn't exist, much to their vexation.

She became dark-haired, since dyes of other shades were unavailable at her unpretentious hair salon. Colored hair first became widely fashionable among young women some years later—a trend led by the *ganguro* or "black face" girls, with their spray-on tan, blonde, pink, green or orange hair and intentionally garish makeup. Isabella frequented a hairdresser in Oshika who kept a pet monkey named Momo ("Peach"). The hairdresser mentioned that Momo's favorite treat was avocado, so the next time Isabella visited she took one to give the monkey, prepared halved, with the pip taken out.

Momo accepted the avocado with her tiny hands through the bars of the cage and nibbled at it delightedly.

"Don't get too close or she'll get your scarf!" the hairdresser warned. Isabella was bending over chatting to Momo as she finished off the avocado. Too late!—the monkey had the scarf in a tight grip. Isabella gently extricated it from Momo's hands, as the monkey gazed at her face with wide eyes full of wonder. From then on, whenever she went to Oshika, she bought an avocado for Momo.

Isabella objected to the way some people treated their dogs, keeping them tethered on a short chain. Other dog owners provided entertainment as she rode her bicycle along the sidewalk. Exemplary about cleaning up after their dog, they wore white cotton gloves and sported a range of pooper-scoopers and containers. One day she spotted an ingenious adaptation: a man was squatting down behind his canine, using a pair of *hashi* to grasp the stools as they emerged and pop them in a plastic bag before they touched the footpath.

In summer, Japanese celebrate the Buddhist Obon Festival, when the spirits of the ancestors return to earth to visit the family home.

"We light incense sticks and put them at the gate to help the ancestors find their way," Yoko explained, "and we make a toy horse out of straw or maybe a . . . *kyuri?*"

"Cucumber," said Isabella, whose domestic vocabulary had grown rapidly.

". . . *Kyukamba*. Make legs out of *tsumayoji* (toothpicks) for the horse, and make an ox out of a *nasu* . . ."

"Aubergine."

". . . *Obajin* . . . Horse is to help ancestors come very quickly. Ox is to take them back to heaven . . . but *very slowly*."

"But these days," Midori laughed, "some families put out toy helicopter and motorbike, instead of horse and ox."

Isabella learned that you should never use *hashi* to pass food to another person, because a particular funeral ritual involves the family members of the cremated deceased using them to pass around the remnants of bones from one to another.

"And you shouldn't stick them upright in your rice," she told me, "because that happens in the funeral rite, too. Oh, and to place them down crossed on the table signifies death, so that's taboo as well.

"A Japanese will marry in a Shinto ceremony and be buried in a Buddhist one. The bride will often change into a traditional white Western wedding gown, too. She might change six or seven times during the reception to show off her various gowns . . .

"Women tend not to wear rings; they leave their fingers unadorned. Very little use of perfume. Natural smells are preferable—part of the value they place on being natural . . . Odd, given how extremely made-up they are . . ."

17

Downtime

Once in a while, we took a day trip to Tokyo or stayed the night in a hotel. We attended an avant-garde *butoh* play or visited the Kabukiza, Tokyo's preeminent kabuki theater. Some years before, we had seen an acclaimed kabuki company when it toured to Sydney. The production entranced us with its artistry, intense, emotionally expressive acting and remarkable onstage illusions. At the Kabukiza, the setting and bustling atmosphere magnified the theatrical experience. Many in the audience bought obento at the theater to eat during the performance. Glamorous women in kimono looked down from their box seats and aficionados cried out whenever the play produced a transcendent moment. A dramatic gesture called the *mié* pose usually elicits these shouts: overcome with emotion, the actor strikes an attitude, turning his head to best display an exaggerated expression of fierceness or grief, crossing one eye and momentarily freezing (kabuki actors are exclusively male). During the

American occupation, Faubion Bowers, General Douglas MacArthur's personal aide and interpreter, organized special performances of kabuki for American soldiers, some of whom burst into laughter at the mié poses. I liked a television commercial for a brand of coffee that poked fun at the convention, in which a trained monkey struck a classic mié pose after taking a sip from a can of the coffee.

Isabella planned our excursions into arts and culture. We might spend the morning browsing the collection of the Metropolitan Art Museum at Ueno Park, and the afternoon at the National Museum, with its magnificent collection of art and archaeological artifacts. Usually I wanted to visit Maruzen bookshop to make some purchases. I decided where we would eat—say, Irish stew and a pint of Guinness for lunch at an Irish pub in Harajuku, sukiyaki for dinner at a Ginza restaurant. We caught the last Shinkansen home to Shizuoka, my seat reclined, my shoes off and feet up on the footrest, head lolling to one side on the spotless linen covered headrest, the vibrant images of the day jostling for prominence before my closed eyelids as I dozed.

As immensely as I enjoyed these visits, in which little by little we made the acquaintance of the great city, the idea of moving to Tokyo failed to attract me. I shrank from the prospect of living among the dense population, dragging myself to work every day in a packed subway car. In the park near Meiji Shrine, Elvis-styled rockers dancing to ghetto blasters struck me as kitsch and exhibitionistic, as did buskers miming in butoh-style on the street nearby. I had the feeling that if you scratched a Tokyoite you would find underneath something not too far from the specimen they liked to consider a hick.

235

* * *

WE WERE cycling on the bicycle track along the coast of Suruga Bay to Shimizu, crossing familiar bridges, making the usual turns, inhaling alternate breaths of sea air from the bay and carbon monoxide fumes from the traffic on our other flank. The track diverged from the road and we skidded through drifts of sand washed up on the pathway; it took us across a Cessna airstrip and up to a concrete promenade, along which we continued.

"What is that over there?" Isabella gestured to somewhere on the beach.

"That is amazing," I remarked. "To think anyone would be dumb enough to drive a car down there."

An abandoned sedan was irretrievably bogged in sand, and the tide was coming in. Probably, the occupants were simply not used to going to the beach and thought they could just drive around on the sand.

"No, there! That little white thing—I think it's a rabbit."

It headed for the sea, hopping haphazardly: hesitantly, then in a burst. On it went, perilously beyond the line drawn by a recent wave—now halting in the region of darker brown sand, where the moisture shone blue for an instant, reflecting the sky. A faint shriek carried to us. Along the beach from the spot where the animal crouched, its owner, a young girl, separated from her family and ran to it, waving her arms. She held a leash in one hand. Her pet bounded farther below the line of the tide just as the swell reared up.

"Oh no!" we gasped.

A wave formed, broke and raced up the incline of

wet sand, foaming white water. The rabbit hopped again, and the girl scooped it up an instant before it was engulfed. The wave whipped up around the girl's knees. Her father was there now, taking her by the arm. Then they had their pet on the leash again where it belonged, hopping beside them contentedly as they continued their outing.

We cycled along for a while, then turned away from the sea and wheeled our bikes down a gentle grass slope. A competition men's baseball game was in progress — one team wearing white uniforms with blue pinstripes, the other in red. We sat in the shade of the trees to watch the action. The red pitcher fired in a fastball, the white batter swung and missed; the ball slapped — *thwack!* — into the catcher's mitt.

"*Sutoraiiii-ku!*" yelled the umpire from his place behind the batter.

The pitcher wound up and fired again.

Thwack!

"*Sutoraiiii-ku!*"

COASTED ALONG the promenade anticipating a swim, though Shimizu Beach had some deficiencies: a buzzing sound from ship propellers irritated your ears when your head was submerged, and you imagined you detected the slight feel and taste of an oil slick. Some things you didn't much see on an Australian beach: volleyball; scuba divers; jet ski races; inflatable rubber sharks and crocodiles; communal pergolas where beachgoers went to eat, drink and recline smoking. Dreadlocked Japanese Rastafarian wannabes in their twenties ran a Jamaican-style cafe. In my single days, I used to relax on the promenade out front with them, drinking rum and cola and listening to Bob Marley albums until the sun set. Shunned by the locals, the shop was most often empty, though every other facility was packed: too *abunai* ("dangerous")—harmless and drug free though the ersatz Rastafarians were.

Isabella braked and pointed over to a copse. "I caught sight of something moving over there. Do you see that pile of garbage?"

"That's disgusting—who on earth could have dumped that stuff there?"

"Something big moved in it."

I hadn't ever seen an unauthorized heap of garbage in Japan. The Japanese were fastidious about how they disposed of it, conforming with innumerable rules and regulations.

"There it is," she said.

A bulk resembling a large sack shifted position, and in doing so, revealed itself to have a human shape. When it became still, an effect of camouflage took hold, and we could see only a pile of garbage again. I got off my bicycle, leaned it against a railing and walked over to have a closer look. A man was sitting in the pile eating a gooey substance out of a fast food carton. He had long matted gray hair and a beard and was dressed in rags. Shocking. I had never seen anything quite like this in my life, let alone in Japan. Here the homeless were generally as punctilious in their housekeeping as everybody else; they kept tidy makeshift cardboard shanties, were quiet and polite, and rolled up and put away their sleeping mats when they weren't using them. Some youths caused a public uproar when they were arrested for burning out some of these poor and peaceful souls from their makeshift homes at Tokyo Station.

The refuse stank in the heat, and flies swarmed all over the wretched individual. He continued to gobble up muck from the carton and rummaged about him in the waste for more foul sustenance.

"Let's go—he's all right," Isabella said.

"He reminds me of Lucky in *Waiting for Godot*," I said, shaking my head. "What an abysmal condition."

We enjoyed our swim, and as we rode back, the breeze blew an opaque, silvery plastic bag across my path. I stopped to pick it up and found two thousand-yen notes inside, equivalent to almost thirty dollars Australian (in those heady days of the "strong yen").

"Well, there's nowhere to put it," I said. "It's been blown here a long way from the beach. If I tie it to the railing, someone else is going to take it, so I might as well keep it."

We cycled on for ten minutes, past the trees that surrounded Lucky and his filthy habitat. We looked over as we cycled past.

"Is he still there?"

"Yes, there he is."

I stopped my bicycle.

"You know, maybe I should give the money to him—it's purely by chance that I have it."

I left her with the bikes and walked across to the man. The closer I approached, the more dreadful his condition appeared. I went up to where he sat hardly distinguishable from the stinking garbage surrounding him, bent over with a smile and extended my hand with the cash.

"I've just now found this. Here, you take it."

He opened his mouth as if about to speak but said nothing. A swarm of flies buzzed around his mouth, and one or two passed in and out without bothering him. Gaping at me through wide, runny, red eyes, he reached out and clutched the banknotes . . .

"I wonder what he'll buy with it," I said as I got on my bike and we started moving.

"I can't imagine him walking into a convenience store and doing some shopping."

"No. But anyway, I guess he seems to have everything he needs."

MIDWINTER, and chilly enough to produce a fine veil of snowflakes that vanished on touching the ground. As my downstairs neighbor Kuma drove us up into the mountains in his green Range Rover, we started to see heavier snow. Isabella and I traveled in the back seat, Noriko in the front.

"We are going to visit an old hunting village," he said. "The traditional hunters there are called *matagi*—bear hunters. That's pretty close to my family name, Matsuki." He smiled contentedly as he negotiated a bend. He loved escaping the city. I admired him for having achieved his relatively freewheeling lifestyle, with nobody to tell him what to do. He was much his own man, if almost *too* nice. Strains of "Puff the Magic Dragon" had begun drifting up through Yamamura Heights of late as he rehearsed with his a cappella group.

We drove for miles through the mountains. Thick drifts of snow were piled up all around. The landscape mused on timeless scenes from *ukiyoe* woodblock prints: the tranquil hush of white-canopied pine forests, and in the villages, snow-covered wooden shops and dwellings jostled together under each other's eaves.

Lulled by the drive, I fell asleep, and when I awoke, the snow had all but disappeared. Kuma was slowing the vehicle. We crawled along a narrow lane that ran beside a river gorge on our right. To our left lay cultivated fields, bordered by forest. Ahead of us, a ramshackle building teetered on the edge of the gorge, looking as if it might topple in at any moment.

"We're here," he announced. "That's where we will be staying—a ryokan, an inn so historical it was the subject of a television documentary, which is how I got to know about it. The hunting community here goes back at least ten centuries, to the Heian Period."

As we pulled up at the building, a door opened and a grizzled old fellow came out to greet us, stepping past a wheelbarrow containing a bunched-up fur. No, not a fur as such . . .

"Oh, look," said Noriko. "There's a monkey asleep in the wheelbarrow!"

"I wonder . . ." Isabella murmured.

My door was nearest. Getting out of the car and going over, I saw immediately that the monkey had assumed the still mask of death. Looking closer, I noticed a trickle of recently dried blood coming from the nostrils. The eyes were inert, gazing blindly at the inner side of the wheelbarrow. A terribly sad sight, the monkey was fully grown and must have weighed forty or fifty kilos.

The innkeeper spoke in Japanese, explaining how he'd shot the animal half an hour earlier. He was a *bad* monkey, he said, always coming out of the forest and eating vegetables from the garden.

The man hacked up a laugh. I wondered why he had put the poor thing there for us to see . . .

"I'd rather have it coming into the garden once in a while and lose a turnip or two," I muttered to Isabella.

"Country people have no choice," she pointed out. "It may have come in more often than you think— probably used the garden as a smorgasbord."

He showed us into the ryokan. The interior was spacious and shadowy, the walls of dark brown wood, rough-hewn beams supporting a high pitched ceiling. The front hall had a split level: after entering, you stepped up onto an open tatami area with a flat, stone fireplace on one side—a shallow pit about five feet square. An iron cooking-pot was suspended from above by a chain. No chimney, but rather, a hole way up in the apex of the roof to let the smoke out. By the wall was a low, expansive, roughly circular table, the tabletop made from a single section of an ancient tree. The surface polished smooth, the color and texture of the dark timber and the growth rings shone out. Sliding doors screened off this dining area from a hallway that led deeper inside.

Alongside an antique desk used for signing in guests were two heavy sideboards, equally age worn. But more eye-catching were the curiosities exhibited about the hall. Stuffed animals stood or perched all around the walls. An eagle, wings spread, beak screaming out a silent cry, settled onto a forked branch. Next to a sideboard, a tanuki posed upright on its hind legs, dressed in a cap and tartan coat, bearing a toy rifle over one shoulder. A glass-eyed fox guarded the entrance way, brush erect and jaws contorted into a corpse-like grin. Another tanuki and smaller furry creatures—weasels, squirrels and others—peered through glass beads, grimacing and snarling, baring tiny sharp teeth.

The room that the four of us were to share adjoined the dining area. It started to drizzle outside, so we went into our room and Kuma brought out a deck of cards. We chatted and played gin rummy for an hour or so.

"Last week I watched a video called *Yes, Virginia, there is a Santa Claus*," Kuma said after we'd finished. "Do you know that movie, Michael?"

"Yes, I think I've seen it."

"The young girl, Virginia, wrote to the editor of the New York Times asking whether there really was a Santa Claus, because her friends said there wasn't. Her father told her that if the New York Times said Santa Claus exists, then it must be true.

"I downloaded a copy of the editor's letter to her." He took a sheet of paper from his backpack. "'Virginia, your little friends are wrong. They have been affected by the skepticism of a skeptical age . . .'" My brain withered as he read it through to the end. "'. . . No Santa Claus! Thank God! He lives and he lives forever. A thousand years from now, Virginia, nay, ten times ten thousand years from now, he will continue to make glad the heart of childhood.'

"I believe that is so true," Kuma said, moist-eyed. "So true, that in a way we can truly say, 'Yes, Virginia, Santa Claus does exist.'"

Perhaps it should have been an easy thing to agree and try to change the subject; but I felt there was too much at stake. It would be somehow to betray our friendship, to pander to such sentimentalism, kindly though he meant it. I owed him the truth — my truth, at least — even over this trifling issue. He seemed to want to share in the myth with me, a foreigner, to affirm what he accepted as an authentic Western interpretation, beyond what he saw as the shallow, commercial significance that most Japanese attributed to Christmas. On the contrary, I found their fanciful notions of the festive season, among other things, to be most engaging, unconstrained as they were by the culture-bound perceptions with which my upbringing had indoctrinated me. One display in a Tokyo department store depicted poor old Father Christmas crucified on the cross. Another year, they erected a tableau of the last supper, but instead of the disciples, Jesus was surrounded by twelve Japanese salarymen. A sign in English read: "Happy New Year! Thank Christ it's over."

I couldn't make myself submit to his uncritical account of the fable. A very Japanese thing, this mania for cuteness and nostalgia. To some extent a national trait, effusive displays of guileless innocence worked to disarm many, maybe most, visitors, though others perceived them as childishness (perhaps their own perception of unfamiliar communicative mannerisms refracted through a cultural prism).

"I see what you're getting at," I said to Kuma, "but I don't agree. I stopped believing in Santa Claus a long time ago."

"No," he said, "I don't mean like that. I mean, in the way that this editor explains in his letter . . . 'The most real things in the world are those that neither children nor men can see . . .'"

"No," I insisted. "A capitalist-manufactured myth. The newspaper wants to affirm those qualities of gentleness

and meek-and-mildness, childlike innocence, generosity
of spirit—qualities it abstracts from the Christian mythology because they are in the general interest of
moneymaking."

If he was offended or hurt he didn't let on. It was driz-
zling heavier outside, so we all dozed for the remainder
of the afternoon. When we woke up, he suggested that
he and I partake of the indoor *onsen* (hot spring bath)—
a customary thing to do in Japan. The bath was
downstairs in the basement. We soaped and rinsed off
with a bucket, before inching ourselves down gingerly
into a tub of steaming water too hot for my comfort.
Later, we climbed back up the stairs, to find Isabella
and Noriko seated on the tatami mat by the crackling
fireplace. A pair of young newlyweds from Tokyo joined
us, and the monkey-slaying innkeeper came in and sat
down with us as well. Smoke filled the room, burning
my eyes out of their sockets, so that the tears streamed
down my face. I was on the very point of leaving, unable
to bear the terrible stinging any longer, when all of a
sudden my eyes and lungs adapted spontaneously.

The innkeeper's wife served dinner, wholesome country fare built around a hearty *onabe* (stew). We drank
saké heated over the fireplace as the innkeeper regaled
us with tales of days gone by. Generations of the man's
family had owned the ryokan and worked as local mail
carriers. One time, he told us, the river rose so high it
filled the gorge and all but washed the building away.
The flood carried down a gigantic tree—a section was
cut from it and this very table built. The Tokyo bride-
groom reacted to the alcohol with increasing
garrulousness, soon becoming volubly drunk. After we
four retired to our room, we listened to him sliding the

doors open and shut and crashing about the place singing and calling out.

Early next morning, we walked from the ryokan along a lane that went down through the village. People around these parts sure had a macabre appreciation of animals. Small stuffed corpses arranged in "lifelike" poses adorned the porches of the simple wooden houses. Some postures were natural, while others mimicked human beings, the animals wearing clothes and brandishing miniature implements: an axe here, a broom there, a rifle over there. Beady eyes stared as our footfalls crunched on the gravel. An eerie atmosphere. No indication of another human being in the early morning stillness, only us four friends and the invisible, ubiquitous hand of the taxidermist.

18

Everyone's a Critic

As I came out through the front door of the Narita View Hotel, an unmistakable red and white Qantas passenger jet, "flying kangaroo" logo on the tail, passed low overhead, nose raised, descending in the direction of the airport. Good timing. The three artists passed through customs and we made our greetings as they came out into arrivals. Laurens Tan, Simeon Nelson and Richard Goodwin. The fourth of the group, sculptor Ari Purhonen, contributed works to the installation, but wasn't attending in person.

We caught the train to Tokyo—the sleek, comfortable Narita Express. None of the three had been here before. They scrutinized the passing landscape as we chatted and I briefed them on some planning details. The flat rural countryside flew by, rice paddies and established old farmhouses with their traditional lines and elegant high roofs, before the urban landscape of suburban Tokyo started to assert itself. Increasingly disordered laneways, crazy webs of power lines, jumble of buildings.

"Look over there, they've had some designer graffiti put in!" Simeon said, pointing. The youngest, he was obviously enthused, despite the flight and early morning. Nice observation of his, I thought. Just one single, lonely piece of graffiti to be seen anywhere around, though you'd expect spray paint to thrive here in this busy metropolitan rail corridor. The lurid 3D kanji had morphed into an ironical icon of conservatism—intended to express an anarchic sentiment perhaps, but . . . conventionally, politely, through what it *said*, not what it *was*. No assault on civil order; not viral as it can become in the West, where graffiti "pieces" and "tags" spread faster than the authorities are able to erase them. Captured, isolated, framed, this one stood out as mere tokenism—*Look, we have youthful rebelliousness here too!* As though some nice young person with fashionably spiked hair, patchy designer jeans and matching chain for a belt, had spray-painted the message from a sense of social responsibility.

"When you ride down the street in a bus here," I said, "you feel comfortable that the people on the sidewalk are exactly where they are supposed to be, doing exactly what they are supposed to be doing. You see a woman pushing a pram, some guy standing on a street corner, two kids riding bikes down the footpath: they are exactly where they should be. There are untold people just like them, doing the same authorized thing. You know they're not up to no good. It's hard to explain. You see a few teenagers in a group passing something to each other, it's not a drug transaction: they're probably swapping *purikura*—tiny decorated photo-stamps of each other—"

"Puri . . . purikuru?" said Simeon.

"From *purinto kurabu*, Japlish for 'print club'—their circle of friends with whom they take photos together in purikura booths. A high school fad . . ."

TOKYO STATION a vast multilevel maze. Helps to know where you are going. Takes a while to develop a knack for following the color-coded overhead signs that guide your way among the human rapids surging in every direction—diverging and converging here and there, backing up at escalators and gateways to teeming subways and above-ground lines. Three thousand trains, carrying three hundred and eighty thousand passengers, pass through the station in an average day. Nothing compared to the peak hour crush at Shinjuku Station, which serves over three million per day: the entire Tokyo subway system transports a mere eight million. You anticipate the paths of other people in terms of collective flows. As two currents merge or cross through each other, the human units interact minutely—exchange glances, instantaneously project co-ordinates of the position a moving body will occupy in the next second. You keep moving. If you stop still to take your bearings, you'll disrupt the flow. If you want to leave the current you are in, you flow with it while making your way to the edge, the way you would escape a riptide at the beach. Slip out and take refuge in a static spot: behind one of the big round columns supporting the ceiling; by a souvenir stand, the wall of an entrance-way or a stair-rail. Much as you might escape from the current in a stream by sheltering behind a boulder or fallen tree.

I'd earmarked a likely spot for storing the artists' luggage while we spent the day in Tokyo. Handy to the departure platform for the Tokaido Shinkansen, a couple of flights of stairs down and around a corner, was an area set aside from the main thoroughfare, with a restaurant, toilets, and rows of coin lockers. We stowed the luggage in some lockers and set off on the itinerary I had planned to give them a glimpse of the city.

Nothing gives the visitor such an acute sense of place as Tokyo Tower. I took us there via the Mita subway line, and we alighted at Onarimon Station and walked the short distance to Zojoji, a Buddhist temple in the Shiba area of Minatoku, close to the tower. Zojoji is a classic example of the function a Buddhist temple or Shinto shrine can play in carving out a truly peaceful space in the midst of city surroundings. We climbed the stairs to the entrance of the Great Hall of the temple. Inside, priests were conducting a ceremony before the ornate altar, their chanting punctuated by the thin, pure tone of a hand-held bell.

In a garden in front of the hall stood rows of humble stone statuettes, adorned with little red knitted caps, scarves and bibs, and decorated with multicolored plastic garlands and pinwheels that spun furiously when the breeze picked up.

"Statues of the bodhisattva Jizo," I said, "the guardian deity of children and travelers. Mothers who have lost their newborn or unborn babies come here to make these offerings to him. A bodhisattva is an entity who chooses not to become a buddha until they have helped all other living beings attain buddhahood."

I led us to a Shinto shrine near the Jizo garden and demonstrated the ritual for prayer: struck the hanging gong, tossed a coin into the donation box, put my palms together, bowed my head and closed my eyes. I could hear the fading knell of the gong, the spinning of the toy windmills amidst the breeze and city buzz.

As we left through a side gate onto the footpath of a shady street, Richard stopped and turned back around to the temple. The oldest among us by a few years, a soft spoken, thoughtful man. He ran the fingers of his right hand through his curly brown hair, while making a sweeping gesture with his left forearm.

"Remarkable," he said, "how the temple's environment extends out into the street. A wall you can step over—not really an exclusive boundary between inside and outside. These trees out by the street are cared for just as much as those in the temple grounds—no absolute line of demarcation between there and the street." He shook his head and looked at me. "I think it's quite different, the way public space is organized here, throughout the city. I've noticed it everywhere."

Five minutes' walk from Zojoji, Tokyo Tower rears up in its brassy red and white ostentatiousness.

"Built to be the tallest self-supporting tower in the world," I said, as we craned our necks to look up at the tip.

"Yes, I understand they made it three millimeters taller than the Eiffel Tower," Laurens joked. He was not far wrong: the difference is about ten meters.

"It does lack something of the romance of the Eiffel Tower, though," Laurens said.

"I guess so, but it is what it is. It sure gives you a good look at Tokyo," I said.

We ascended to the high observatory. Far beneath, Tokyo raced in all directions to the circle of the horizon.

Close on one side, the skyscrapers of Shinjuku reached up. To the other side, far away, we could barely discern Mount Fuji through its veil.

Approaching noon we happened across a restaurant on the way to the subway station. We piled in and the shop master brought us cool oshibori, moist towels. I used mine to wipe my hands and face, and the artists followed suit.

"Have you tried sashimi before?"

"Yeah, sure," said Simeon, and the others nodded.

"Really? I never had it before coming to Japan."

"Heaps of Japanese restaurants in Sydney now," Simeon said.

Shop master served us dishes of tuna garnished with green and purple seaweed, some *miso* soup and boiled rice with a pickle.

I separated my chopsticks.

"Just pull these apart like this and rub them a bit to get rid of any wood fibers—" The shop master interjected in Japanese: you did not have to do that with good quality hashi like these. He picked a set up up and stroked its length with his finger to demonstrate its smoothness. It was clear they were reasonably good quality *waribashi* ("splittable chopsticks"): smoothly rounded and joined with a bridge at the top.

"You've insulted his chopsticks?" Richard laughed.

"Oversensitive." Actually it is quite a rude thing to do in a restaurant of a certain standard, understandably. My bad.

Simeon watched me prepare some wasabi, rubbing

the light green root against a white crockery grater and dissolving it in soy sauce.

"So you grate your own wasabi here." He pronounced the word wasabi strangely, with a long 'a' vowel in the second syllable.

"In this shop you do, anyway. More often than not it comes from a tube—wasabi." I couldn't help correcting the pronunciation.

"In Australia everyone says it like 'woss-*ar*-bi.'"

"Japanese gives pretty much an equal emphasis to each syllable: wa-sa-bi." I noticed the waiter continuing to eye us with interest. "*Kore wa nan to iu mono desu ka?*" I asked—what is this called?

"*Wasabi desu ne*"—Wasabi, isn't it?

I HAD planned two more stops for the day: Sensoji Temple at Asakusa and the electronics district of Akihabara. Riding the immaculate subway cars and treading the broad footpaths alongside affluent Tokyoites, first-time visitors are sometimes forced to reevaluate some inherited Eurocentric biases. My new friends were well-traveled, progressive thinkers, but mingling with the Japanese populace can have a humbling effect. Japan does not present Westerners with evidence to support ingrained, if unwitting, ethnocentric illusions.

At Asakusa in the traditional *shitamachi* ("downtown") district, we joined the throng visiting Sensoji, the oldest temple in Tokyo. We passed en masse through the entrance to the grounds, beneath the famous giant red lantern suspended from it, bearing the kanji characters for Kaminarimon—Thunder Gate—and between two protective deities, the gods of wind and thunder, who stared through us angrily into infinity. Tourists of all ages, shapes and sizes, including a notable percentage of foreigners, packed the scores of souvenir stalls lining Nakamise Dori, an avenue running 250 meters or so straight up to the main hall. Progress fell to a snail's pace. The sweet aroma of incense hung thick in the air.

Laurens took out his video camera.

"This is good. I want to collect images for a video project about souvenirs."

"Here's the perfect place then," I said. "The most popular tourist spot in Tokyo. And of course, the Japanese love souvenirs. At work, whenever anyone goes on a trip, they'll bring back something for their co-workers from wherever they've been — usually a food or other product of that area; so many of these stalls have cakes and snacks made here in Asakusa. But as you can see, a lot of souvenirs are intended for foreign tourists."

The stalls were bursting with their wares, the gamut of the Japanese souvenir: t-shirts and yukata emblazoned with Japanese emblems and characters; kimono, happi coats and *geta* (traditional wooden sandals); *sensu* (folding fans); statuettes of the Goddess of Mercy, Kannon, to whom the temple is dedicated; replica ninja starknives and *katana*; toy cartoon characters, daruma dolls, folding fans, lanterns and geisha wigs; traditional cakes and rice crackers; and all kinds of trinkets and gewgaws.

Laurens veered off through the crowd, his eye to the viewfinder. He crouched over the display counters and moved along them from a few inches away for the closest possible view. Some of the tourists in the vicinity noticed him coming and obligingly got out of his way. A Japanese teenager giggled, while jostling his friend to have a gawk at the eccentric tourist. Laurens's physical attitude and concentrated fixation on the stalls differed markedly from the other tourists' with video cameras, who were taking occasional shots of the crowd and their friends and panning the scene. Supreme single-mindedness—someone who knew how to focus on his work, how to abstract from the situation what he wanted from it. Admirable aplomb.

We straggled back through the late afternoon throng of Tokyo Station. Still sounding in my ears, the din of Akihabara—the bowels of the Tokyo electronic market, which ring like the innards of a giant pachinko machine.

Richard dragged himself forward like Scott of the Antarctic—backpack on his back, awkward package under one arm, glazed stare into nowhere. We were a strange looking bunch of foreigners with our luggage and brown paper packages. The artists had shipped most of their artworks and component parts ahead, but brought a few necessary articles with them on the flight, so we were sharing the load.

Passing by one of many faux marble columns supporting the high station roof, I turned my head and found myself at the focal point of a searing stare. Mori, the vice-principal at Central Japan Business College. Glaring straight at me, standing rigid like a ghost amongst the swirling throng of commuters, who floated to and fro between us like shadow puppets. I returned his glowering look for a few seconds and then dismissed it. Interesting, I thought. His insidiously burning, piercing stare was strangely potent—bordering on the psychotic. Whew. Well, that's behind me, I thought to myself. Thank you, thank you, O ghost of Nobunaga!

"Not far to go," I said, unloading my packages beside

another column a few yards on, stretched my back and looked back at the other three, who were doing the same. We rested for ten minutes there, between an obento stall and a glossy advertising billboard depicting some penguins. I glanced back over to where Mori had stood, but he was gone.

Our perfectly air-conditioned Shinkansen rolled out of Tokyo on its elevated track, overlooking the rooftops in the low-rise districts, giving the impression we were gliding aloft between the taller buildings and neon signs. After ten minutes, the rear door of our carriage slid open and a young, uniformed woman entered, pushing a re-freshment cart. She bowed and made a greeting before moving down the aisle. I treated us to a whisky and we leaned back to imbibe it as the night deepened outside.

An hour and a quarter later a shudder and drop in acceleration told me it was time to get ready to alight, and I informed my companions. We stood up and gath-ered their bags and packages. I started to move toward the doors.

"Where are my templates?" Laurens asked, with a hint of desperation. No one knew. "A brown cardboard parcel about so big by so," he said, tracing out the shape of the item in space. He examined each of his col-leagues, going over their luggage item by item, went down on his knees and patted around and underneath our seats.

Richard said tentatively, "Was it flat and fairly thin and taped up with orangey colored tape?"

"It was you! I remember . . . I gave it to you when we got the stuff from the lockers. Where is it?"

Richard wracked his brains.

"I don't think I brought it onto the train."

Laurens was fast losing composure.

"What did you do with it? My installation is pointless without those templates!"

"We've got to get off," I said. The Shinkansen emitted a low hum as it pulled up at the platform.

"Pointless . . ."

"Let's not worry about it now," I said, summoning my most reassuring voice and giving Laurens a pat on the shoulder. I was in problem-solving mode: the immediate issue was to calm him down. So much work, preparation and distance traveled—unraveling in a single negligent moment. It was like a nightmare.

Terminal Hotel was ten minutes' walk, during which time we established that Richard, in his exhausted state, must have left the package behind when we had our breather by the obento stall at Tokyo station.

We booked into a room and I telephoned the Tokyo stationmaster and explained our situation: about our international art project supported by the Australian Embassy and how we left behind a critical component of the installation at his railway station. There should be a package at the base of a support column standing between an obento stall and a glossy advertising billboard depicting a row of penguins before a blue sky.

Mad gaijin. He assured me he would do his best. I put down the receiver.

"Not sure it's fixed," I said. "I'd better call Shirata-san, one of the other organizers, and tell him what's happened . . ."

He phoned me back the next afternoon.

"Everything is okay," he said. "We are lucky. I called the Tokyo Police Department and explained the problem. A female officer from a police box near Tokyo

Station walked around the station and finally found the package in the early hours of the morning. They will dispatch it by express courier, so it will arrive tomorrow."

"Was it where I said, near the obento stand and billboard with the penguins?"

"No, not in such a place. Maybe someone moved it."

SO THINGS worked out, thanks to the humble diligence of that police officer, her lonesome footfalls echoing in the pedestrian passages of Tokyo Station into the early morning. We fulfilled our plans, holding exhibitions and seminars on Australian public art in Shizuoka, Tokyo and Kyoto. The media covered our event: on television, newspapers and a documentary video series of contemporary art, *Kyoto Art Today*. In Australia, the project was covered by the magazine *Architecture Australia*, in which the reviewer Michael Hedges wrote: "The title *Distance* relates to the desired overlapping of architecture, sculpture and urban planning as explored by all four of these sculptors. Their understanding of the special needs and purposes of public sculpture gave this exhibition sensitivity, relevance and empathetic authority."

Some hiccups along the way though. A few of the sculptures were large metal objects that the artists had to assemble at each site, so they arrived from Australia as bizarre, industrial looking bits and pieces. Richard's main piece *Parasite/Follicle III* resembled an organic ultra-light helicopter on legs, and Purhonen's "Hollow Men" were polished, elongated metal prisms, six feet tall, with oblique eye-slits the spectator could peer through; Laurens's installation included crematorium hoppers, computer drawings of sewage treatment water-testing bottles and plastic microfiche cards containing images of sewage maps.

A customs officer telephoned to notify us that there was a problem with these objects and materials and they were not going to allow them in, so we had to go to Tokyo to sort things out.

"They say it is not art!" Shirata said, throwing up his arms.

"Everyone's a critic," I replied. I wasn't sure he appreciated the humor, but eventually we succeeded in getting everything through.

On the return trip from the Kyoto opening, two of the artists got off the Shinkansen with the aim of running along the platform to the next carriage. The doors closed and the train left them behind, so they had to wait there stranded for an hour.

But it was fun to work with the artists and see Japan through their eyes. Sometimes they got it quite wrong. We were walking down Sleaze Street in Shizuoka after a bowl of ramen, on our way to spend an evening at Kentos nightclub, where a Japanese Elvis and Andrews Sisters performed their "Oldies but Goodies." Hair-oiled young men in cheap, flashy suits stood on corners handing out brochures advertising girlie shows. We wove our way through the sidewalks full of tipsy evening revelers in their glad rags.

"Oh, you are Italiano yes?"

Curly haired Richard laughed.

"I've been getting that a bit. It's this white t-shirt."

I laughed and nodded: "I guess they think it's a singlet."

The artists did a double-take at some of the young

women, whom they mistakenly thought to be "hookers": made-up, laughing, chattering girls in their twenties, wearing thigh length leather boots, fur stoles, and provocative mini-skirts and hot-pants, draping themselves over youthful and not so youthful men.

"No," I assured them. "Not a hooker in sight. It's all quite innocent."

Satisfying, to make possible these artists' first glimpses of Japan and to enable a cross-cultural collaboration with Japanese artists, which was a key aspect of the exhibition. Laurens was a consummate networker, and thanks to him, a year later the University of California, Berkeley and Davis invited me to attend their international conference on Pacific cultures and speak on the "figure of the Outsider in Japanese culture."

19

Music City Blues

The government restructured national universities and dismantled the liberal arts system. We at Shizuoka University disbanded Liberal Arts and founded a new faculty, which had the aim of equipping students for the burgeoning information revolution. Half the Liberal Arts members joined faculties that hosted the disciplines they studied: physicists moved to the Science Faculty, educationalists to the Education Faculty and so on. The other half, those who were deemed to have the background to adopt social information studies — including me — joined with computer engineers based at the university's second campus, at a city called Hamamatsu, at the western edge of Shizuoka Prefecture, half an hour by Shinkansen toward Nagoya. Our Hamamatsu faculty would be known as the *Johogakubu* or Faculty of Information, the first faculty of informatics established in a national Japanese university.

Bancroft didn't approve of all this upheaval, so he resigned and left for Paris to live the good life and pursue further studies. Munakata retired from Shizuoka University as an emeritus professor to concentrate on his passion for noh Shakespeare.

I was assigned to translate the name of the faculty into a suitable English one and settled on the Faculty of Information, designating its two departments as Information Arts and Information Science; the computer scientists, however, preferred Department of Computer Science for the latter. Initially I elected to move into the Humanities Faculty, but Dean Soga, the driving force behind the new faculty, had other plans. He assured me that I would be provided with better resources and more funding for research there, and my academic interests in media, culture and the Internet would be useful. I complied with his wishes and submitted some subject descriptions to the national Ministry for Education, Science, Sports and Culture (Mombusho) as a component of the university's submission. They ratified the subjects I designed, "Culture of Tourism" and "the Human Body and Culture," and I commenced work on them within a Culture and Communication division of the Information Arts Department.

I taught media, film and cultural studies—fields that had connections, if sometimes tenuous connections, with my research into modern literature and theory. English language subjects now came under the heading of Communication Skills, and to help me teach the subject, I adapted a brand new learning laboratory, equipped with the latest in information technology and multimedia capabilities. The laboratories enabled a "blended learning" approach, combining computer based and face-to-face teaching techniques of pair- and group-work, role-play, simulation gaming and debate. I contacted English language teachers in Swedish and German universities, who collaborated with me on cross-cultural, web-based projects; these were innovative at the time and gave many of my students the first communication they had ever had with foreigners their own age.

Because we started the faculty from scratch, we founding academics needed to design an expanding curriculum that took the initial cohort of students up year by year into higher, yet untried courses of study. The sempai-kohai system worked to advantage in addressing this challenge, for it provided cohesion and student leadership. The faculty heads knew the value of this system and took measures to engage and reinforce it from the outset. We formed committees and held countless meetings to try to formulate an appealing "identity" for our faculty, which would appear in public relations brochures for distribution to high schools throughout the country. In the inaugural year, we held an orientation weekend at a fitness camp at Gotemba, a town located on the flank of Mount Fuji, a lengthy bus journey from Shizuoka campus. New students took part in team building exercises such as baseball and orienteering, along with lectures and discussion groups aimed at forming beneficial relationships of the sempai-kohai sort.

The weekend promoted too much upbeat togetherness for me, though I generally sought to contribute to faculty esprit de corps. The process of mustering chatty, eager-eyed freshmen and staff at seven o'clock on the morning of departure was out of keeping with the emotional disengagement instinctive to me at that time of day. Our committees had planned every detail of the outing over the prior weeks, and now in its realization, everyone melded in harmoniously. As they took their seats in the tour buses, most of my colleagues effortlessly adopted sociable attitudes and joked familiarly with the students despite the hour. I found the paternalistic undertone hard to take, however, and would have preferred to leave our charges to their own devices, to allow them to develop their independence and me to snooze in peace. But this was the Japanese way, and the weekend ran like a well-oiled machine, bespeaking years rather than weeks of programming. After all the proceedings, I reflected again on the mechanisms of socialization, while bivouacked in a Gotemba dormitory among my male colleagues after the staff beer party, curled up in our futons on the tatami floor like a brood of gumnut babies, some snoring grittily in multiple keys the whole night long.

For two years after the restructure, we ex-liberal arts members traveled a daily half-hour trip to and from Hamamatsu by Shinkansen and an extra twenty minutes by bus on both ends of that. When the fortnightly faculty meeting came around, the day was long and tedious. Committee meetings occupied the morning; the meeting started at one o'clock in the afternoon and could finish as late as eight or so at night. It soon became clear that the halcyon age was over for us, and we had entered the workaday academic world of the late twentieth century.

Hamamatsu is comparable in size to Shizuoka City, both in the region of half to three-quarters of a million.

However, the economic base of Shizuoka is quaintly rural, that of Hamamatsu definitely industrial, with an emphasis on musical instruments, cars and motorcycles; Kawai, Suzuki, Yamaha and Roland all have head-quarters there. The city fathers promote Hamamatsu as "Music City" because of the large number of these music-related companies. Indeed, the city is the center of the musical hardware and technology industry in Japan, and commands a one-hundred per cent monop-oly on the manufacture of pianos in the country. Certain cultural benefits attach to this status: since 1991, the city has hosted a triennial international piano competi-tion and boasts concert and theater facilities of the highest standard for all genres of music and drama. A forty-five story skyscraper named Act City is the city's ar-chitectural centerpiece, if a building of doubtful appeal, a colossal phallic protuberance in the middle of an otherwise level city skyline. It houses four auditoriums, including a four-level hall seating over two thousand, used for opera, ballet, drama, and traditional theater, and a thousand-seat concert hall, along with shopping malls, restaurants and a five-star hotel.

In contrast with the more laid-back attitude in Shizuoka, the people of Hamamatsu are supposedly more *genki*—energetic or spirited. They like to think of a phrase in their local dialect as accurately character-izing them: *"Yaramaika!"* ("Let's go for it!") In their favorite annual festival, teams from a hundred and sixty-four town blocks go to the sand dunes to compete with huge fighting kites, each team trying to cut the cord of their rivals' kites. The kites are up to four or five meters square and can fly out over the sea for kilometers on a thick line. Teams of ten people anchor and maneuver the kites, and the contest may become even more violent on the ground than in the air.

The city lacks the natural beauty of Shizuoka City, and the university campus is small and unattractive, a plain rectangle on flat ground, where the army used to keep its tanks during the Second World War (thus the earth there, I heard, is especially hard and compacted). Like Shizuoka, Hamamatsu was the target of bombing attacks, which destroyed sixty per cent of the city; one incendiary attack in June 1945 killed eighteen hundred people. Wartime Hamamatsu accommodated armament factories and an airfield that served as a base for the imperial army air force and its flight school. From the point of view of American bomber crews on their way from Saipan to Nagoya or Tokyo, these installations made the city an attractive secondary target.

The airfield is now the Air Training headquarters of the Japan Air Self-Defense Force (JASDF). There are squadrons for early warning and flight training, so on most days one sees radar-carrying Boeing E-767 AWACS (Airborne Warning and Control System) planes taking off and landing and Kawasaki T-4 training jets circling like mosquitoes.

A BRONZE statue of Professor Kenjiro Takayanagi (1899–1990) stands at the front gate of Hamamatsu campus. A pioneering scientist in the development of television, Takayanagi conducted his groundbreaking research at this very place from 1924, when it began life as Hamamatsu Industrial High School. At Hamamatsu in 1926, he engineered the first transmission of a televised image in Japan using the world's first all-electric television set—that is, one with no essential mechanical parts—and followed up this development in 1933 with his own iconoscope, the critical component of a television camera. In 1937, two years before domestic sets appeared, his television system was the world's most advanced. Other inventors such as the Scotsman John Logie Baird and Russian-American Vladimir Zworykin had demonstrated crucial elements of television technology earlier than he did. No exaggeration though to refer to Takayanagi as "the father of Japanese television," in acknowledgment of both his inventions and his subsequent work with NHK, where he worked to foster television broadcasting in Japan.

Takayanagi was, understandably, the hero of the electrical and computer engineers. They were far more industrious than us liberal arts refugees with whom they now had to cohabit. They researched and published insatiably, regularly producing research papers with five or six authors, and to be expected, they considered us something of a joke. Their projects did indeed attract quite good funding from industry, in contrast with our less practical endeavors in topics like phenomenology, Hitler, the Celts, proverbs, transformational grammar, Japanese verb forms, Malory, Thoreau, Beckett, et cetera—topics with none too compelling connections with social informatics. But personally I felt that some of our computer scientists had an inflated idea of their accomplishments if they viewed themselves as treading in Takayanagi's footsteps. The historic engineering of television was some distance from the designing of a remote control with some added functions of questionable utility.

One arrogant remote control developer was in his

thirties, fresh faced and full of self-confidence, often making long, articulate speeches in faculty meetings—his star was much in the ascendant. The first contact I had with him was when someone advised me to consult him about some student administrative issue or other I needed to solve, since he was the relevant committee head. I sent him an email and received the straightforward reply, "Please do it yourself." I said to myself, Well, there's one person I don't have to worry about being nice to.

Then, what do you know? in a faculty meeting one evening, while someone was standing giving a report, he made a show of coming over to me, squatting down beside my chair and shoving a group research paper in front of me on the tabletop to proofread. I knew that to comply meekly would be to seal my fate as a proofreading lackey, so I ignored him and attended studiously to the professor delivering the report. I didn't enjoy being rude, but experience had shown me that the best way to handle pushy individuals was to be firm and show them you were an animal that might bite—otherwise they would quietly steamroll you.

After a pregnant pause, my imperious young colleague felt compelled to speak to me again, if rather less imperiously.

"Are you going to check our paper?"

"Not during the meeting. If you visit my office at an appropriate time, I will help you."

He brought his article to my office and I did help him, but he hated me ever after. Yet I did not feel that my treatment of him was gratuitously mean. Even apart from the rod for my own back I would make by performing publicly as an English proofreading minion, it would amount to acknowledging that it was beyond my ability to comprehend and contribute to the meetings. I fully recognized how important the faculty meetings were as a font of knowledge and hence power. To fail to understand the intricacies of the goings-on around me would be to surrender my autonomy to those from whom I would need continually to seek assistance. Thankfully, this was about the time Japanese electronics companies developed PDAs ("personal digital assistants" or hand-held computers) with the capability of recognizing kanji characters inputted by hand using a stylus. I spent hours on end in meetings consulting my pocket PC and translating sheaf after sheaf of documents into English, to keep in touch with administrative matters.

Some found the new, busier and more intense university structure an emotional strain. One professor needed to take time off to cope with a nervous ailment, and another stopped giving classes and going to meetings. The students were not exempt from the stresses and strains of university life either, despite our efforts to guide and even cosset them. Three students had committed suicide in the first few years—one jumped from a window along my corridor on the fourth floor. Following each instance, the student's *shido kyokan* (guidance instructor) would stand up in the regular faculty meeting and report dejectedly, apologizing for not having had the foresight to prevent the incident.

UNFORTUNATELY, given the micro-political opportunities that arose, some of my comrades in Information Arts became infected with a competitive urge to advance themselves, causing them to lose charm. Alas, all too soon they forgot the languorous aspirations to a life of culture that had underpinned our previous activities.

"We may have trouble getting Mombusho, the Education Ministry, to ratify our new Graduate School of Informatics," my colleague Miki-san informed me. "It seems there won't be enough of us who are qualified to be full postgraduate research supervisors. Of course, that was the reason we had to send our documents off to Mombusho some weeks ago."

"Yes, of course."

I wasn't much bothered any more to have things I already knew explained repeatedly. Most colleagues implicitly assumed I was unable to comprehend political and administrative minutiae. It may have taken me twice as long as my colleagues to prepare my submission to Mombusho, but I approached tasks like this as a form of exercise in language study and invariably got there in the end.

I believed I had a fair idea of the sort of academic accomplishments Mombusho would be looking for as they restructured the university on a more up to date, Western model. Weeks before, Professor Hashimoto's offer to assist me with my submission had strengthened my determination to do it myself. He was now my section head.

"I have some publications I think may be useful," I said when he raised the subject, "such as these journal articles that involve Michel Foucault and postmodernism—"

"Oh . . . Michel Foucault. He is a . . . philosopher, isn't he?"

"Yes, that's right. He's thoroughly relevant to topics such as the structure of contemporary society and themes like information, surveillance and social power."

"Hmm . . . Mombusho don't want us to teach philosophy to postgraduates, only information." He sucked his teeth audibly and shook his head, both actions combining in an expression of grave doubt.

"What?!" I shrieked silently—an inner shriek of disbelief. I would find it intolerable to capitulate to such an opinion. But I was mindful of the implications of Japan's being what cross-cultural theorists call a high power-distance culture, in which seniority carries a lot of weight in organizations because of the perceived distance between rungs on the ladder. You don't get far by standing up and contradicting your superiors.

I went on testing the water.

"Well, I have given some conference papers on the use of film and information technology in teaching language and culture—"

"Mmm . . . conference presentations do not count in Mombusho's assessment."

"But these are international conferences—they must be worth something?"

As fine and honorable a person as he was, I wondered whether a subliminal agenda might not be at work, one inclined to reinforce our relative standings in the hierarchy. "How would *you* know what counts in their assessment?" I wondered. I was convinced that my doctorate, research, conference papers and edited book would carry weight, and if he failed to share that view—perhaps because of not entirely appreciating the interdisciplinary possibilities that were opening up—then it would not be in my interest to take advantage of his offer.

"Well, thanks," I said, "that would be good. I'll try to

put it together and bring it to you to check for me, if you wouldn't mind." Ever scrupulously prompt with my work earlier on in my career, I had by now developed the guile to complete my submission at the very last minute, allowing no possibility for any checking by any third party. Instead, I sent it directly to the administrator responsible, an amiable man named Goda-san.

When the results came back Goda-san summoned me and said cheerfully that Mombusho had ratified me as a *marugo*: virtually unknown outside universities, the term refers to an elite qualification as a postgraduate research supervisor. He showed me my documentation to explain the term, pointing to a symbol consisting of a kanji character, *go*, with a circle printed around it. *Go*, he said, meant that the recipient met the requirements of teaching in the graduate school. Putting the circle (*maru*) around it indicated the further qualification needed to supervise higher degree research.

A week later Miki-san and I were in her office discussing one thing or another and, in passing, she mentioned the graduate school submission.

"I don't know what we will do in the Culture and Communication group, because the government regulations state that we need two marugo to assess the other members each year for promotion."

"I believe it turns out I'm one," I said.

She stifled a titter.

"Oh, I think not." She opened a desk drawer, brought out her own letter of certification and repeated what Goda-san had told me about the ranking system. "So, this symbol"—she pointed to the character *go* on her document—"merely means you are able to teach postgraduates, but not supervise research. It needs a circle around it for you to be a marugo. You see how even my letter has no circle?" She smiled condescendingly, as she might to a child with a learning difficulty.

"Oh, I see. I'd better go and get my letter so that you can double-check it for me."

When I returned with my notification she scanned it and stiffened for a second, her face blanching visibly.

"Is that the character there, with the circle around it?" I asked innocently, pointing at it.

"That does . . . *seem* to be it," she half-muttered, half-hissed, tight-lipped.

RELOCATING to Hamamatsu severely affected my activities of tennis and *gomi* (garbage) disposal. We were no longer free to play tennis except during lunch or outside business hours. Fewer keen players worked at Hamamatsu; a group of eight or so, we played socially most days and competed as a team in city-wide tournaments. Once or twice a year we recruited extra players for a Sunday tournament against players from Shizuoka campus, carrying on the festivities that attended our former tennis events.

At Shizuoka campus, the disposal of gomi had been straightforward: put it in a big plastic bag and, any time I wished, drop that in a large, heavy wire-grille container that stood near my building. Now, however, each faculty on the campus was assigned a weekly lunch hour for staff members to get rid of their gomi. The plastic bags had to be transparent and you had to write your name and office number on them using an indelible ink marker so they were traceable back to you. Then you carried them over to a padlocked container, where special armband-wearing gomi officers inspected the contents. (Another embarrassing armband-wearing task was traffic duty, when a small group from the traffic committee patrolled the campus one day annually, cautioning students who had parked their vehicles or bicycles in prohibited areas.)

If something was in a bag that shouldn't be, such as a drink can, or cardboard sheets in wider than two-inch strips, then theoretically you needed to rectify the fault before the gomi officers could accept your bags. Though sifting through gomi was a task memorable for its tediousness, sometimes I managed to forget my correct day or was playing tennis. I missed the gomi disposal for that week and perhaps the next week or two, until the garbage bags started to mount up in my office alarmingly.

The duty of gomi officer transferred to different faculties on a rotating basis so that everyone had a turn. Academics treated the duty as an unfunny joke and were not overly particular about the contents of the bags—a "you scratch my back" attitude prevailed. Once, though, I encountered a mid-level administrator in charge of campus gomi who had me undo my garbage bag, take out the bits of plastic secreted therein and place them in their correct container while he supervised. Consequently, I started disregarding the rules when it suited me and conducting a casual campaign of civil disobedience, or what I referred to privately as "gomi terrorism," riding on my bicycle down to the containers any old day after work under cover of darkness, carrying my garbage bags. Although the container for wastepaper was locked, there was also an open iron container for old computers and furniture and suchlike, so I would toss my bags in there and ride off into the darkness whistling.

Many foreigners found it a problematical task to get rid of their domestic gomi properly. Firstly, they were not used to having to take it to a special pickup point on a particular day, depending on the type of gomi: nonburnable gomi on two designated days per month; burnable gomi twice a week; recyclable gomi two designated days per month; recyclable plastic containers once a month. Secondly, they weren't crazy about the fastidious way the Japanese classified their gomi for disposal. This was an art form almost as complicated as the tea ceremony, and by the time most foreigners had understood the nuances, they were so frustrated and found the process so annoying they were apt to resort to their own particular form of "gomi terrorism," however mild:

PET (polyethylene terephthalate) bottles: remove the cap and label and dispose of separately; shake out left-over contents; squash bottle with foot. Paper diapers: remove dirty matter. Sticks: cut to sixty centimeter lengths and tie up in bundles of maximum diameter five centimeters. Bathmats: cut into pieces less than sixty centimeters. Rubber hose: sixty centimeter lengths. Tubes of mayonnaise, toothpaste, ketchup: empty of contents. Dialysis bags, tubes: consult personal physician. Bamboo skewers: snap ends. Glass bottles: remove caps and dispose of appropriately, depending on whether metal or plastic; wash out bottles and jars. Place bottles and cans in designated, color-coded receptacles: clear glass (white), brown glass (brown), miscellaneous (gray), PET bottles (yellow), cans (blue).

If there are not enough receptacles, please consult the Neighborhood Association.

Yeah, sure.

Thirdly, short-term foreigners had a habit of rummaging through the bulky items the Japanese put out for recycling—including perfectly good furniture, stereos and televisions—and scavenging serviceable pieces to furnish their apartments. This custom did little to improve the popular stereotype of the gaijin as intrinsically undesirable, a conception that in my experience was not altogether misplaced.

20

Gaijin House

Time came to move house to Hamamatsu, so I contacted a real estate agency. A female agent drove Isabella and me around to look at some rental properties. The first was near a highway, with no front fence and absolutely zero privacy once you walked out the door; the second was a wreck and miles from campus. The third place was in Fumioka, a comfortable walk away. It was a 3SLDK (three bedrooms with living-dining-kitchen space and storeroom); a detached, single-story residence, with brown metal outer walls, a ceramic-tiled roof and a tall brick wall that enclosed the roughly triangular block on two sides.

The agent opened the front door and beckoned us in; we left our shoes in the *genkan* and stepped up into a parquet hallway. The house was old but clean and roomy. Dim and stuffy, but with the warm aroma of fresh tatami. The owners had sealed it up with heavy hurricane doors and shutters. When the agent slid open the hurricane doors at the back, light flooded in through sliding glass doors and *shoji* (paper screens) into the large, timber-floored, Western-style living room. Traditional *fusuma* (sliding screens) divided this from a newly matted tatami room, and another fusuma divided that space from the kitchen. Opening all the doors created a spacious open-plan area. A second tatami room adjoined the kitchen, and a bathroom-toilet and a storeroom connected to the hallway.

The woman opened the rear glass doors and air streamed in. We went out to the garden, which was expansive by Japanese standards, if in want of maintenance. *Niwaki* ("garden trees")—pruned into bulging, globular shapes in a traditional style supposed to make them look more "natural"—lined the area, and there were one or two big trees too, including a fig with branches that stretched out over the house. At the border of the property away from the street, trees and bushes merged into thick foliage that covered the neighboring block like a jungle. Amidst the dense vegetation was a dilapidated dwelling, an overgrown corrugated iron shack that looked like it could fall over at any minute.

The sight astonished the woman, who had obviously never been here before, and she stood there mouth agape. Suddenly a small black cat leaped down from a branch onto the roof of the shack with a tinny bang, scrambled across the corrugated iron and disappeared over the far edge.

"*Sugoi wa!*" ("Amazing!") she murmured in an undertone, shaking her head incredulously.

Clearly the situation demanded a Japanese-style statement of the bleeding obvious, so I raised my eyebrows.

"*Neko desu ne,*" ("It's a cat") I observed. "Does anyone live in there?"

"*Zenzen wakaranai . . .*" ("I have absolutely no idea") the agent said, still shaking her head at the mind-boggling sight.

Back in the house, I asked about the rental, sure it would be too high, but it turned out to be the same as I was already paying for our somewhat cramped apartment. To live in a traditional house with an attractive and private walled garden was something I hadn't dared to dream.

"It's beautiful," I said to the agent. "We'll take it."

"I think we have that place next door and their black cat to thank for the price," I said to Isabella as the three of us set off back along the quaint winding lane. "Not too many Japanese will want to live next door to them."

"No, too *abunai* (dangerous)," Isabella joked—the word was sometimes used to describe innocuous taboos or departures from the expected norm.

"But perfect for us."

"It's ideal."

As we passed the neighboring block, the agent stopped to peer through the thicket at the little shack, still agog. The overgrown garden had no front fence or any cleared space except for a well-trodden path that led through the trees and thick bushes. The chaotic vegetation was incongruous with the neatly trimmed neighborhood, as though a fragment of some supernatural forest had magically descended on the spot. She mouthed a single silent "*Sugoi!*" ("Astonishing!")

NEWCOMERS GENERALLY knock on their neighbors' door, introduce themselves and present them with a modest offering—towels and tea-towels are popular. I first en-

countered the custom while living at Yamamura
Heights, during a more dissolute phase. The doorbell
shattered my slumber and I opened the iron door half-
asleep, bleary eyed, unshaven and wearing a pair of
undershorts that served me as pajamas. A casually
dressed middle-aged man and woman stood there holding a package. They went into a spiel that eluded me
in my hung-over condition. Misperceiving them to be
salespeople or missionaries, I cut them short.

"*Ie, iranai,*" ("Don't need any") I said and closed the
door with a hasty combination wave-smile-bow. "*Domo.*"
("Thanks.")

On my way back in to fall on my futon, it occurred
to me they may be new neighbors—as indeed they
proved to be. When I went back and opened the door,
the couple were still standing there, nonplussed. I apologized profusely and, to be polite, accepted their present
of a bath towel, hand towel and face washer set—exactly
what I needed, in fact—and disappeared behind my
iron door again. A poor attempt at cross-cultural communication on my part, and they didn't present me with
another chance to improve on it.

Soon after moving into our new home in Fumioka,
we became aware that the shack next door housed a
frail old widow. She always wore the same ancient, faded
kimono and was bent over with osteoporosis like many
of her contemporaries—testament to hard work in the
rice field and a diet poor in calcium. She could be
glimpsed wandering like a ghost in her unkempt grove.
Early each morning, wisps of smoke curled out from a
space between the wall and roof of her abode, as she
heated up her pot of tea on a fire fueled with twigs and
old newspapers. The risk posed by her cooking method

was not lost on her neighbors on the far side, who'd placed a red fire-bucket prominently atop the brick wall between their two properties. Well, she has to eat, I said to myself, and started to take a little notice around meal-times in case her fire got out of control and incinerated our house.

The woman was hard of hearing and kept her television on at high volume day and night for company. She had a heap of moldy cardboard boxes at the rear of her home to stop the wind whistling through. She was such a tremendously stoic figure that I decided to do the right thing this time in terms of the neighborly gift giving ritual. I bought an expensive box of *matcha manju* (fine green tea flavored, soft mochi rice cakes filled with sweet bean paste) at a department store and had it gift-wrapped. Next time I saw her in her unruly garden I pushed through the undergrowth and introduced myself, to a pleasant enough reception. When I proffered the box of rice cakes, however, she refused it.

"*Iranai*," ("Don't need it") she said flatly.

Thinking she was just being polite (and still unaware of the fatal risk of choking that eating the gooey mochi can hold for the elderly) I tried again. "*Tsumaranai mono desu ga . . .*" ("It's nothing much, but please accept this humble gift . . .")

"*Ie, ie—iranai*," she said forcefully, leaving no doubt that she meant it. I excused myself and left her to her business.

I was pleased she had vindicated my behavior in Shizuoka, and I enjoyed eating the treat by myself, Isabella having no taste for either mochi rice cakes or sweet bean paste.

The widow had lived there alone for many years,

having lost her husband in the war and never remarried. Our neighbors on the other side were a middle-aged working class couple who lived with their son and daughter-in-law and the husband's mother. Isabella referred to their place as "the compound," because it consisted of contiguous domiciles that housed the three family sub-units, erected within a wide gravel parking area. The man was as proud as Punch when a grandson was born into the family. When the Children's Day festival came around on May 5, he flew carp banners and streamers as is the custom, the carp being a symbol of success. On the night of the first Children's Day festival after his grandson's birth, a party of about thirty merry-makers paraded along our winding lane dressed in indigo happi coats with thick white insignia and head-bands, blowing on bugles. They made a left turn into our neighboring "compound" to honor the grandfather, who returned the compliment by treating them to re-freshments. Then they took up their bugles once again and jogged off down the lane, continuing on their mission of crisscrossing the neighborhood to frighten away evil spirits.

One day the man's wife and a woman from across the lane knocked on our door and introduced them-selves to Isabella, their mission being to inform her about the system of gomi collection, but they adopted such an overbearing manner they alienated her for good. A week later, when the two women were on duty at the disposal point, they forbade her from leaving our bag of gomi by making the dreaded X-sign, crossing their fore-arms at her: *"Damé!"* ("You can't do that!") She looked them in the eye and placed the bag on the heap without saying a word. In future, we did our best to decipher and comply with the rules for sorting and disposing of gomi but had nothing more to do with the women, nor they with us.

This element of officiousness abounded among the obasans (middle-aged women) at the helm of the neighborhood association, which managed the gomi collection. Police officers, on the other hand, were most affable. Soon after we moved in, a knock sounded at the door, which we opened to find the local constable there, his bicycle propped up behind him on its stand. He introduced himself politely and bowed briskly. Just making sure, he said, that everything was all right and we knew the police telephone number in case we ever needed it. He gave us a sticker to attach to our doorjamb to show he had called and that we were now under his jurisdiction.

"Be careful when you go downtown, there are a few bag snatchers getting around these days," he told Isabella, winning her with his caring attitude. Then he bowed farewell and was off on his bike.

Thoroughly characteristic. Once I was walking along in Shibuya, Tokyo, at midday, when a young man staggered past me and collapsed inebriated into a long row of bicycles lined up alongside a police box, knocking them all over like dominoes. He flailed about swearing for about a minute, until a policeman emerged, extricated him from the bicycles and had an amiable word with him, then sent him on his way tottering along the sidewalk and set the bicycles back upright.

Another time, Isabella and I were chatting over a nightcap in a cocktail bar after a meal of teppanyaki; we were the only customers at the time. Two policemen shuffled in, caps in hand, all smiles, bows and apologies.

"Excuse us!" an officer announced. "We are searching for members of the group Aum Shinrikyo." The religious cult that carried out the sarin gas attack on the Tokyo subway. Their headquarters was in Shizuoka Prefecture.

"Thank you very much," I said, bowing my head. "As you can see, there's no-one from Aum Shinrikyo here."

"No, we can see that," one officer said cordially, returning my bow. "Please take your time and enjoy yourselves. Goodnight."

"Goodnight. Look after yourselves!" we called after them.

From then on, we referred to them as the "politeness police," convinced they must be the nicest police force in the world.

ONE SUNNY mid-morning, Isabella, wearing her summer kimono, called me to the garden. I was sitting reading in my tatami room. The glass doors were open, and as I came out, I noticed her looking down at the ground and heard for the first time Smudge's distinctive *nyaa*, the call of the domestic cat, to whom the Japanese refer affectionately as Nyaa-chan.

She smiled at the tiny, cheeky being, who stared back up at her intensely, its coat covered in black and white patches, its head and, most conspicuously, its ears too large for its skinny body. It opened its jaws so wide to cry out that the interior pink mouth and gullet seemed about to engulf the head.

I was completely won over.

"What's this?" Vaguely suspecting complications.

"Hello puss," Isabella said. "You've been visiting us for a while now, haven't you, gorgeous?" She bent over to set the residue of a can of salmon on the cement path before the kitten, who scoffed it down without ceremony.

"You know we can't keep a cat here," I said. "We'll be kicked out. Don't feed it."

The kitten lapped at the tin, looked up, widened its jaws and eyes, and sounded a gentler *nyaa*. "She can talk," Isabella said. "You're very talkative, aren't you, sweetie?"

Nyaa-aa!

"Has it been here before? How do you know it's female?"

"I don't know, her face."

"Aren't they the ones that have more kittens?"

"Possibly."

"It hasn't been going into the house, has it?"

"Of course not."

"You know, the rental contract is serious when it says 'no pets.' It means *us*—especially us."

The kitten crouched and glared. A black streak cut diagonally across its white muzzle, smudging its face and merging into a half-mask and bandana. It cried out again—*nyaa!*

"Oh Smudgy," Isabella said. "Yes, Smudge, that's right, isn't it?" They continued their talk and I returned to my book, less worried than I had made out.

Before long, Smudge confirmed her gender by producing a litter. She had set up her den among the squashed cardboard boxes our neighbor, the bent, elderly woman, kept behind her house. One morning Isabella found the newborn kittens huddled dead in the frost. The only responsible thing was to have the animal spayed.

"You fed her," I said virtuously, "you fix it."

It took Isabella a fortnight to catch her—in a game of cat and mouse, so to speak—by propping up a cardboard box using a stick with a string attached and placing sardines underneath. Eventually the cat fell into the trap, and she tied up the cardboard box and took it by bicycle to the veterinary clinic.

Glossy coats, chic collars and leads on display, the dogs and cats bided their time, in self-possessed conformance with the dictates of etiquette, like their Japanese owners themselves. The spectacle of Isabella entering with her cardboard box sent a ripple of unease through the waiting room. Inside the box, the cat was venting its fear and fury, alternating low growls with plaintive wails. The vet summoned Isabella into the surgery and she explained what she wanted. He directed her to put the box down on an examination table.

"Is she tame?" The cat was screaming and trying to punch its way out.

"Yes, she's fine," Isabella lied, determined to have the job done.

The instant the box was open, the cat flew out snarling and hissing like a demon from hell, ears flattened and teeth bared, eyes raking the room as though seeking out a victim, and sprang up onto a high shelf. The vet and his nurse didn't want to tangle with it, but pressed themselves back against the wall. Noticing a leather gauntlet on a shelf, Isabella pulled it on and managed to grasp and restrain the cat. The vet found a netting bag and stuffed the animal in. Next day, when Isabella returned to collect her, the cat was uncommonly tranquil—and more importantly, desexed.

My heart went out to the little cat eking out a harsh,

solitary existence in her den. She preferred this spot to the cozy nest of old jumpers Isabella fixed up for her in our garden shed. Isabella now fed her openly, but I insisted we not allow her inside—so that became their little secret when I was out. Our rental contract specified "no pets," but no clause specifically prohibited the feeding of a neighborhood cat, I supposed. She was an independent entity, technically as much our neighbor's cat as ours. But as time passed, the animal imprinted herself on us. Whenever we went out in the morning or came home at night, she'd meow from one of her strategic spots on the roof, an affectionate call of recognition. If I was coming home late after work and didn't hear her greeting call, I wondered where she might be and hoped nothing had befallen her.

A dozen of them occupied the immediate vicinity— a rag-tag mixture, domestic and feral. At night, they made appalling demonic howls, fighting and courting in the tree branches that spread out like an alternate universe over our roof. Some bobtails roamed among them. Apparently, in earlier times, superstition held that you should amputate a cat's tail to stop it turning into a goblin at night, but a bobtail breed exists as well, which I presume accounts for the ones around these days, rather than that gruesome practice. Smudge caught the wrong end of the neighborhood cat-fights and was sometimes afraid to climb down to the front window for her breakfast because of a formidable ginger tom who prowled around. I acquired a water pistol to protect her meals, but some nights, sleep had no defense against the goblins on the roof.

One night we were roused out of sleep by a sudden shuddering of the house. Not the goblins, they were silent . . . an earth tremor! We headed for the nearest door, unsure whether to go out and risk being killed by falling tiles or remain in the house and be crushed under the roof. We waited there on the step, watching seismic ripples pass through the very earth: the earth itself rose, fell and eddied as though transformed into liquid. Astounding. I don't know about the physics of such a phenomenon, but that's how it looked, anyway.

A DEFINITE change in the wildlife of Fumioka occurred over time. In the beginning, some varieties of small birds had twittered among the trees in the old woman's and our gardens and hopped about on the grass pecking at seeds. Their numbers fell as the cats took over, until a time came when none but the bravest or most foolhardy sparrow dared alight on the spreading branches of the big tree.

I hosted a cosy barbecue get-together in the garden, inviting a friend of Isabella's, Larissa, and her husband Yuichi. Inspired by Ojima-san, the Shizuokan fisherman, I bought a small *shichirin* clay charcoal-burner of my own, shorter than knee height, with a square wire grill on top. I prepared meat, king prawns and mushrooms on bamboo skewers, along with various species of shell-fish, and diversified the cuisine with experimental grilled enchiladas. While I stoked up the shichirin, we drank champagne and munched on the assorted hors d'oeuvres I'd picked up at an imported foods retailer in the city.

Isabella had met Larissa at the local health and fit-ness club. Isabella introduced herself to the graceful, long-legged, blonde vision of glamor and discovered that she too was Russian. They became fast friends, and we three met for lunch from time to time at a Russian restaurant in the city. The two women would chat on in their native tongue while I enjoyed my shashlik and glass of vodka. In her late twenties, Larissa brimmed with poise and self-confidence. She held a degree from an institute of technology in Russia but had been working here as a nightclub hostess. "It is not an ordinary nightclub," she told us more than once, "but a *very* high-class place."

She was typical of the beautiful young Russian expats who saw Japan as an escape from the social and financial doldrums that life in Russia then promised. Even her degree didn't guarantee the quality of life to which she aspired. She was much more at home with the money and luxury available in Japan than bickering in a Belgorod marketplace. Besides, she told Isabella, Russian men were hopeless drunks who beat up their women, and she wanted nothing to do with them. A good looking young man back home in Russia adored her, but he had no job, and he did nothing more to woo her other than come around with a bottle of wine when the whim struck him. He declared his desperate love and desire to marry her, but she refused him.

Larissa was a single mother. Her parents were raising her son, Sasha, in Russia. Her father was a truck driver, but his health was failing, so she needed to send money regularly to help support the household.

"Yuichi used to come to the club often after I began working there," she said.

Yuichi grinned bashfully. I learned over the course of the evening that he had been a successful entrepreneur in the business of organic cosmetics and now owned a company that imported and distributed health products. He drove a late model Mercedes Benz and took Larissa for holidays abroad. He indulged himself in the hobby of collecting antique hurricane lamps.

"He didn't even drink. He would come just to see me," she continued. "He was already married, but not happily. He and his wife divorced, and he sold his company and gave her all the money so he could be with me. Then he started a new company in health products."

She needed Isabella to translate her Russian at times during our conversation, but even so, her English was not too bad; nor was her Japanese for that matter, for someone who had been here for the short time she had. She picked up a lot from Yuichi and from clients at the club where she still worked. She carried a notebook with her everywhere she went, and was always jotting down English or Japanese expressions. Isabella encouraged her to study Japanese more formally and both now attended classes at HICE: Hamamatsu Foundation for International Communication and Exchange.

"Mike . . ." Larissa had a distinct and disarming accent. She pronounced the diminutive form of my name something like "Ma-eek." "Thank-you for arranging the interview for me at the university with the Japanese professors of Russian. I think they were speaking Russian to me, but hard to tell. Anyway, I enjoy teaching the students Russian. They are nice but very quiet. It's not easy to get them to speak. Oh—when I came into the classroom, I heard a boy student say to his friend, 'Kawaii!'" ("She's cute!") She giggled girlishly.

I served a sizzling shellfish onto her plate using my pair of cooking hashi.

If the skittish professors were any guide, I could imagine how the male students must have responded to this blonde Russian bombshell, the likes of whom they must not have seen beyond the movie or television screen. Larissa knew how to make the most of her female graces and kept men from her "high-class club" on a leash despite being married to the long-suffering Yuichi—it became clear that theirs was a union of convenience for her. Day or night, if she needed a lift, she would phone a client up on her mobile and in no time he would be there to drive her. No strings attached—the exclusively Japanese customers were simply besotted and crazy for her company whenever they had the slightest chance of it.

I may have found her a touch narcissistic but sympathized with her and admired her enterprise in making a life for herself and, presumably, eventually her son. Like Smudge, she was a survivor. Because of that—and perhaps because being a male I had no choice in the matter—I was happy to help her out when I could.

After our guests left and Isabella went in to her futon, I stayed outside in the darkness for a while, sipping on a glass of wine and nibbling leftovers. In a perfect state of mind for a snooze, I lay down on a rug I had spread out there and dozed off. Deep into the night I opened my eyes again. Feeling comfortable and secure, I rolled over on my back, thinking I might spend the rest of the night underneath the stars. There up above me, settled on a bough of the fig, was a dark silhouette, unmistakable for its size. The big ginger tomcat stared down at me through his wide, confident eyes and contemplated whether to assume his goblin body. His henchmen lurked nearby, their senses trained like laser beams on the scraps of food I hadn't yet cleaned up. Preferring to err on the side of discretion in supernatural matters, I immediately gathered up my cushion and rug and went into the house to retire, leaving the scraps to them.

21

Becketteers

Rieko Suzuki and I arranged to meet at Tokyo Station. She suggested we stroll across to the Imperial Hotel, close to the Emperor's palace. Founded in 1890 for the royal household, the Imperial was classy digs. The original wooden building burned down in 1919, and the owners commissioned the brilliant American architect Frank Lloyd Wright to design a new one. That building, the most famous of his six in Japan, survived the Great Tokyo Earthquake of 1923 and the American bombings of the Second World War, but was demolished in 1968 and replaced with a modern high-rise.

Rapid elevator ride up to a waiter, who led us to a private dining cubicle with a view of the imperial gardens. Rieko was an impressive, intelligent woman. Intense personality, artistically and ideologically dedicated. We communicated easily thanks to our mutual enthusiasm for the work of the Nobel Prize-winning Irish author Samuel Beckett.

She produced and acted in innovative performances in Japanese of Beckett's radical late plays. She was a veteran actress of the *angura* ("underground") avant-garde theater that grew out of the 1960s in Japan. Beckett had a strong influence on the angura movement: the first Tokyo performance of his groundbreaking play *Waiting for Godot* in 1960 was a momentous event for dramatists such as Tadashi Suzuki (b. 1939), Minoru Betsuyaku (b. 1937) and Shogo Ota (1939–2007). Literary critic Yasunari Takahashi (1932–2002) described this "first generation" of theater innovators as striving for "a 'revolution of theater' that would be total and far-reaching, aiming at no less than a revolution of the consciousness of the audience."

Rieko performed in Ota's company, Theater of Transformation, from 1974 until it disbanded due to financial problems in 1988. She acted in his best known works, *Tale of Komachi Told by the Wind* and *Water Station*, when they toured Europe, the United States, Canada, Australia and Korea.

We discussed her current project over a light lunch. She and her company were in the process of mounting a modest Tokyo production of a short Beckett play, *Not I*, in which the sole character would be a disembodied mouth, surrounded by darkness and illuminated by a spotlight. I'd been asked to find a Japanese production that might be appropriate for a Beckett festival that was being planned as part of the Festival of Sydney 2003. Rieko's *Not I* seemed ideal. Her fascinating career embodied an important era of modern Japanese theater, and this new production of hers was portable and inexpensive. Moreover, the play was not produced terribly often because of its brevity and the problem of creating

its theater illusion, an effect at once spectacular yet min-
imalistic.

"Of course," said Rieko, "I perform it in Japanese . . ."

"But that may be as much an advantage as a problem,"
I said. "The audience will be mostly scholars and en-
thusiasts familiar with the monologue in English or
French. It might seem an odd thing to say, but I think
they'll find it intriguing to watch the play in what to
them is an alien language. I mean, an intention of
Beckett's *is to be alienating*, and most know the play
well anyway. Watching a performance in an unknown
language, the emphasis will be even more upon the
mystery of the human utterance, rather than the content
of what's spoken. They'll hear the pure music of the
Japanese language, unadulterated except for the meaning they bring to it."

Waiters discrete but meticulous. To top off the meal,
I ordered a Courvoisier and she an iced tea.

"What size do you expect the theater to be?" she asked.

"Quite big," I said. "It's the Sydney Theatre Company's main stage, which will be the central venue for
the symposium. I'm wondering whether your *Not I*
might be performed there, so perhaps it could be linked
with some discussion of the play."

"I am considering using an idea from my Tokyo production that may be effective, then—a stage prop in
noh called a *tsukurimono*, a boxlike structure made of
a framework covered with beautiful material, whose dramatic function is to conceal an actor."

"I once saw a play performed in the noh theater at
the Atsuta Shrine in Nagoya, in which a big hanging
bell was lowered to enclose an actor," I said.

"Yes, that is a famous tsukurimono in the play *Dojoji*

(Dojoji Temple). There are others, too, though they are relatively uncommon: props that may represent a hut or other dwelling, a boat, or a tomb or suchlike. Sometimes they allow an actor to change costume on-stage without being seen. In *Not I* that can be a useful trick, because we do not want the actor's body to be seen by the spectators before the lights go down and after they come back up. Before the play starts, the actor can be sitting on a platform in the tsukurimono. When the lights fade and the theater is in complete darkness, the material on the top of the box is taken down, and then the tiny spotlight will come up on the character, Mouth. After the spotlight goes out at the end, the box is covered up again. This way, the actor's body will never be visible, only the mouth."

A brilliant idea—to use a traditional device from noh to solve theatrical problems in such a modern Western work. Absolutely appropriate, since the Japanese avant-garde, anti-realistic theater in the 60s had dramatic roots in noh and kabuki.

I was optimistic. Beckett's work was so important to the development of contemporary Japanese theater that specialists were sure to find the various artistic strands informing Rieko's *Not I* intriguing.

"We start to rehearse next week. When we are ready, I'd like to invite you to come and see our dress rehearsal," she said.

"I plan to go to Australia in a month's time," I said, "so I'll meet up with the organizer and see if we can obtain some funding. I'll come to Tokyo and meet with you again before then."

Walked with Rieko to the entrance of Hibiya subway

station, minutes away, before heading back to Tokyo
Station.

I HAD contacted the Samuel Beckett Research Circle
of Japan some years earlier at the suggestion of Enoch
Brater, a leading first-generation American Beckett
scholar. I struck up a correspondence with him, hoping
to hook up with international Beckett studies. I sent him
copies of some published articles and he replied by
email, encouraging me to get in touch with the
"Japanese Becketteers," as he called them, and their
leader, Yasunari Takahashi, who was known among the
Japanese literati, Brater wrote me, as "the Great
Takahashi."

Beckett had an enormous intellectual impact on
young, revolutionary dramatists in 1960s Japan. The
Japanese Becketteers, among the brightest, most progressive Japanese scholars of English literature,
welcomed me into their circle as a kindred Beckett ad-
herent. Takahashi was a renowned expert on
Shakespeare as well as modern English literature, on
top of traditional and modern Japanese drama and literature. Such a marrying together of the culturally
far-flung, I had sometimes heard, reflected a national
history of hankering after Western culture.

I joined the group and met regularly with the
Becketteers in Tokyo, enjoying their rarefied discourses
on Beckett in English and Japanese. They were among
the elite of Japanese literary scholars, so it was an airy
release from my workaday faculty chores. I now held a
post of full professor, which I appreciated as an honor,

but one that brought some time-consuming and challenging tasks, such as heading the public relations committee and the editorial board of the faculty research journal, published mostly in Japanese.

At first we used to meet at the University of the Sacred Heart (Seishin Joshi Daigaku), the alma mater of Empress Michiko, located in Shibuya, Tokyo. Our host, Junko Matoba, a most likable and genteel woman, was a senior professor at the university and among the very good friends I made in Japan.

After our scholarly meetings, everyone repaired to a fine restaurant for a social get-together. The Great Takahashi occasionally missed the meeting itself but showed up at the restaurant, where he held court with good humor, modesty and erudition. It became clear after a while, however, that his health was deteriorating with a serious illness, so I attributed his attitude to the meetings to that, rather than lordliness. He was extremely gracious toward me. An article I wrote about the Samuel Beckett Research Circle of Japan appeared in a periodical published by the international Beckett society, prompting him to send me a note thanking me for "declaring to the world the existence of our Society"—which definitely was to overstate my contribution. The first time we met, he mentioned the edition of Blyth I'd worked on:

"Of course, I know the accomplishment of your co-editor, Professor Munakata, in adapting the plays of Shakespeare for noh," he said, smiling. "I have myself adapted Shakespeare for *kyogen* plays" (a genre of plays that generally function as a comic interlude between two serious noh plays.)

"Yes, I've heard that."

"So actually," Takahashi purred with a sly overtone and chuckled, "I suppose you could say that he and I are to some extent . . . rivals in that field . . ."

I did as much as I could to assist my Beckett colleagues, consulting, proofreading, rewriting for publications, theses and international conference papers, and clarifying nuances in Beckett's work that were sometimes elusive to the Japanese scholars. Some of my own research subsequently appeared internationally and in the leading Japanese literary journal *Studies in English Literature.*

Now and then, a foreign Beckett scholar engaged in a lecture tour of Japan gave a talk at our meeting and took part in our get-together. One was Dr. Gottfried Büttner, a medical doctor and expert literary critic who'd had a twenty-year friendship with Beckett. We were on the second floor of a classy if somewhat rickety restaurant in a Shibuya backstreet, where Dr. Büttner was entertaining us over our meal with some anecdotes. One story—something of a parable—highlighted Beckett's compassionate nature:

"Beckett's seventh-floor apartment in Paris was across from La Santé prison," Büttner said. "His friend and German translator, Elmar Tophoven, described to me how he entered the apartment one day and found Beckett at the window looking down over the prison exercise yards. Tophoven saw flashes of sunlight reflecting into the room around Beckett and realized that a prisoner must be using a mirror to communicate with him—the author felt a particular compassion for people deprived of their freedom, and he communicated regularly with the inmates using a mirror and semaphore. Tophoven then saw Beckett signal to the prisoner that it was time for their conversation to end. He raised his arms just like this . . ."—Büttner demonstrated— "Tophoven said the gesture looked exactly like that of the Pope blessing a crowd below."

Büttner paused for his audience to assimilate the story. Inoue-san, an associate professor from Meiji University, clarified the thrust of the tale in Japanese—the word "Pope" was unanticipated and the implication unclear. I squirmed a little: I didn't relish the inclination of some Beckett fanciers almost to deify the man.

"Ah, the Pope . . ." someone said, and the group simulated its comprehension of the punch-line with affirmative *ah so*'s, nods and polite laughter, more pleased with the breaking of the communicative impasse than the point of the story itself.

Right at that moment there was a slight jolt in the room, and a vibration ensued. Everyone but Dr. Büttner and his wife was instantaneously aware of what was happening, for we had all experienced many such tremors.

"*Jishin da!*" ("Earthquake!") someone declared in a restrained but agitated tone.

Misconstruing the activity at the table as an appreciative reaction to his anecdote, Dr. Büttner chortled heartily in response. The earth tremor strengthened correspondingly, and in a few seconds the glasses, china and cutlery on the joined tables—indeed the tables themselves—were engaged in a sustained, seance-like shudder, as if in appreciation of the entertainment. My colleagues and I entered a particular tense state of awareness in which one's senses were focused on the vibrations—trying to detect whether they were strengthening or subsiding, alert to see what was about to happen. Dr. Büttner's merriment increased in proportion with the intensity of the tremor, along with our anxiety. The eyes of the man across the table from me rolled around, and he had on a fixed nervous grin as he continued to nod at Dr. Büttner, too well-mannered to interrupt.

Fast approaching a sensible time to dive under the tables, so I raised my voice and said emphatically to the Büttners:

"We're having an earthquake!"

But as if on cue to humiliate me, the tremor halted abruptly right then. Their hilarity faltered for an instant as they glanced at me quizzically, wondering what on earth I was blathering about. The Japanese were looking around at each other with frozen open-mouthed grins and raised eyebrows.

"Excuse me," I said, "it's nothing." I smiled and joined in the sigh of relief that passed furtively around the table, and Dr. Büttner set sail on another anecdote.

IT WAS AT an international Beckett conference and festival held at Hümboldt University, Berlin, that Anthony Uhlmann, my fellow doctoral alumnus, had invited me to convene a Japanese component of a Sydney Festival Beckett symposium that he was then planning and to try to find an appropriate Japanese production. He had already published an excellent book on Beckett; with that work behind him, the Sydney event would launch him into deserved prominence in the Beckett world.

Isabella accompanied me to Berlin for the conference. Several companies were performing Beckett plays in theaters around the city, but enough Beckett was enough, and I had no problem sacrificing them in favor of Isabella's preference to attend the Berlin State Opera's production of Wagner's *Lohengrin*. After the interval, I occupied the wrong seat, the one directly in front of mine, only realizing my mistake minutes later, when a mature, decorously outfitted German woman approached and stood in front of me, looking down on me imperiously. I turned and saw Isabella sitting in the row behind me, head inclined and eyes closed. I rose to my feet and bowed instinctively to the woman, Japanese style.

"I do apologize, madam, it must be the champagne," I said, smiling idiotically.

Mirthful embodiment of incredulity, the woman occupied her seat and turned away from me grandly, with a dismissive gesticulation for all the public to see. I've never been belittled with such hauteur, so artfully done it was oddly exhilarating.

Our trip to Berlin had been brightened for me by the foil of my Japanese acculturation, such that even the most trivial of interactions became memorably aesthetic: life in Japan seemed by contrast monochrome and two-dimensional. Color of a gray rat?

Next day, a similar experience. My Beckett presentation was heartily received, so relieved and elated, I ducked into a Mexican cafe a few doors from our hotel, with the idea of celebrating privately over a tequila. Glorious morning, and the cafe society was filling the tables on the footpath; inside the restaurant several tables were still empty. The tall, lithe young waitress possessed lustrous black skin and the poise of a leopard. She glanced over my way but continued to chat with the bartender for a while before sashaying to my table. I ordered a shot of their best tequila with salt and a slice of lime, but she returned languidly with a shot-glass of tequila, a slice of orange and a shaker containing a brown powder.

"Um . . ." I piped up, indicating the little serving tray she set before me. "I think I asked for a tequila with salt and lime. What's this?"

"I thought you would prefer it with cinnamon and a slice of orange, since you ordered 'tequila *oro*,'" she explained, with an impartial look. Eyes clear, fathomless pools.

"Oh, I see . . . Well, fair enough." Didn't mind her telling me what to drink. Teutonic version of the Fantastic Shop.

I downed the shot, marveling both at the waitress and the difference between the German and Japanese service cultures, both of which struck me as sublime in each its own way. I've since learned that Germany is one of few countries in the world where they drink "tequila gold"—in Spanish, *oro*—in that fashion. Had another for good measure and repaired to the hotel.

After the conference, Isabella and I traveled by train to Prague via Dresden and along the Elbe River, arriving just in time for a major riot. Six-thousand anti-capitalist demonstrators descended from around Europe to protest against the annual International Monetary Fund and World Bank summit. A sinister looking black taxi shuttled us to our hotel, Klasterni Dvur, on Bartolomejska Street. Dusk. Along the route we noticed groups of armed police in black uniforms marshaling together on street corners to prepare for the demonstrators.

Next morning we wandered the city, spellbound by the beauty of its architecture and mystery of its labyrinthine alleys. I stumbled across a quaint, richly stocked bookshop, where I bought some works by Czech authors in English translation and some CDs of Martinu symphonies. We visited Franz Kafka's house in the Jewish Quarter, and the Museum of Medieval Torture Instruments, before crossing Charles Bridge to climb the picturesque, uncommonly steep Nerudova Street to Prague Castle, stopping along the way for me to buy a marionette of Kafka, fashioned as a gloomy looking clerk in a dark gray office suit and blue necktie.

Rioting kicked off early that afternoon; fortunately, we were back in our hotel room. A peaceful march turned ugly when roaming bands of protesters started hurling missiles and Molotov cocktails at the armored police lines, setting some policemen alight. Police responded with batons, water cannon, stun grenades and tear gas. We watched the action unfold live on television from the point of view of a CNN news helicopter. Anarchists were digging up cobblestones from the streets and hurling them at the riot police, along with cars, buildings and anything capitalist-looking—especially the McDonald's franchise in Wenceslas Square, which they trashed.

Isabella stood by the window.

"That must be the helicopter out there," she said.

Sure enough, through the window we could see the CNN helicopter televising the riot, hovering overhead. I turned back to the live aerial images of the rioting that were showing on the television screen, then to the window, which happened to frame the helicopter outside.

"Pretty good example of what Baudrillard calls the 'hyperreal,'" I said, "where the media image becomes more real than reality. Too real for me."

Our hotel was once a medieval Jesuit cloister,

bequeathed to the Sisters of Mercy in 1856. The secret police commandeered it during the Communist regime and routinely jailed political prisoners here—including Vaclav Havel. Nice Beckettian touch. Beckett dedicated a play to Havel, having heard that the Czech was forbidden to write when he was in prison for subversion; and after his release, Havel dedicated a play to the Irishman in return.

LOCATED RIEKO'S apartment building in a northern Tokyo suburb, climbed the stairs and knocked on her door. Hauled my wheeled suitcase behind me: later that night I'd be off to Tokyo Narita Airport to fly out to Sydney the next morning. She greeted me and introduced me to the director of her Tokyo production, a young woman, Hatsumi Abé. Half Rieko's apartment had been converted to a rehearsal studio to prepare for *Not I*. The three of us drew up chairs around a small table in the kitchen area. Hatsumi spread out a plan that covered the tabletop.

"This is the tsukurimono box we intend to use in the play," Rieko said, "but we have to know what these different viewing angles will be in the theater. For example, where precisely will the spectators be placed at the extreme sides and at the top rows? Then we can make the box the right size and place it in the correct position for everyone to see Mouth. If you get us those measurements, we will design the box and fax it to the theater in Sydney, and the producers over there can build it."

In the studio a chair was placed, to which had been added a simple wooden structure, with a device on which Rieko could rest her chin and keep it in position for the duration of the performance. Hatsumi showed me to a single spectator's chair, before moving to the control booth behind me.

Lights off, and the room fell into such darkness that I couldn't see my hand in front of my face. Rieko's voice began the monologue, a quiet stream of Japanese hard to follow, gradually growing in volume. As the spotlight faded up to create a circle of light just big enough to illumine the actress's mouth, her speech simultaneously grew increasingly loud and insistent, until it was a rapid-fire muttering and spewing forth of the stream of words, the monologue of the lone character translated into Japanese:

> . . . *out into this world . . . this word . . . tiny little thing . . . before its time . . . in a godfor – . . . what? . . . girl? . . . yes . . . tiny little girl . . . into this . . . out into this . . . before her time . . . godforsaken hole called . . . called . . . no matter . . .*

The spotlight isolated Mouth precisely, and maintained the same position throughout the monologue. Not easy to do that: various contrivances had been required in historical productions to keep the actress's head stock still. Amid the pitch blackness, Mouth being the sole reference point, my perception started to become distorted. Startlingly, the disembodied mouth seemed to float in the darkness and even grow and shrink in size, as my eyes moved involuntarily and their focus shifted. Mouth's voice poured out in staccato Japanese: the mad narrative of a woman who was walking in a field and suddenly found herself fallen into an infernal state. As observer, I was immersed in the strange illusion. The darkness removed any frame of reference: the mouth struck me as being the mouth of the darkness itself—a limitless, raving emptiness. Bordering on the frighteningly, maddeningly real. I became disconcertingly aware of the mouth/voice reverberating in my mind, as though the darkness of the imagination—the environment within which imagined visions manifest themselves—converged with the all-enveloping real darkness of this real place. Rieko's performance was the most powerful I'd ever seen.

A week or so later, I met with the conference organizer, Anthony Uhlmann, in Sydney, and we went together to pitch the idea to a cultural officer from the Australian branch of the Japan Foundation. She heard us out cordially about Rieko's *Not I*, but informed us that their funding program was finalized for the year and they would not be able to extend us a grant. Funding for the Sydney Festival was all earmarked as well, with a substantial amount needed for a fiftieth anniversary production of Beckett's most famous play, *Waiting for Godot*, to be performed at the Belvoir Street Theatre under the direction of Neil Armfield. The Oscar-winning movie star Geoffrey Rush had agreed to play one of the two lead roles. Unfortunately, no funds left over for Rieko's project.

Arriving back in Japan, I notified her about the outcome. Her *Not I*, nevertheless, went ahead successfully in Tokyo. I turned my efforts to organizing the Japanese section of the academic symposium. First I phoned Yasunari Takahashi to invite him, but he was too ill to join in. He thanked me and wished me luck. Sadly, he passed away some months later, but several of the Japanese Becketteers participated.

* * *

Enjoyed playing host to my Japanese Research Circle colleagues, chairing a panel in which they presented research papers and helping them find their way around. A week into January, so the flight brought us from one extreme of climate to the other, from bitterly cold Tokyo to a Sydney bathed in glorious sunshine. Our plane banked over the harbor, presenting us with a breathtaking panorama of the city—spacious, green and sparkling like a gem.

A quick look at the opera house, then three of us shared a meal of Sydney rock oysters at a stall on the eastern side of Circular Quay, enjoying the view of the harbor bridge and the spectacle of the yellow and green ferries coming and going at the quay.

"Iconic spot indeed," Inoue said approvingly as he consumed an oyster Kilpatrick.

Passengers clambered across the deck of a ferry not twenty meters from us, which was maneuvering to leave the quay, bobbing up and down in the wake of another vessel. Adults laughed, children squealed as they jockeyed for the best positions.

"People here know how to enjoy the harbor," I said. "Everywhere has its pros and cons; but if you compare this with Tokyo Harbor or Yokohama, here the place is bursting with energy—people sailing yachts and really immersing themselves in nature. The intoxicating influence of nature distinguishes Sydney Harbor—transforms it into a playground."

The Beckett festival had an impact on the Australian cultural scene and vice versa. The symposium, "After Beckett / Après Beckett," was described as the largest, most important humanities conference ever held in Australia. As for the theatrical side of events, Geoffrey Rush decided to pass up Company B Belvoir's production of *Waiting for Godot* in favor of playing a pirate captain in the Hollywood movie *The Pirates of the Caribbean*, alongside Johnny Depp and Orlando Bloom. Understandable for many, I guess, disappointing for me. Armfield made do by casting two well-loved Australian actors as Didi and Gogo (Vladimir and Estragon): John Gaden and Max Cullen brought sincere Aussie warmth and nuance to these existential tramps.

A thirteenth fairy, however, arrived in the form of Samuel Beckett's estate. Beckett's nephew, Edward Beckett, who participated in the festival, threatened to bring an injunction to close Armfield's production down because it included improvised music in some scenes, an unauthorized innovation. Controversy surrounding authorial control spilled over into the front pages of the major Australian newspapers. In an impassioned speech he made on the final day, Neil Armfield roundly denounced the estate as "an enemy of art."

"If there is something to hope for at this watershed fiftieth anniversary of the play that broke the rules," he said, "it is that Edward Beckett gives his uncle's work back to artists to work with. After all, if he doesn't let go, he's consigning it to a slow death by a thousand hacks." Memorable line.

Don Anderson, one of Australia's best-known and respected literary critics, summed up Australian feelings toward Edward Beckett's attempt to derail the Aussie *Godot*: "Bugger this for a joke!" A senior lecturer at the University of Sydney, he had supervised my postgraduate research on Beckett. Stanley Gontarski, a professor at Florida State University and world famous Beckett specialist (international examiner of my PhD thesis) took the opposite view:

"It's a storm in a billy-tea cup," he said to the packed symposium, and he was probably right. "Problems like this go with the territory of being an artist," he insisted.

Later I enjoyed mingling with these characters, whom I'm happy to remember as my teachers and mentors.

"Freedoms are earned," Gontarski said over a coffee. "If you've got confidence in your work, let it stand."

Over a beer, Don Anderson likened certain literary executors to those of the post-war East German Stasi.

"Political police of intellectual debate and performance," he said. "They are behaving in illiberal ways that completely contravene the spirit of the people whom they represent."

22

Weightless

On past New Year's Eves we lay on our futons at midnight, listening to the chimes of two distant bells waft up from Buddhist temples by the lake. They rang out a hundred and eight times to symbolize the hundred and eight human sins, in a ritual called *joya no kane* ("the watch-night bell"). One sounded with a celestial peal, while the other carried a jarring overtone. They died away together, to a pleasing, vaguely dissonant echo. Our year would fade into the depths of Japanese myth as we sank into sleep, the soft echo merging with its trace in the memory.

This time, Isabella's elderly father was ill and she needed to go to Australia soon, so we decided to walk down. The locals were gathered around a bonfire in the temple garden. Some stood waiting for a turn to ring the big bell, which you did by swinging a horizontal beam forward to strike it. Sparks swirled as the bonfire spat and sputtered, and we mingled in with the smoke and tranquil chitchat.

* * *

A GANG of laborers arrived and cut down every tree in the old woman's garden next door and mine, clearly a stage in someone's plan to develop the properties. I could see the time was nigh when my lease would not be renewed, and here I was with my outdoor privacy stripped away, living in a wasteland, waiting to be told to leave. Nothing to do but work long hours every day, go out to dine and drink, then come home and crash on the couch in front of the television. On weekends when I was not working in my research room, I went out walking, occasionally played tennis or stayed at home with the curtains drawn. Nearly fifteen years in Japan, and the exercise was losing its point, despite opportunities for stimulating academic projects and travel to Asia, Europe, Russia and the United States. Fumioka was fast becoming depressing. The man who used to fly the carp banners had lost his wife and mother and now lived alone, shuffling around in his compound like the lost soul I imagined he had indeed become. The solitary old woman had passed away too. Because real estate was being developed and improved across the suburb, the cats were becoming scarce as well, like the birds before them, though Smudge hung on.

Sometimes Tsuji and I met for a meal at an izakaya near his apartment. The place had a warm, vibrant atmosphere and catered for students and locals, so the menu was varied and cheap: varieties of sashimi; all manner of *yakitori* (grilled chicken skewers), pork or beef skewers; grilled squid, mushrooms, peppers, *asupara bacon* (asparagus wrapped in bacon), shrimp, salmon fillet; fried chicken, potatoes, garlic — in short, the delicious gamut of izakaya fare. We sat near the counter, where we had immediate access to the obliging chefs in their aprons and headbands, who worked vigorously over their sizzling, smoking grills while parties of students quaffed draft beer and shouted conversations. I often had a serving of *basashi* among our multiple courses — a Chinese delicacy, thin slices of raw horse meat smothered in garlic and soy sauce. The Chinese will eat anything with legs except tables and chairs, so it's said. I finished my meal with grilled *iwashi* (sardines), served on a bamboo leaf, and *yaki onigiri* (grilled rice-balls): such a beautifully simple dish that it gave me an echo of the thrill I used to feel — *This is Japan*. We would share some *atsukan* — heated saké — pouring it for each other from a ceramic saké flask into our little cups, before making our farewells:

"Sayonara!"

"All things in moderation!"

But a constant thread ran through these outings: I could see I was in danger of heading down a well-worn path of dispirited expatriates who overdid the alcohol. Even worse, I starting smoking again — a habit I had beaten twenty years earlier after a struggle. The hours I spent hanging out in nightspots for company and joining in passively with the incessant cigarette smoking of the patrons and hostesses took their toll. Cigarettes were cheap — the equivalent of two dollars fifty Australian for a packet of twenty — and neither social stigma nor government regulation restricted where one could smoke. Once again, unthinkingly, stupidly, I allowed myself to slip under the domination of tobacco.

Underneath it all, I'd lost the motivation to go on. Isabella was in Australia indefinitely, and while living here for two years alone had been an adventure when I first arrived, now it was becoming repetitive and plain lonesome. I was sinking. We talked over the possibility of my returning home.

"I would follow you anywhere if I could, but my father needs me here," Isabella said on the phone. "You're fifty now. What do you intend to do—stay there alone and work till retirement, then come back to Australia when you're sixty or sixty-five? The sooner you move, the more you'll benefit from the lifestyle here in Australia. We'll be able to enjoy our time together."

"I'm not going to be able to continue my academic career in Australia. The systems are too different. I probably won't meet the requirements for a full-time university job."

"It doesn't matter. We can cross that bridge when we come to it. You've earned enough money to invest and live off the interest. You'll get casual work of some kind or perhaps do some freelance writing again."

She was right. I was afflicted with pangs of anxiety about the loss of salary and status I enjoyed in Japan, but life had more to it than that. I made up my mind not to procrastinate any longer. The next day I gave the faculty dean a year's notice.

NEEDED TO travel to New Orleans for a conference but didn't think to take any measures for the cat's well-being in my absence. She was, as I may have mentioned, a vagrant, an independent agent with her own rules and destiny. I arrived home at night after a week away. Opened up the hurricane doors and the front window, expecting her to leap up on the windowsill, but saw no sign of her. Left cat food in a saucer by the window, and when I looked around an hour later, there she was, hunkered over it. Something was seriously wrong. Her tail was crooked, and she could hardly keep her head up. It drooped forward until it rested on the windowsill. She'd received a sickening gash to her tail end, and the skin around her hips sagged like a pair of loose pantaloons. Her tail hung on by exposed muscle and sinew, and she looked ready to die right there in front of me.

I confined her in the bathroom while I went to the university the next day, reconciled to the likelihood she would be dead when I got home. Little battler that she was, though, she pulled through. She moaned pitifully to get out, so I moved her to the garden shed. Tried feeding her some raw egg yolk and milk, which she refused. Next I checked, her saucer was undisturbed and she had gone—gone off to die, I guessed. She came home again after I had given up all hope; renewed appetite and looking stronger. She amputated her own tail by chewing it off at the base, and I buried it behind the house.

"What could have happened to her?" Isabella asked when I rang her.

"Her injury looks too localized to have been caused by a car," I said. "More likely she drove someone mad whining at their door for food while I was away, and they threw something heavy at her."

"I'm so glad she's survived. She's a beautiful creature and a wonderful companion, the way she calls out when you leave for work each morning and welcomes you home again at night."

"She's come to rely on me for food. She's become my responsibility—or she already was, and I've only now realized it. I'm going to have to figure out what to do with her when I leave."

A neighbor was pottering in her garden a short distance down the lane, and I went in to speak to her. Her property was quite big and next to an empty block. I'd sometimes seen the cat heading off in that direction, her piebald coat standing out conspicuously against the green of the woman's garden like crazy anti-camouflage.

"I wonder," I ventured, after the usual pleasantries, "whether you might be kind enough to feed the cat after I'm gone?"

The woman frowned. "But I have a dog . . ."

"I'd be happy to pay someone to feed it."

"No-one wants cats around here anymore, you see . . ."

TUXEDO MOON was a karaoke dive and watering hole for neighborhood residents. The owner, a heavy-set fellow named Jimmu, mentioned having been a bosozoku outlaw biker in his teens. Imposing name, that of the legendary first emperor, but I just called him "Jim," since it sounds pretty much the same. Though mild-mannered, he looked the classic manga tough guy: barrel chest, ample paunch, beefy shoulders and biceps, an already thick nape broadened even more by a roll of fat, and oiled hair combed back in the style the yakuza borrowed from their mobster heroes in old Hollywood movies. Trimmed his eyebrows immaculately and wore a spotless white shirt and black waistcoat, with an apron tied around his middle. Cooked an excellent yakisoba, serving it on a sizzling cast iron platter, with the fried soba noodles, cabbage, bacon and ginger heaped up on top of a fried egg.

Jim introduced me to the folk-romantic side of the yakuza, with stories about Shimizu no Jirocho (1820–1893), a Shizuokan version of Robin Hood, the most famous yakuza in history, expert swordsman and the subject of more than a hundred movies. I asked him to teach me some proper *enka* songs—the Japanese blues-like genre—to take my Japanese karaoke repertoire beyond the ubiquitous *"Ue o Muite Aruko"* ("Let me look up as I walk," known in the West as the "Sukiyaki Song"). I wanted to be able to sing something sad and bluesy about drinking saké alone in a run-down dive in a freezing, windswept port somewhere—a classic enka theme. But a happy drinking song as well, please. He put his hand to his forehead to help him think.

"Ah. *'Yuki Guni'* ('Snow Country') and *'Sake Yo!'* ('Oh Saké!')" he exclaimed. These songs by the enka Elvis, Ikuzo Yoshi, were just the ticket. Jim took his role as my karaoke sensei in earnest and exercised it theatrically on busy nights when I performed as his trained gaijin, as he conducted and corrected me, to a sometimes embarrassing and irksome degree.

Gracing the bar were the Takeshitas, a flamboyant middle-aged couple who seemed to be there whenever I called in, giving the impression they came every night. Their chihuahua, Sakura-chan ("Miss Cherry-blossom"), was sitting up on a stool beside Mrs. Takeshita, who was using chopsticks to feed her dog tit-bits. Sakura-chan traveled with them everywhere in a Louis Vuitton handbag, her head sticking out with a haughty air.

In his early fifties, Mr. Takeshita was ten or twelve

years older than Jim but also affected something of the gangster look. He used to sport an old-style combed-back hairdo but had recently changed it to a close cropped, spiky one, in line with a current yakuza trend. A *hebii dorinka* ("heavy drinker" or boozer), he often behaved overbearingly and foolishly as a result. He dressed like a mid-level salaryman and more than likely was one, perhaps in a dubious firm. Mrs. Takeshita was strikingly beautiful and poised, probably from an upper-class family — she was attractive enough to have been a geisha and could pass for a model or film star. Both Takeshitas were formidable karaoke singers and hence the glamor figures of Tuxedo Moon. To my mind, she was the better singer, with a versatile, soulful voice that she could color with the nuanced vocal catches and shifts in timbre — from honeyed to husky to mezzo — that mark a good female enka voice.

Jim said he didn't need another cat, particularly a wild one, even with the five hundred dollars I offered as an inducement. He already owned a handsome Persian tom that occasionally presented itself in the club, slinking about the floor among the shadows or posing on the bar. A luminous purple-green aquarium, about six by four, was set on a stand against a wall. The tom would sit staring up at the fish intently, the tip of his tail flicking spasmodically.

"By the way," Jim cautioned, "you'd be a fool to give someone that much money — they'll keep it and get rid of the cat."

Needless to say, the Takeshitas weren't too interested either.

"Sakura-chan hates cats!" Mrs. Takeshita said passionately and cooed at her pet. On the key word *neko* (cat) the mutt's ears were up and she was scanning the floor for a trace of Jim's tom.

I DID some reporting as a freelancer for the Australian ABC's Radio National. Their documentary guru the late Tony Barrell approached me to undertake some research and field recording for a program on Japanese folk religion. I visited the 19th World congress of the International Association for the History of Religions held in Tokyo in 2005, where I met a leading authority on folk religion and Shugendo, Professor Hitoshi Miyake. Shugendo is an indigenous tradition of magic and mountain worship. Miyake agreed to be recorded in an interview with me, along with an expert scholar on Japanese religion, Dr. Gaynor Sekimori.

We arranged to meet at a library near the professor's home at Roppongi, where we would do the recording. I hadn't counted on it raining and noted with chagrin that Miyake appeared to deem me unworthy of sharing his umbrella, as I fumbled with my briefcase slung over one shoulder, while trying to shelter my expensive recorder under my dampening coat. We reached his building at Roppongi Hills, standing among the phenomenally upscale high-rise buildings there. Rental could run to fifty or sixty thousand US dollars; a prime penthouse could be worth up to twenty million.

As we went up in the elevator, he related a brief history of his home. For many decades his traditional family house had occupied the site of what became proposed as the Roppongi Hills residential development. He sold the property for a nice sum, with the proviso that he could keep possession of a penthouse on top of the high-rise building, on the same site where the family home had stood—an elegant way to placate the ancestors.

A stylish apartment indeed. A gracious hostess, Mrs. Miyake made us tea. I recorded the interview with Miyake alongside Dr. Sekimori's English interpretation. One of those otherworldly experiences.

> *"The Japanese tradition is that everybody has a soul or a spirit as well as a physical body, and the spirit is bestowed upon a baby at birth by the deities and the ancestor spirits. The first cry of the baby is the sign that the spirit has entered the child. The spirit then matures in the same way as the body, and eventually—when a person grows old and dies—leaves the body. The Japanese define death as the moment the spirit leaves our body. If the descendants memorialize a dead relative, say prayers and perform rites, then the spirit is purified. But if that doesn't occur, a spirit becomes a ghost, and in the case of people who die violently in conflict or who die resentful, they can bring curses on society . . ."*

My gaze wandered the Roppongi skyline as the hypnotic voices of Miyake and Sekimori in simultaneous Japanese and English filtered through my headphones with crystal clarity.

> *"Aborted fetuses—children who should have been born—are now the center of a widespread cult, based on a mother's belief that her unborn fetus may curse her. Moreover, a person who dies before they are married is thought to be unhappy, and may curse their parents from beyond the grave. Ghosts are always*

seeking to be remembered and memorialized by their descendants. They will appear in places where people gather, at riverbanks or graveyards, and in recent times there have been many stories about ghosts who appear in schoolyards and lavatories . . ."

However, inadvertently I spoiled the rare moment for my companions. As we sipped our tea after finishing the interview, I espied Miyake and his wife cast me one or two odd, seemingly disparaging glances, but they said nothing. Not until I was back at Tokyo Station refreshing myself at a lavatory washbasin did I see that my cheeks and throat were covered with what looked like enormous poxy black freckles. I hadn't seen it when I picked them up, but the headphones I brought were in a decrepit condition and had shed portions of the thin black plastic membrane covering the padded earpieces, and these fragments still adhered to my skin. At first I felt surprised nobody had said anything to me, but let me walk off into Tokyo looking like I had a dose of the Black Death. I concluded that, from a Japanese perspective, they may have found it too embarrassing to draw the detail to my attention—or who knows, perhaps beneath their dignity. Or an evil omen . . .

For all that, Tony Barrell broadcast the interview, and I set my sights on some more radio projects. ABC Radio National commissioned me to record and mix a report on the World Exposition, Expo 2005 in Aichi, Japan. I took some days away from campus to wander the spectacular Expo site, recording vox pop interviews to present a sample of the Japanese public's responses to the Australian pavilion. At the university, I mixed these with recordings I made of "Australia's national day" at

Expo: ambient sound and music from the Australian pavilion, Prime Minister John Howard's address, and various grabs of live choral and instrumental music by Australian performers. ABC broadcast my finished piece on its national program *The Deep End*.

I SYMPATHIZED with Mrs. Takeshita, who entered Tuxedo Moon alone early one evening when I chanced in on the way home from work, shortly after opening time. No Mr. Takeshita, no Sakura-chan. She wore dark glasses and had a silk scarf pulled forward over her head. She came directly up to me. Unusual—most often, she and her husband passed me with a cursory nod.

We exchanged greetings. "Where is your husband?" I asked.

She sighed.

"I suppose he is still in Tokyo." She lifted her glasses to reveal a purple mark that lined her cheek on the curved ridge below the eye, and she bent her face closer to me so I could see her disfigurement under the dim light.

"What do you think of this, Michael?"

I knit my brow and peered at her bruise, aware of her pupil, blurry in the periphery of my vision, regarding me detachedly. I wondered what she wanted of me, what she expected me to say, why she was directing this demonstration at me—as representative of all men? I looked into her eyes but failed to interpret any particular expression.

"That's no good," was all I could think to say, trying my utmost to extend a sincere feeling of kindness and concern, while making it clear to her and any observers that any warmth that passed between us was strictly within the bounds of decorum. After a second, she replaced her glasses and moved along the bar to sit alone with her drink, silhouetted by the luminous purple-green aquarium.

AMONG MY duties as head of the faculty public relations committee was the task of leading some delegations to high schools from which our students had graduated, in order to strengthen our institutional relationships and thereby recruit more of their graduates. We supplied school principals and career advisers with the glossy brochures we produced as part of our PR duties, and informed them of how their graduates were doing in their university studies. The faculty had spent the past year overhauling the curriculum, so we used the brochures to explain our new master plan for information studies. Two committee members and I scheduled ourselves to go to the city of Kanazawa, the capital of Ishikawa Prefecture. Apart from international research conferences, this was my most extended official trip so far, necessitating an overnight stay.

The tall, mild mannered Yamaguchi-san and I traveled together, standing in the aisle of the packed Shinkansen carriage during the first leg of the trip but finding a seat on the limited express when we changed trains at a town called Maibara. Our journey took about three and a half hours. Yamaguchi usually wore jeans but was in woolen trousers and a tweed sports coat for the occasion, his longish but thinning hair brushing over the collar. We conversed casually, ruminating on what promised to be a long day ahead, resigned to these tiresome extra duties. We met our colleague Sasaki-san at Kanazawa station in time for an early lunch and to plan our strategy for the day, dividing our targeted schools into two groups. Sasaki would take one group, Yamaguchi and I the other, the unspoken reason being not to disturb any of our hosts by presenting them with an unaccompanied foreigner. Privately, I doubted that this would be the most effective method, because I found Sasaki to be a somewhat off-putting character so-cially—brusque and intense, reminiscent of the nostril-hair trimming Mr. Saza in Nagoya. Of course, the intricate formalities of social intercourse, minutely adjustable to the context, served to reduce the friction that any annoying personal idiosyncrasies may cause. This was not so with foreignness, for a foreigner's mastery over social subtleties could be a conspicuous spectacle in itself and did not make him any less of a foreigner. At any rate, though I believed I was fluent enough in Japanese to have handled the job alone, and had hitherto taken on tasks equally as difficult, the arrange-ment made things much easier for me by lessening the amount of preparation I had to do.

We found the job the less onerous the more the day progressed. It was quite uplifting, in fact, to see these carefree young students flocking in their corridors. Yamaguchi and I chatted with principals and career ad-visers, taking turns to describe our curriculum and explain its rationale with reference to happy looking graphs and tables that appeared in the brochure. The teachers would make appropriately appreciative gestures, and we would announce our departure at the reception counter with a spirited *"O jama shimashita!"* ("Sorry about the interruption!") Very soon the day was done and we were on our way to meet up with Sasaki at a business ryokan where we had booked a room to share.

We rested on the tatami floor for some fifteen minutes, until a kindly middle-aged woman knocked at the door and came in to serve us green tea. We shared some immaculately polite conversation with her about the state of the weather, where we hailed from and why we had come to Kanazawa. My colleagues were, of course, adept communicators in this sphere of what the Japanese refer to as *omote*, outer form, as opposed to *ura*, inner substance. Analogous terms are *tatemae*, or the presentation of appropriate appearances for public consumption, and *honne*, the expression of one's actual feelings.

Steeped in elegant communicative conventions herself, the woman betrayed not the slightest hint ever to have met three such illustrious gentlemen-scholars. And from Hamamatsu! Our city seemed to strike her as some kind of distant, mythical Shangri-La, presumably the direct opposite of her true — and accurate — opinion.

"*Ah so desu ka!*" ("Really!") She gushed in wonder at our tale and giggled prettily at a witticism on the gallant Yamaguchi's part, modestly covering her mouth with her hand. She played the engaging hostess to a tee, providing us with details about where to take a bath if we wanted and where dinner would be served.

When she left, the formality dropped instantaneously to the level of *ura*, and the comfortable communicative style appropriate to our *uchi*, our in-group.

"We had better go and get some beer and saké to drink after dinner," Yamaguchi said, finishing his cup of tea and getting up from the tatami. "*Ikimasho.*" ("Let's go.")

"I noticed earlier on there's a bottle shop down the street," said Sasaki.

"But look, here's a mini-bar," I said, opening the small refrigerator to reveal its alcoholic contents.

"No, no," said Yamaguchi. "Too expensive. But we'll have to be careful bringing liquor in from outside, because you're not supposed to."

"Well, it won't look right if we go out with a backpack and come back again ten minutes later," Sasaki murmured contemplatively.

"Let's smuggle it in under our jackets," Yamaguchi said with a grin.

So off we went for a brisk preprandial constitutional, we three gentlemen-scholars, bowing cordially to the woman when we passed her coming in through the door. *Splendid evening for a bit of a walk, hey-ho!* Returned fifteen minutes later laden with a big bottle of saké and a healthy supply of canned beer, along with packets of rice crackers, dried squid, pretzels and potato chips to sustain us.

Before dinner, Yamaguchi and Sasaki took baths and I showered. We dined over several courses of a traditional meal in the tatami dining room before repairing to our own room for a private drinking party.

On the following day, Yamaguchi went to one final high school while Sasaki and I took in some of Kanazawa's attractions. The city had much to recommend it culturally and historically. Originally a temple town of the Ikko sect of Buddhism in the fifteenth century, after 1580 it became the base for the Maedas, the most powerful warrior clan after the Tokugawas. In its day, the culture of Kanazawa rivaled those of Kyoto and Edo.

We visited Myoryu-ji, the "Ninja Temple," so named in reference to the cunning devices—secret doors and trapdoors, pitfalls and peepholes—installed to combat intruders when the temple was built in 1643, during the Edo period. After that, we called in at the fabulous twenty-five acre Kenrokuen garden and the nearby remnants of Kanazawa Castle.

Kenrokuen is, they say, one of the three most beautiful gardens in Japan, possessing as it does the six elemental charms of a perfect garden, according to an ancient Chinese text on landscape theory: spaciousness, seclusion, artifice, antiquity, watercourses and wide views. Those who know consider these attributes as mutually exclusive, for an impression of vastness overpowers one's sense of intimacy and seclusion; artificiality weakens the effect of antique elegance; and flowing water interrupts distant views. Only in a transcendent garden such as Kenrokuen may the six sublime attributes coexist; and such a paradoxical coincidence of contrary qualities will occur in a state of absolute harmony.

NO LOCALS wanted the cat. I had no option but to send her to Isabella in Australia before returning home myself. After fifteen years, I'd started phasing down my life in Japan. In the process of establishing my life and career here, a web of habit and attachment seemed to have propagated in all directions, solidifying and entangling me. Now the threads were dissolving and falling away, with every residual idea and plan aimed towards a finite point of departure. I could visualize it. I would have managed the red tape to do with terminating my job and domestic life, discharged all my duties and social obligations. Research books reallocated, computers and equipment decommissioned, office cleaned out, belongings packed for transportation or disposal, arrangements made with international removalists. My final lecture in Japan behind me, I would go out through my front gate towing a single suitcase—as I had arrived in the country those years before, almost entirely unencumbered.

But this absurd complication threatened the streamlined progress of my actions. The problem of how one went about exporting a tail-less feral feline to Australia was superfluous to the many other extremely sensible and necessary things I needed to do. Everything thrown out of kilter.

I took her to the vet to be examined for fitness, vaccinated and microchipped. First trip in a car, and she raged all the way, growling and hissing from her brand new, airline approved carry-cage, while the taxi driver chuckled and made wry comments. The vet still remembered her, and he and his young female assistant were wary. He obviously considered me mentally deficient to want to send this obnoxious creature abroad, and he questioned me condescendingly. Did I understand there were several official requirements? I told him I knew better than most, but he refused to comprehend my Japanese. He shook his head and smirked but eventually agreed to do as I asked. I wrestled the cat out onto the examination table, where he managed to carry out the procedures. When he was done, he signed the necessary documents, and Smudge was on her way to becoming an international entity, recognized by two governments.

Although she was recovering well, she wasn't an exemplary specimen, so I took a liberty or two filling out the forms, fearing her alley-cat pedigree might not go down very well with the customs and quarantine agencies. Where the forms requested her breed, I decided it might be best to invent one, "Japanese domestic bobtail," hoping to minimize any scrutiny of her posterior. I had an idea of how she would react if the airport vet conducted the pre-flight examination too closely. I was afraid that if the vet deduced the obvious—she was an untamed cat who had lost its tail sometime during recent months—she would be judged unfit to travel. What could I do then? There would be nothing left but surrender her to the local council officers to be destroyed.

One day the pet removals agent phoned me.

"You have written on the quarantine form that the cat is five years old. However, on the veterinary form you sent us, you say she is seven."

Curses. Hadn't thought anyone would give a damn about a cat's age, so I didn't bother to keep track of what I put on the forms. Of course, in hindsight, obviously the information needed to be consistent to ensure that I was trying to transport the correct cat. (I suspect now she may have been a bit older.)

"Oh yes, I recall now, I must have miscalculated somewhere there."

"So what is it, five or seven?"

"What was the age on the vet's form again?" I asked, deciding that it would be better to defer to the guess I had made on the Australian government's form.

"Seven years old."

"No, no. Well, it's actually five. Yes, that's right, five."

"So I will change the age to five years old?"

"Yes, thanks." I stifled a sigh of relief. Fortunate that he had noticed the discrepancy, instead of a bureaucrat somewhere further along the line.

Flight booked for the next evening and her mandatory month's stay at the quarantine center in Sydney due to start. The plane ticket and quarantine cost about three thousand Australian dollars. Plus five dollars for a cat's ticket on the Shinkansen and Narita Express. In the evening, when she came for her supper at the usual time, I lured her into the carry-cage and snapped the door shut, unwilling to risk her not showing up next morning. She yowled her displeasure through the night.

Tokyo station at its busiest, and she must have been traumatized: swung around at knee height, buffeted amid a forest of human legs, her senses assaulted by a million strange sounds and smells. Alerted by her cries, people looked anxiously about at the ground, thinking there must be a lost cat—something unheard of at Tokyo station. Then they would see me, point, laugh, and put each other's mind at ease: *"Bikkuri shita!"* ("Goodness me, so surprised!")

When we got to the platform for the Narita Express, I put the cage down beside a column and stepped away for a breather. From nowhere, two young girls darted over and peered in; one bent over, the other dropped down on her haunches:

"Kawaii!" ("How cute!") Flurry of venomous hissing and muffled thumps as the cat hurled herself against the plastic bars at the girls. They snatched their fingers away and turned to me as I went over.

"Kowai!" ("Scary!") one girl squealed, wide-eyed.

"She's off to see the world," I said laughing, but the girls scampered off along the platform.

My agent from the pet removals company had given me directions to their operations center in the remote cargo section of the airport. I walked down a road shuddering with trucks and semi-trailers and passed through a security checkpoint, where a guard examined my foreigner's identity card. This was a completely different world from that of the human airline traveler—no glitzy departures complex but a busy hive of warehouses. Delivery trucks and forklifts roared about everywhere, and the air was thick with exhaust fumes and rubber dust. I found the building and went upstairs, past an unmanned reception counter exhibiting the pet removal company's sign and through open double doors. Inside was a roomy office-area-cum-storage-space, full of busy office workers and stackers. My agent's desk was close to the doors. He easily identified me, came over and introduced himself.

He had me place the carry-cage on a long bench, so he could make sure that all was in order. I had prepared the bottom of her cage with special materials for absorption and insulation against the cold of the flight, but unfortunately, the journey proved too much, and she had soiled the lot. I asked the agent whether he had anything to make do, and he went to get me a sheet of flannel. I fixed up the cage while the agent restrained her. She had lost her usual ferocity and huddled limp between his hands. I paid the bill and headed home, fingers crossed that the official veterinary check would go without incident.

By the scheduled time of the veterinary check, I was waiting by the telephone, willing it not to ring. By flight-time I had still heard nothing. I pictured poor Smudge in the midst of her adventure, her rite of progress: wide-eyed, flattening herself against the floor of the cage as it clattered over conveyer belts or as cargo-workers heaved it about. She would find herself in the dark cargo hold, overwhelmed by the roar of the engines. She would experience the sudden surge of acceleration, pressing her back and playing tricks with her senses until the take-off was complete. At the tip of the ascent, as the aircraft settled into its cruising speed, she would relax her pent-up tension. Would she perceive a sensation of flight, from the changes in motion and air pressure? If the aircraft ran into any turbulence, she might experience a moment of weightlessness. Sighing with relief that the day was behind me, I leaned back and sank into the quiet of the empty house.

WE THREE reunited in Australia, to reside on a property of eight acres in a bushland valley, where Isabella and I still live today. The cat had six good years until her injuries caught up with her and she died from a digestive blockage. I tried to be as good a friend to her as she was to me in Japan, where a foreigner's life has its stresses too. She had many adventures over here and encountered beings such as horses, cattle, wallabies, eagles and foxes, whose existence she never imagined. The exotic bird-life fascinated her, but we belled her and kept her indoors at night to thwart her predatory instincts. She refused to be petted but chose to enjoy our company at an appropriate distance, making up the third corner of an intimate triangle. In the winter, she might crawl under the wood stove in our parlor for a snooze, but she always took her night's sleep on a bottom corner of our bed. Whenever any other humans showed up she disappeared — even our closest neighbors weren't aware we had a cat. We buried her near the bedroom balcony and marked her grave with a few terracotta tiles. Isabella placed a jar there containing a clump of fur from Smudge's hair brush. After we went into the house, I happened to glance over that way, just in time to see a black snake glide over the grave and disappear in the bush.

CPSIA information can be obtained
at www.ICGtesting.com
Printed in the USA
LVHW031835170220
647200LV00001B/22